# ACCESS TO JUSTICE IN RURAL COMMUNITIES

This book offers insight on access to justice from rural areas in internationally comparable contexts to highlight the diversity of experiences within and across rural areas globally.

It looks at the fundamental questions for people's lives raised by the issue of access to justice as well as the rule of law. It highlights a range of social, geographic and cultural issues which impact the way rural communities experience the justice system throughout the world, with chapters on Australia, Canada, England, Ireland, Kenya, Northern Ireland, South Africa, Syria, Turkey, the USA and Wales.

Each chapter explores three questions:

1. How do people experience the institutions of justice in rural areas and how does this rural experience differ to an urban experience?
2. What impact have changes in policy had on the justice system in rural areas, and have rural and urban areas been affected in different ways?
3. What impact does the law have on people's lives in rural areas and what would rural communities like to be better understood about their experience of the justice system?

By bringing in the voices and experiences of those who are often ignored or sidelined by justice systems, this book sets out an agenda for ensuring social justice in legal systems with a focus on protecting marginalised groups.

# Access to Justice in Rural Communities

*Global Perspectives*

Edited by
Daniel Newman
and
Faith Gordon

•HART•
OXFORD • LONDON • NEW YORK • NEW DELHI • SYDNEY

HART PUBLISHING

Bloomsbury Publishing Plc

Kemp House, Chawley Park, Cumnor Hill, Oxford, OX2 9PH, UK

1385 Broadway, New York, NY 10018, USA

29 Earlsfort Terrace, Dublin 2, Ireland



First published in Great Britain 2023



A catalogue record for this book is available from the British Library.

A catalogue record for this book is available from the Library of Congress.

ISBN: HB: 978-1-50995-164-2
ePDF: 978-1-50995-166-6
ePub: 978-1-50995-165-9

Typeset by Compuscript Ltd, Shannon

To find out more about our authors and books visit www.hartpublishing.co.uk. Here you will find extracts, author information, details of forthcoming events and the option to sign up for our newsletters.

# FOREWORD

RUSSELL HOGG

The rural typically holds a special, if varied, place in the life and traditions of most nations. It is a cultural space as well as being a material or physical space, a place of the imagination that is widely shared in the psyches of urban as well as rural dwellers. Proximity to the soil, and to the essential pillars of life, not infrequently underpins images of the rural as stable, caring, resilient, a refuge from the troubles and disorders of the city, and a crucible of national ideals and virtues. Rural communities enjoy high levels of face-to-face recognition, internal trust and what commentators call social capital. These provide the foundations of well-developed informal social controls, what are often assumed to be high levels of social cohesion and a sort of natural justice.

There is, however, a downside to these rural virtues that bears directly on the issues with which this valuable collection is concerned. Research has noted the pressures that can exist in small, tightly-knit communities that place a high value on self-reliance and resilience to suppress problems affecting personal and civic reputation, to even avoid accessing services like those relating to mental health or drug and alcohol dependency when they are available, and to internalise one's personal troubles. This contributes to a situation where, contrary to certain images of rural harmony, we often find significantly higher rates of suicide, violence (especially domestic violence), substance abuse and other problems in many rural communities.

The widespread investment in idealised images of rural life can therefore obscure the many realities and problems confronting life in rural settings. This may be especially so at the present time, as rural ways of life are increasingly disrupted by novel global economic, political and technological forces, including the challenges of climate change and new social movements and cultural currents (green politics, gender and sexual politics, indigenous rights). This is also an era in which many governments have cut services and public provision in favour of allowing market forces to determine the fate of local economies and communities. Change has brought to the surface some of the contradictions and tensions that were long erased in mythic accounts of rural life.

This collection addresses what one author (Kool) refers to as the 'rural justice gap', what amounts to a crisis in the provision of legal services and the delivery of justice in the rural context. A major strength is that it does so in relation to a wide variety of national settings: England, Wales, Ireland and Northern Ireland, Kenya, South Africa, Turkey, Syria, Australia, Canada and the United States. Chapters engage with the formidable impediments to accessing justice in these diverse rural settings as well as many of the initiatives directed at overcoming some, if not all, of them. Many of the contributions also demonstrate the close inter-relatedness of the legal needs that remain unmet in rural localities. Civil and criminal law problems compound each other and the wider patterns of disadvantage that underlie them.

Injustice – and thus access to justice – has an important geographical dimension that is often obscured by the ideology of law that tends to depict law as a spatially invariant practice: a system of rules whose writ runs the length and breadth of a given territorial entity or jurisdiction and delivers equal justice to all who reside within it. But as the anthropologist Clifford Geertz has stressed, law is 'local knowledge', not 'placeless principle'. A central theme running through all the otherwise diverse contributions to this collection is that living in a rural community can – and all too frequently does – give rise to serious disadvantage in accessing appropriate legal services and thus the equal justice promised by the system. Moreover, this compounds, and is in turn compounded by, other forms of disadvantage, discrimination and exclusion, including disadvantage stemming from the deficient provision of other services in rural settings (health, family, employment, education, financial, etc). Legal justice is not hermetically sealed off from the wider questions and challenges of social justice.

There is also a more subtle aspect to the question of justice in the rural context. Constructions and perceptions of rural place are often conjoined with perceptions about the type of people who (rightfully) reside in them and those who are regarded as out-of-place, what Chris Philo referred to as 'discrepant *other* rurals'. Disadvantage in relation to the law and much else is frequently related to a presence that is treated as disturbing the imagined rural. This poses deeper questions about the law and the definition of justice, as well as the meanings of rural belonging and identity. The contributions point to striking examples of those who are in, but not necessarily treated as being *of*, the rural: Irish Travellers, Indigenous Australians, the mentally ill and often young people where they rub up against local civic norms. It can also include victims of certain forms of violence, like family or homophobic violence. These forms of exclusion or marginalisation are hardly confined to rural communities but they are often accentuated there because of the more assiduous policing of the boundaries of civic life. Personal identity is more closely bound up with civic identity than it is in the 'soft', highly segmented and impersonal city.

The various deficits in the fabric of rural governance and civic life also feed into more general concerns about effective representation, political legitimacy and social justice. The question is posed of how an equitable and inclusive economy and polity (one that comports more closely with rural myths) is to be attained in the face of spatial disparities and the novel challenges and sources of tension and conflict to be found in many contemporary rural settings.

The restrictions on movement and association caused by the Covid-19 pandemic both highlighted and aggravated the disadvantages flowing from distance, but the widespread recourse to technology (Zoom meetings and the like) seemed to point to apparent solutions. The chapter by Adisa, James and Newman warns of the dangers of a too-ready adoption of such measures to overcome the problems of remote justice and to justify further legal service cuts in rural areas. Most importantly, the authors stress the loss of 'the client's voice' and the erosion of empathy and accountability in the administration of justice – what would amount to a further disembodying of the meaning of justice.

With its wide-ranging and critical examination of the issues of rural justice, this impressive collection is a welcome addition to the literature on an important, often neglected subject.

# ACKNOWLEDGEMENTS

An edited collection project provides an exciting and unique opportunity to engage with scholars globally who are working at the cutting edge of their subject. We are grateful to all of the amazing authors from all around the world, who accepted our invitation to contribute to this collection. Their contributions truly represent part of the collection's title – global perspectives.

We would like to sincerely thank all of the contributors we have met through this process for their excellent scholarship and enthusiastic correspondence throughout the life of this project. They have made this collection a joy to work on. We both have been fascinated, inspired and educated by their scholarship. We hope that those who read the collection will also learn from their contributions and the new key insights contained in each chapter.

Special thanks to Professor Russell Hogg for writing an excellent Foreword, and to Assistant Professor Michele Statz for writing an excellent Afterword for this collection. Their pieces really draw out important messages in relation to the collection as a whole.

We sincerely thank everyone at Hart Publishing, who are always such a pleasure to deal with. Thanks especially to Kate Whetter: she is such a fantastic editor and made the whole process of producing this collection so enjoyable.

Daniel would like to thank his wife, Rhian, and his two children, Betsi and Iolo, for always being a wonderful distraction at the times when he needs a break from work. And thank you also to Faith, with whom it is always lovely to work.

Faith would like to thank her parents, Kenny and Isobel; her sister and brother-in-law, Serena and Jonathan; niece, Esmé Grace; goddaughter, Iona; her close friends and several colleagues at the ANU and the IALS, for always showing a keen interest in this project and for celebrating its completion. She would especially like to thank Dan for his friendship and for remaining an inspiration in his scholarship and advocacy.

Daniel Newman and Faith Gordon
*Cardiff and Canberra*
*June 2022*

# CONTENTS

# LIST OF CONTRIBUTORS

**Olumide Adisa** is a Senior Research Fellow and Head of Centre for Abuse Research at the University of Suffolk.

**Fiona Allison** is a Senior Research Fellow working at the Cairns Institute, James Cook University (JCU) and at Jumbunna Institute for Indigenous Education and Research, University of Technology, Sydney, and holds a Doctorate in Law from JCU.

**Kelly V Beskin** is a 2021 graduate from the University of California, Davis School of Law. During her time there, she was a research assistant for her co-author, Lisa R Pruitt, who piqued her interest in examining rural lawyer shortages across the United States.

**Kevin J Brown** is a Reader in Criminal Law and Criminal Justice at Queen's University Belfast, UK.

**Emmanuel Bunei** recently received his PhD from the University of New England, Australia. He is a multidisciplinary researcher, drawing from the disciplines of economics, criminology, law, psychology, political science, agriculture, and sociology.

**Christy Craig** is an Assistant Professor of Sociology at Fort Hays State University.

**Chris Cunneen** is Professor of Criminology at Jumbunna Institute for Indigenous Education and Research at the University of Technology Sydney.

**Fiona Donson** is a Senior Lecturer in the School of Law, UCC, and Director of the Traveller Equality and Justice Project based in the Centre for Criminal Justice and Human Rights.

**Kim Economides** is Professor Emeritus and Honorary Professor of Law, University of Southern Queensland.

**Faith Gordon** is an Associate Professor in Law and Deputy Associate Dean of Research at the ANU College of Law, The Australian National University.

**Hannah Haksgaard** is a Professor at the University of South Dakota Knudson School of Law where she teaches courses in the areas of Property and Family Law.

**Russell Hogg** is Honorary Professor in the Centre for Crime, Law and Justice, Faculty of Law. University of New South Wales.

**Sue James** is CEO of Legal Action Group.

**Amanda L Kool** is Director of Legal at Sharebite, a US-based social enterprise that leverages corporate food ordering to donate meals to people in need.

**Murat Madenüs** is an Officer in the Turkish General Command of Gendarmerie.

**Witness Maluleke** is a Doctor of Policing, graduating from Tshwane University of Technology, South Africa; he is rated as a Y2 Rural Criminologist/Stock Theft researcher by National Research Foundation (NRF), 2021–26, and is a senior lecturer in the Department of Criminology and Criminal Justice of University of Limpopo, South Africa.

**Jess Mant** is a Lecturer in Law at Monash University, and an expert in access to justice, legal aid and family law.

**Lisa Moore** is the Director of the Canadian Forum on Civil Justice (CFCJ), a research organisation affiliated with Osgoode Hall Law School and the only national not-for-profit organisation in Canada with a mandate to advance access to justice through empirical research.

**Samantha Morgan-Williams** is a Post-Doctoral Researcher for the Traveller Equality & Justice Project at the Centre for Criminal Justice and Human Rights in the School of Law, University College Cork.

**Adnan Mouhiddin** (LLB, MSc, PhD) is a law and policing tutor at Coventry University and a Fellow of the Higher Education Academy in the UK.

**Daniel Newman** is a Reader in Law at Cardiff University with extensive research expertise on access to justice, legal aid and the legal profession.

**Lisa R Pruitt** is Martin Luther King, Jr Professor of Law at the University of California, Davis.

**Ziwei Qi** is an Assistant Professor in the Department of Criminal Justice at Fort Hays State University.

**Joseph K Rono**, PhD is a Senior Lecturer in the Department of Sociology and Psychology at Moi University in Kenya and former Head of the Department.

**Michele Statz** is an Assistant Professor at the University of Minnesota Medical School and affiliated faculty with the University of Minnesota Law School.

**Charles Watkins** is Professor of Rural Geography and Head of the School of Geography, University of Nottingham.

# 1

# Rural Access to Justice

DANIEL NEWMAN AND FAITH GORDON

> Sometimes a rural life … it means that you're a very long drive from everything … The geography of where people find themselves situated, both in metropolises and in the heartland, really starts to matter. (Debra Granik, 2015)[1]

This edited collection focuses on rural access to justice. We are both so proud to be able to be a part of publishing it, because as editors we both strongly believe that rural communities have been too often ignored in access to justice scholarship. We think there is a need for this global collection and for the diverse authors within it to be heard on significant areas affecting people in rural communities. One of the main aims of the collection is to help stimulate a change, and bring more attention internationally, to rural access to justice as a research area.

Neither of us comes from the city. Perhaps this underpins our interest in the rural; it may have helped us understand the specific differences of rural life and the need to take the rural more seriously. Daniel is from a village on the edge of the South Wales valleys. While his home was only 12 miles from the capital city of Wales, Cardiff, that seemed a distant land in his childhood; the place of occasional trips with his parents on special occasions such as birthdays or Christmas. His reality was his village, the handful of other villages within walking distance and the small towns a little further away that dot the post-industrial landscape in these former coal-mining communities. Moving away to attend university – the only member of his family to do so – in an English city was a culture shock that has always stuck with him. Faith is from the small rural village of Annaclone in County Down, Northern Ireland. Faith's father is a third-generation blacksmith, and the blacksmith's forge was a central gathering place in most rural communities. First out of all generations to attend university, Faith was acutely aware of gaps in service provision for those living in rural communities, with many neighbours turning to her for assistance to complete application forms. We both work in cities

[1] 'Debra Granik on "poverty porn", self-worth, and her new film, *Stray Dog*', interview with Sam Fragoso, 11 July 2015, available at www.avclub.com/debra-granik-on-poverty-porn-self-worth-and-her-new-1798281922.

now (and capital cities at that), but we are acutely aware of our rural roots and rural needs – and our families still live outside of the city.

In *The Country and the City*,[2] Williams reveals the way that rural life has been simplified, stereotyped and sanitised. His analysis reveals the conservative way in which rural life has been viewed through an urban lens; one that sees the countryside, as it is conceived, as natural and pristine. Such an idealisation works to evoke a 'Golden Age' that assumes rural life is free of the social and economic struggles experienced by those live in the city. For Williams, what we get is 'a myth functioning as a memory' that frames the countryside as nostalgia and overlooks the struggles of those living in rural poverty, such as he grew up in. Williams teaches those from outside rural areas that the reality of the countryside is not simply that of childhood camping holidays or day-trippers' picnics; it is more than the excitement of spotting a cow or the jolly frustration of being stuck behind a tractor in a narrow lane. Williams sheds light on the way rural life is more complicated than such romanticism; that it entails a diverse range of experiences, and may contain many hardships – just like city life. While Williams' focus was on English literature, what we want to do with this volume is to shed light on the reality of access to justice in rural communities, which we demonstrate can also include such variety and similarly entail all manners of difficulty. We want to show that this is the case for England and Wales as a legal jurisdiction, but we also intend to capture how it is true across the globe.

The typical focus of access to justice scholarship is on urban areas; research has tended to look at what occurs in cities, perhaps in larger towns. This may reflect where scholars are based; it might stem from the location of many institutions of the justice system; and it could involve a judgement based on where most of the activity occurs. There is also the possibility that some scholars overlook rural areas and do not consider these communities relevant or interesting. The result is that while we have a great deal of knowledge on access to justice, which has long been a focus of legal scholarship – and is especially prominent in the rise of socio-legal studies in recent years – most of what we know relates to urban areas. There is less understanding of access to justice in rural communities, and rural access to justice does not form a significant part of wider knowledge bases on access to justice. But we believe it should. And there are accomplished scholars conducting compelling research on rural access to justice. This volume is about highlighting (and celebrating!) their work to encourage greater insight into rural access to justice and – it is hoped – to persuade more academic researchers to look at rural communities in their scholarship.

The collection examines access to justice in rural areas in internationally comparable contexts. It explores criminal, civil and family law contexts to highlight rural access to justice in the round. It highlights the diversity of experiences within

[2] R Williams, *The Country and the City* (Spokesman Books, 2011).

and across rural areas globally. The collection covers a range of social, geographic and cultural issues that affect people in accessing justice in rural communities. We have a truly global span to our contributions. They include chapters on Australia, Canada, England, Ireland, Northern Ireland, Kenya, South Africa, Syria, Turkey, the United States of America and Wales. By bringing in the voices and experiences of those who are often ignored or side-lined by justice systems, this book will set out an agenda for ensuring social justice in legal systems, with a focus on protecting marginalised groups.

This collection utilises a framing device of setting the authors questions that need to be addressed to ensure that the contributions fit tightly together into a cohesive whole. Despite the variety of rural experiences, we are keen to communicate, there will be a clear and purposeful narrative of addressing the gap in knowledge around rural access to justice that runs through every chapter. Our aim has always been to provide a definitive book on the state of rural access to justice, so – even considering the diversity of our contributors and their subjects – it is our intention to use this framing device to ensure the collection works on a unified whole that advances knowledge in the round.

There are three overall framing questions that bring the chapters in the collection together. Every author has been asked to consider one or more of the three framing questions in their individual chapters. This allows for consistency of vision and an interconnectedness that links together some markedly different contributions. The three framing questions are:

1. How do people experience the institutions of justice in rural areas, and how does this rural experience differ from an urban experience?
2. What impact have changes in policy had on the justice system in rural areas, and have rural and urban areas been affected in different ways?
3. What impact does the law have on people's lives in rural areas, and what would rural communities like to be better understood about their experience of the justice system?

The authors signpost their engagement with these questions in more or less explicit ways in each chapter.

As editors, it is our privilege to share these chapters with the world. We hope that readers of this volume will be inspired to conduct further research on rural access to justice, responding to the topics here or complementing them with work in new or evolving areas. We want to thank everyone who has contributed and everyone who reads and engages with this collection.

The book begins with a Foreword by Russell Hogg that sets up the rural as a space holding an important value in the life and traditions of many nations. He sets the context that underpins this collection, that rural life can contain many difficulties that need to be taken more seriously. This Foreword thus tees up the material to follow by highlighting the need for wider examination of the often neglected problems around access to justice that can exist in rural communities.

In chapter 2, Kelly V Beskin and Lisa R Pruitt provide us with an overview of rural access to justice initiatives in the United States of America. In particular, they offer deep insight into the shortage of rural attorneys and the approaches taken over the past decade in various States to tackle the problem. They also discuss the impact of the Covid-19 on the legal profession and consider the implications for the delivery of legal services in rural America.

In chapter 3, Joseph K Rono and Emmanuel K Bunei take us to Kenya to consider alcohol use and abuse in rural areas of the country. They argue that criminalisation of alcohol in Kenya has encountered cultural, administrative and law enforcement resistance, and has exacerbated problems with alcoholism. They conclude that there is a need for greater sensitivity in the development of law and policy to better take account of local cultures and traditions.

In chapter 4, Witness Maluleke highlights rural crime in South Africa by exploring stock theft amongst livestock farmers. The chapter shows that farmers have a lack of trust in the justice system and can feel isolated from courts, so do not engage fully. He argues that those charged with working on cases of stock theft need greater knowledge of livestock and livestock theft as they play out in distinctive rural settings.

In chapter 5, Murat Madenüs uses a socio-cultural analysis of a fictional work on a rural murder investigation to develop a more nuanced understanding of how rural communities experience crime and justice. His chapter focuses on Turkey and Sabahattin Ali's short story, *Kağnı*. This case study is offered in order to increase the visibility of rural villages in discussions around access to justice in Turkey.

Fiona Allison and Chris Cunneen turn in chapter 6 to exploring First Nations peoples' experiences of access to justice in Australia. They discuss the high levels of unmet legal need in the regional and remote, often rural, areas in which First Nations peoples tend to live. The need to improve access to justice for these communities is shown to be important in its own right, as well as in order to tackle wider social disadvantage for First Nations peoples.

In Ireland, Fiona Donson and Samantha Morgan-Williams detail the high levels of discrimination in accessing goods and services faced by the Traveller community. Chapter 7 draws out the barriers Travellers face in challenging such discrimination due to the current legal system failing marginalised minority groups in process and provision. The impact of the present situation is that Travellers become re-victimised.

Chapter 8 sees Faith Gordon and Kevin Brown explore older people's victimisation. The chapter focuses on victims of crime in rural communities in Northern Ireland, drawing upon the voices of those older people who have been victimised. The authors call for more resources to be allocated to older people in rural communities, and for reforms to be introduced that are tailored to their circumstances.

Jess Mant looks at how people in rural areas of England and Wales experience the family court process. In chapter 9 she explores issues such as the emergence of advice deserts and the limitations of pro bono advice. The chapter highlights the importance of understanding that legal-aid policies impact those in rural areas differently, due to variations in travel and support, compared to those living in urban areas.

Chapter 10 sees Lisa Moore analyse the importance of location in Canada, considering justice in relation to the urban–rural dichotomy. Focusing on rural justice, the chapter includes a case study of mobile legal service delivery to address geographic barriers in the justice system. The chapter draws out the importance of adapting the delivery of legal services to their location, which has the potential to improve access to justice.

Amanda Kool and Hannah Haksgaard look at the rural justice gap that results from the rural lawyer shortage in the United States of America through a lens of supply chain management. Chapter 11 involves the authors in conceptualising the problems resulting from the lack of rural legal services as those resulting from a poorly calibrated supply chain. The authors show how this supply chain can be transformed to better service the justice needs of rural communities.

In chapter 12, Adnan Mouhiddin looks at the rise in crime since the civil war in Syria and the particular increase amongst young people. He considers the value of restorative justice as a means of alternative dispute resolution for young people in rural areas. The chapter develops understanding into whether and how restorative justice may correlate with the values and norms of the Syrian rural and tribal communities, and explores it in the context of similar practices that already exist among these communities.

In chapter 13, dedicated to their friend and collaborator Mark Blacksell, Kim Economides and Charles Watkins explore changes in rural legal service provision over the past three decades. This is a retrospective chapter, in which the authors consider developments since their ground-breaking work on rural lawyers in the United Kingdom from the 1980s and 1990s. The chapter is also comparative, taking in work done in Oceania, and North and South America, as the authors set out an agenda for future research and policy in rural legal services.

Ziwei Qi and Christy Craig consider domestic violence in chapter 14, which they outline as a significant public-health problem facing women in rural areas. They offer an insight into both the tangible and intangible costs of domestic violence victimisation in these communities. Their chapter looks to develop greater understanding of victimisation to help promote the change that is needed to better protect women in rural areas.

In chapter 15, Olumide Adisa, Sue James and Daniel Newman look at the impact of the court reform programme in England and Wales and the wider implications for provision of advice. The authors consider the implications of advice deserts, remote access, and the experiences of those seeking access to justice outside large towns and cities. The chapter expands discussions of access, emphasising the necessity to consider the rural experience in future policy.

The book ends with an Afterword by Michele Statz, in which she reflects on the – often overlooked – importance of rural place. She draws out the significance of understanding that rurality is heterogeneous and that all places are particular, which thus pulls out a main theme of this collection. Drawing the book to a close on an appropriate note, she makes a powerful call for more research on diverse rurality realities.

We hope this book will encourage more recognition of the rural – more urge to understand the range of rural experiences – when it comes to access to justice.

# 2

# A Survey of Policy Responses to the Rural Attorney Shortage in the United States

KELLY V BESKIN AND LISA R PRUITT

Rural communities in the United States lag behind their urban counterparts with respect to most measures of well-being and quality of life, including access to health care,[1] education[2] and digital technology infrastructure.[3] Another significant rural deficit – until recently overlooked, as discussed in this chapter – is access to legal services. Rural America suffers a painful shortage of lawyers, a deficit that has grown more acute in recent years. Further, current institutional responses – most in States dominated by urban populations and urban-centric policymakers – provide little hope for reversing this trend.

This chapter surveys the short history of policymakers' and scholars' attention to the rural lawyer shortage in the United States, discussing this phenomenon as a key aspect of a burgeoning rural access-to-justice (A2J) crisis. A number of initiatives to narrow the rural-urban justice gap are currently afoot in the United States, including the expanded use of paralegals and various interventions based on artificial intelligence and other technologies. These, however, are beyond the scope of this chapter, which focuses on the rural attorney shortage. It goes without saying that the absence of lawyers has an impact on how rural residents experience the justice system and, indeed, the state more broadly. Rural residents may be reluctant to engage the legal system if they do not have an attorney to help them navigate it, and that reluctance may predispose them to distrust government more generally.

[1] JD Reschovsky and AB Staiti, 'Access and Quality: Does Rural America Lag Behind?' (2005) 24(4) *Health Affairs* 1128.

[2] JD Ulrich, 'Education in Chronically Poor Rural Areas Lags Across Generations' (2011) 24 *Carsey Institute* 1.

[3] L Runyon, 'Rural Areas Still Lag Behind in Digital Technology Adoption' (Harvest Public Media, 26 May 2017) at www.kmuw.org/agriculture/2017-05-29/rural-areas-still-lag-behind-in-digital-technology-adoption.

We categorise policy responses to that problem into several overlapping strands: (i) programmes that provide financial incentives and other supports for lawyers to practise in rural locales; (ii) programmes that channel urban attorney resources to rural areas; and (iii) programmes focused on cultivating and expanding the pipeline to rural practice. Where possible, we provide status reports on initiatives in an effort to document and publicise their progress, thereby informing future policymaking. Finally, we discuss briefly the medium- to long-term impacts of the Covid-19 pandemic that may change the legal profession and delivery of legal services in rural America.

## I. The Rural Attorney Shortage by the Numbers

Even under the miserly definition of the US Census Bureau (population clusters smaller than 2,500 or living in open territory), 19.3 per cent of the US population – some 46 million residents – live in rural areas.[4] This is a mismatch for the 2 per cent of small law practices operating there.[5] The severity of the crisis varies from State to State and from region to region within many States. Rural California, for example, averages one attorney for every 626 residents, compared to urban areas of the State, where the ratio is one to 175.[6] The situation is even more dire elsewhere. In rural areas of Arkansas, the ratio can be as low as one attorney to 1,562 residents.[7] In nearly 40 per cent of US counties (1,217 out of 3,141), the ratio is one lawyer to more than 1,000 residents.[8] Indeed, as of 2020, 54 US counties had no lawyers, and 182 counties were home to just one or two attorneys.[9]

In addition to the paucity of attorneys in many rural areas, most such places are also experiencing a 'graying of the bar', a reference to the higher median age of attorneys practising in rural areas.[10] Across the country, the average lawyer is five years older (47) than the average American worker (42), and one in seven lawyers is aged 65 or older.[11] This trend is more dramatic in rural areas. In Maine,

[4] 'Urban Areas Facts' (United States Census Bureau, 2010) at www.census.gov/programs-surveys/geography/guidance/geo-areas/urban-rural/ua-facts.html.

[5] LR Pruitt et al, 'Legal Deserts: A Multi-State Perspective on Rural Access to Justice' (2018) 13(1) *Harvard Law & Policy Review* 15.

[6] ibid (utilising data mapped by Professor James Meeker of UC Irvine in 2016).

[7] 'Rural Practice Incubator Project Benefits' at www.ualr.edu/law/clinical-programs/rural-practice-incubator-project/.

[8] Webinar Video, 'Legal Deserts in America: A Threat to Justice for All' (American Bar Association, 28 July 2020) at www.americanbar.org/news/abanews/aba-news-archives/2020/07/webinar-video---legal-deserts-in-america--a-threat-to-justice-fo/.

[9] ibid.

[10] W Davis, 'No Country for Rural Lawyers: Small-town Attorneys Still Find It Hard to Thrive' *ABA Journal* (1 February 2020) at www.abajournal.com/magazine/article/no-country-for-rural-lawyers; Pruitt et al (n 5).

[11] Webinar Video (n 8).

for example, nearly half of the members of the bar in 2016 were over the age of 55, and fewer than 12 per cent were under 35.[12] With many rural lawyers nearing retirement and relatively few younger lawyers coming forward to serve those communities, attorney deserts will likely proliferate in coming years, and the sprawl of those deserts will probably expand.[13]

The alarming dearth of lawyers in rural communities often has dire repercussions for both civil and criminal justice systems. Without access to legal advice and assistance, rural residents may be unaware of their legal rights or potential legal claims.[14] They may struggle to navigate the complex judicial system, which could 'lead to the loss of a home, children, job, [and] income'.[15] Indeed, like the availability of housing, food and safe employment, attorney deserts are themselves a social determinant of health.[16] Beyond identifiable and concrete injustices, 'a lack of access to justice can evolve into a greater and entrenched lack of agency in one's life, effectively snowballing to become a much greater handicap than the original unaddressed legal issue(s)'.[17] These challenges exist alongside, and are aggravated by, other deficits associated with rural life: poor public transit, unreliable cell phone service, inadequate broadband internet and material distance from institutions of justice.

Given the challenges endemic to rural life – economic marginalisation, absence of fundamental infrastructure and spatial isolation – rural lawyers play an outsized role in their communities. When lawyers are absent from rural life, the knowledge gap between (would-be) litigants and institutions of justice is heightened. Indeed, an attorney is not only a 'problem solver', she is also an advocate trained to assist people in times of crisis. Rural A2J scholar Michele Statz frames the attorney's role as 'bear[ing] the burden of the problem – the crisis – so that it may be solved in a dignified and just way'.[18]

We do not know much, beyond anecdote, about why recent US law graduates are not choosing rural practice. The only survey of lawyers and law students exploring attitudes toward rural practice, from Arkansas in 2014, suggests a range

[12] Pruitt et al (n 5).

[13] ibid.

[14] ibid; R Buckwalter-Poza, 'Making Justice Equal' (Center for American Progress, 8 December 2016) at www.americanprogress.org/issues/criminal-justice/reports/2016/12/08/294479/making-justice-equal/.

[15] L Wills, 'Access to Justice: Mitigating the Justice Gap' (American Bar Association, 3 December 2017) at www.americanbar.org/groups/litigation/committees/minority-trial-lawyer/practice/2017/access-to-justice-mitigating-justice-gap/.

[16] 'California's Attorney Deserts, Social Determinants of Health, and COVID-19' (California Access to Justice Commission, 2020) at www.calatj.org/wp-content/uploads/2021/01/2020-Attorney-Deserts-Social-Determinants-of-Health-and-COVID-19.pdf.

[17] Pruitt et al (n 5) 23.

[18] M Statz, R Friday and J Bredeson, '"They Had Access, But They Didn't Get Justice": Why Prevailing Access to Justice Initiatives Fail Rural Americans' (2021) 28(3) *Georgetown Journal on Poverty Law and Policy* 321, 375.

of reasons.[19] Some of these reasons are professional and fiscal, as discussed further in section IV.D. Others are social and personal, including the widespread desire to live in places with more cultural amenities (eg, restaurants, theatre) and better infrastructure (eg, good schools for children, better healthcare access). Some express concern about job opportunities for life partners or, for those not already in a committed relationship, the ability to find a life partner in a rural community.

These concerns remind us that the rural lawyer shortage is a problem that has been decades in the making, as the United States has become increasingly urbanised.[20] Rural areas have suffered not only broad population loss, but also particularly acute loss of the developed human capital represented by the professional class, including physicians and lawyers.[21] Indeed, the withering of institutions associated with population loss, such as hospitals, schools and even grocery stores, has been in an unfortunate feedback loop with population loss itself. The challenges represented by the rural lawyer shortage thus go beyond those that justice-system stakeholders have within their power to fix. The well-being and viability of broader rural ecosystems is implicated, as is the reality of rural-urban interdependence.

Until about a decade ago, the word 'rural' and the phrase 'access to justice' rarely appeared in the same publication, let alone in the same paragraph or the same sentence. One early publication that addressed rural A2J was published in 1969 by the *Duke Law Journal*. 'Legal Problems of the Rural Poor' was collectively authored by the journal under a grant from the American Bar Foundation.[22] Three decades later, the American Bar Association (ABA), the pre-eminent professional association of US lawyers, created the Rural Pro Bono Consortium and a few years later published a 'Guide to Pro Bono Services in Rural Areas'.[23] Then, in 2010, the California Commission on Access to Justice released a report titled, *Improving Civil Justice in Rural California*.[24] The next year, the American Bar Foundation published *Access Across America: The First Report of the Civil Infrastructure Mapping Project*, drawing unprecedented attention to spatial inequalities in A2J, including intra-State and State-to-State variations.[25]

[19] LR Pruitt, JC McKinney and B Calhoun, 'Justice in the Hinterlands: Arkansas as a Case Study for the Rural Lawyer Shortage and Evidence-Based Solutions to Alleviate It' (2015) 37(4) *University of Arkansas at Little Rock Law Review* 573.

[20] M Statz and J Bredeson, 'Concerned about Rural Access to Justice? Start Here First' (Northland Access to Justice, 2020) at www.northlandproject.org/the-rural-a2j-guide.

[21] PJ Carr and MJ Kefalas, *Hollowing Out the Middle: The Rural Brain Drain and What It Means for America* (Beacon Press, 2009); H Haksgaard, 'Rural Incentive Programs for Legal and Medical Professionals: A Comparative Analysis' (2014) 59 *South Dakota Law Review* 585.

[22] 'Legal Problems of the Rural Poor' (1969) 3 *Duke Law Journal* 495.

[23] 'Rural Pro Bono Delivery: A Guide to Pro Bono Services in Rural Areas' (American Bar Association, 2003) at www.americanbar.org/content/dam/aba/administrative/probono_public_service/as/aba_rural_book.pdHof.

[24] *Improving Civil Justice in Rural California Executive Summary* (California Commission on Access to Justice, 2010) at www.calbar.ca.gov/Portals/0/documents/accessJustice/2010%20Improving%20Rural%20Report%20Executive%20Summary.pdf.

[25] RL Sandefur and AC Smyth, *Access Across America: First Report of the Civil Justice Infrastructure Mapping Project* (American Bar Foundation, 2011) at www.americanbarfoundation.org/uploads/

The first explicit attention to the rural lawyer shortage as a component of rural A2J came two years later. It surfaced as stakeholders at the State and local level became aware of the problem, initially in specific regions around the nation. In 2012, the ABA's House of Delegates addressed the issue by calling on governments and bar associations to address the loss of lawyers in rural areas.[26] Since then, the *ABA Journal*, the organisation's national magazine, has provided high-profile attention: two cover stories on the rural lawyer shortage, in October 2014[27] and February 2020.[28]

In July 2020, the ABA's updated 'Profile of the Legal Profession' for the first time highlighted the so-called 'attorney desert' problem and mapped precisely where lawyers are in each US State.[29] This was no small feat, because it required the ABA to access attorney address data for each State, data held in various forms by the salient body governing the legal profession in a given State, for example the State supreme court or other institution that admits attorneys to the bar and disciplines them.[30] While the California Commission on Access to Justice and Georgia State University's Center for Access to Justice had already mapped the location of lawyers in their respective States, the ABA project was the first national undertaking to assess the presence of lawyers in relation to geography. That ABA publication threw into sharp relief how widespread the rural lawyer shortage is, as well as how dire it is in particular places. On the occasion of that report's release, the ABA held a national webinar on so-called 'legal deserts', a term increasingly used to refer to places experiencing a shortage of attorneys.[31]

This ABA report and webinar, to date, represent the apex of attention to the rural lawyer shortage in the United States. What remains to be seen is how State and local stakeholders across the nation will respond to the ABA's call to ameliorate the escalating challenge of attorney deserts. Also unknown is what impact the Covid-19 pandemic will have on the rural lawyer shortage. Given the advanced age of many rural practitioners, it would not be a surprise if the pandemic drives many to retire earlier than they had previously planned, thereby accelerating and aggravating the shortage. This is because limitations on in-person interactions and the attendant shift to online communication with courts and clients may prove to have been more than some aging practitioners were willing to take on to stay in business.

cms/documents/access_across_america_first_report_of_the_civil_justice_infrastructure_mapping_project.pdf.

[26] L Laird, 'In Rural America, There Are Job Opportunities and a Need for Lawyers' *ABA Journal* (1 October 2014) at www.abajournal.com/magazine/article/too_many_lawyers_not_here._in_rural_america_lawyers_are_few_and_far_between.

[27] ibid.

[28] Davis (n 10).

[29] 'Profile of the Legal Profession' (American Bar Association, 2020) at www.americanbar.org/content/dam/aba/administrative/news/2020/07/potlp2020.pdf.

[30] LR Pruitt and A Davies, 'Investigating Access to Justice, the Rural Lawyer Shortage, and Implications for Civil and Criminal Legal Systems' in R Weisheit, J Peterson and A Pytlarz (eds), *Research Methods for Rural Criminologists* (Routledge, 2022) ch 6.

[31] Webinar Video (n 8).

Even before the ABA's 2020 report, several State bar associations and other professional governing bodies had begun to address the lawyer shortage and its broader implications for access to justice. Rural-focused task forces were already at work in Alaska, California, New York and South Dakota. Other States, including Michigan,[32] Indiana,[33] Wyoming[34] and Illinois,[35] had acknowledged the shortage, and some were taking steps to improve rural lawyer placement and retention. Meanwhile, some legal scholars and practitioners had also turned their focus on this issue, through symposia and publications.[36] At the same time, the issue was catching the attention of national media outlets, including the *New York Times*,[37] National Public Radio,[38] The Pew Charitable Trusts[39] and *The Atlantic*.[40]

A community's status as a 'legal desert' or 'attorney desert' necessarily influences how all aspects of its civil and criminal justice system function, and indeed how the entire community functions given the human capital represented by attorney presence. In the following sections we consider two particular contexts in which the rural lawyer shortage plays out: legal aid and criminal justice. Beyond that, we turn to a discussion of various State-specific initiatives to increase the number of lawyers practising in rural areas.

## II. Legal Aid Lawyers

Legal aid attorneys are an important piece of the rural A2J puzzle because in 2017 '71% low-income households experienced at least one civil legal problem, including problems with domestic violence, veterans' benefits, disability access, housing

[32] JM Grieco, 'Addressing Our Aging Population of Lawyers (aka Lawyers Are Mortal)' *Michigan Bar Journal* (July 2019) at www.michbar.org/file/barjournal/article/documents/pdf4article3705.pdf.

[33] M Odendahl, 'Too Few Pro Bono Attorneys in Indiana Rural Communities' *The Indiana Lawyer* (6 November 2012) at www.theindianalawyer.com/articles/30039-too-few-pro-bono-attorneys-in-rural-communities.

[34] A Romero, 'Efforts to Encourage and Support Rural Law Practice in Wyoming' (2022) 22(1) *Wyoming Law Review* 155, 158; P Peasley, 'Ensuring the Survival of Wyoming's Newest Endangered Species: Rural Attorneys' (2022) 22(1) *Wyoming Law Review* 161.

[35] R Saunders, 'ISBA Seeks Input from Attorneys Whose Practices Include Rural Areas and Small Towns' *The Bar News* (26 August 2020) at www.isba.org/barnews/2020/08/isbaseeksinputfromattorneyswhosepra0.

[36] 'Rural Practice Symposium' (2014) 59(3) *South Dakota Law Review* 614; 'Ensuring Equal Access to Justice in Maine's Rural Communities Symposium' (2019) 71(2) *Maine Law Review* 209.

[37] E Bronner, 'No Lawyer for Miles, So One Rural State Offers Pay' *New York Times* (8 April 2013) at www.nytimes.com/2013/04/09/us/subsidy-seen-as-a-way-to-fill-a-need-for-rural-lawyers.html.

[38] G Gerlock, 'Lawyer Shortage In Some Rural Areas Reaches Epic Proportions' (National Public Radio, 26 December 2016) at www.npr.org/2016/12/26/506971630/nebraska-and-other-states-combat-rural-lawyer-shortage.

[39] A Simpson, 'Wanted: Lawyers for Rural America' (Pew Charitable Trusts, 26 June 2019) at www.pewtrusts.org/en/research-and-analysis/blogs/stateline/2019/06/26/wanted-lawyers-for-rural-america.

[40] J Pishko, 'The Shocking Lack of Lawyers in Rural America' *The Atlantic* (18 July 2019) at www.theatlantic.com/politics/archive/2019/07/man-who-had-no-lawyer/593470/.

conditions, and health care'.[41] Of these civil legal problems reported, 86 per cent received inadequate or no legal help.[42]

The Legal Services Corporation (LSC), an agency of the US Government, provides some funding for legal aid organisations across the nation, including in rural areas. Organisations funded by the LSC are limited, however, in various ways, including by the restriction that they can provide services only to residents who meet a miserly income threshold, 125 per cent of the federal poverty line.[43] For a family of four, this equals just $32,188 in the 48 contiguous States and the District of Columbia, slightly more in Alaska and Hawai'i.[44] Thus, many who need legal assistance do not qualify for legal aid and must get the help they need elsewhere, such as from a private practice attorney. Alternatively, they must navigate their legal problems with no professional assistance, which has increasingly become the norm.[45]

When LSC-funded organisations are charged with serving rural populations, they face practical, economic and spatial obstacles to doing so. One barrier is the recruitment and retention of attorneys, as already discussed. Another barrier is that the organisations typically use a hub-and-spoke model of service delivery, with lawyers based in a small city hub. Legal aid attorneys thus typically do not live or regularly work 'on the ground' in the spokes, the most rural counties and communities surrounding the regional centre.[46] This spatial challenge prevents legal aid attorneys from being part of the communities they serve, which further undermines the ability of these organisations to meet the needs of rural residents who qualify for their assistance.

## III. The Criminal Justice System

While the phrase 'access to justice' typically refers to the civil justice system, it is important to acknowledge that the rural attorney shortage has significant negative implications for criminal defendants and the State and local government entities responsible for trying them.[47] Since 2013, rural jail populations have climbed

[41] 'The Justice Gap: Measuring the Unmet Civil Legal Needs of Low-Income Americans' (Legal Services Corporation, June 2017) at www.lsc.gov/sites/default/files/images/TheJusticeGap-FullReport.pdf.

[42] ibid.

[43] Income Level for Individuals Eligible for Assistance, 84 Fed Reg 1408, 1408 (Feb 4, 2019) (to be codified at 45 CFR pt 1611).

[44] ibid.

[45] 'The Justice Gap' (n 41); 'Handling Cases Involving Self-Represented Litigants' (Judicial Council of California, 2019) at www.courts.ca.gov/documents/benchguide_self_rep_litigants.pdf.

[46] LR Pruitt, 'The Affordable Care Act in Rural California: A Report on Barriers to Health Care Access and Enrollment in Path2Health, with Proposed Solutions' (2013) UC Davis Legal Research Paper; Legal Services of Northern California, 'How to Contact Us' at www.lsnc.net/how-contact-us.

[47] 'Greening the Desert: Strategies and Innovations to Recruit, Train, and Retain Criminal Law Practitioners for STAR Communities' (Southern Methodist University Deason Criminal Justice

27 per cent, more steeply than in urban areas.[48] Additionally, those in rural jails can expect longer stays than those cited for the same crime in urban areas.[49] The shortage of lawyers is a key factor in these rising rural jail incarceration rates.[50] This is because a person arrested in a rural area can wait for days or even weeks for an attorney to appear before a judge to negotiate the detainee's release.[51] Residency requirements that compel prosecutors or public defenders to live within the county that employs them can aggravate the problem when attorneys are uninterested in residing in a rural place.[52]

When State and local governments cannot employ local lawyers because none are present, or those who are present have conflicts of interest, those government entities incur greater costs because of the rural lawyer shortage. This is partly because of the Government's duty under the US Constitution to provide speedy trials and other aspects of due process, as well as to pay for counsel for indigent defendants. Government entities must therefore pay attorneys to travel from neighbouring jurisdictions, thus increasing the costs that are ultimately born by taxpayers.[53] Indeed, this practical, fiscal concern was a significant consideration for South Dakota when it became the first State to pay lawyers to move to and work in rural areas under the auspices of its Rural Attorney Recruitment Program,[54] which we discuss further in section IV.

# IV. State-Specific Initiatives to Increase Rural Practice

## A. Financial Incentives to Rural Practice

The perception that rural practice may not be fiscally viable deters lawyers from undertaking it. In a 2014 survey of law students at the two law schools in Arkansas, the two most commonly cited disadvantages of rural practice were 'the perception

Reform Center, 2020) at www.smu.edu/-/media/Site/Law/Deason-Center/Publications/STAR-Justice/Greening-the-Desert/Report-Greening-the-Desert-FINAL.pdf.

[48] 'People in Jail in 2019' (Vera Institute of Justice, December 2019) at www.vera.org/publications/people-in-jail-in-2019.

[49] RA Oppel, Jr, '"A Cesspool of a Dungeon": The Surging Population in Rural Jails' *New York Times* (13 December 2019) at www.nytimes.com/2019/12/13/us/rural-jails.html?action=click&module=News&pgtype=Homepage.

[50] P Metzger, 'Rural Justice Systems Low on Pretrial Resources Leave Some to Languish, Die' *USA Today* (13 December 2019) at www.usatoday.com/story/opinion/policing/spotlight/2019/12/13/rural-justice-systems-low-pretrial-resources-leave-some-languish/4415770002/.

[51] ibid.

[52] 'Greening the Desert' (n 47).

[53] A Davies and A Clark, '*Gideon* in the Desert: An Empirical Study of Providing Counsel to Criminal Defendants in Rural Places' (2019) 71(2) *Maine Law Review* 245; LR Pruitt and BA Colgan, 'Justice Deserts: Spatial Inequality and Local Funding of Indigent Defense' (2010) 52(2) *Arizona Law Review* 219, 316.

[54] Pruitt et al (n 5).

of earning a lower income' and 'the perception that rural locations have fewer career and economic opportunities'.[55] It is thus not surprising that a few States have considered offering financial initiatives to get lawyers to 'go rural'. To date, the only success story among these is South Dakota's Rural Attorney Recruitment Program.[56]

Pursuant to that Program, South Dakota began investing in rural communities' justice infrastructure in 2013 by providing stipends to attorneys in exchange for five years of continuous practice in an eligible rural county.[57] Recognising the financial burden associated with legal education, the stipend is $13,288 a year, which represents 90 per cent of the annual tuition at the University of South Dakota School of Law.[58] The Program also has a robust mentorship component; of the 15 initial participants, 10 joined existing law firms, and the five who started solo practices were matched with mentors, sometimes in another county.[59] The wider community provided assistance and networking too: participants were connected with clerks and courts, and at least two counties provided free office space in their courthouse for lawyer participants.[60]

The South Dakota Program was initially limited to 16 participants but has since expanded to accommodate a total of 32 attorneys.[61] As of 2019, the Program had contracted with 24 lawyers.[62] Of those, around half are in rural solo practices, while the other half are working for small law firms or with lawyers who will be retiring soon.[63] Only two attorneys have failed to fulfil their five-year commitment.[64] It is too early to tell whether South Dakota's efforts will produce a long-term net gain of rural lawyers. Among participants who have completed the Program, some have stayed in the rural county while others have moved to metropolitan areas.[65]

While South Dakota was the first State to pay attorneys to engage in rural practice, other States have taken up legislation that would provide some form of financial incentive. In late 2021, North Dakota adopted a Rural Attorney Recruitment Program very similar to that of its neighbour to the south.[66] In

[55] LR Pruitt et al, 'Access to Justice in Rural Arkansas' (Arkansas Access to Justice, March 2015) at www.arkansasjustice.org/wp-content/uploads/2017/04/AATJPolicyBrief2015-0420.pdf. But see Pruitt et al (n 19).

[56] 'Rural Attorney Recruitment Program' (South Dakota Unified Judicial System, 2020) at www.ujs.sd.gov/Attorneys/RuralRecruitment.aspx.

[57] Davis (n 10).

[58] 'Rural Attorney Recruitment Program' (South Dakota Legal Self-Help, 2020) at https://ujslawhelp.sd.gov/rarprogram.aspx or ujslawhelp.sd.gov/rarprogram.aspx.

[59] Pruitt et al (n 5).

[60] ibid.

[61] 'Rural Attorney Recruitment Program' (n 58).

[62] Simpson (n 39).

[63] ibid.

[64] Davis (n 10).

[65] ibid.

[66] North Dakota Century Code, Title 27, Ch 27-02.2; 'Administrative Rule 62 – Rural Attorney Recruitment Program' (State of North Dakota Courts, 2021) at www.ndcourts.gov/legal-resources/rules/ndsupctadminr/62.

addition, the Maine legislature considered, but ultimately rejected, bills that would have provided tax breaks to rural practising attorneys.[67] Legislators in Georgia[68] and Wisconsin[69] have also tried and failed to pass legislation that would assist with tuition reimbursement to lighten the load of law school debt. Similar Loan Repayment Assistance Programs (LRAPs), which are often sponsored by law schools, are discussed in further detail in section IV.E.ii.

## B. Incubators

A legal incubator is typically a one- to two-year programme that provides new attorneys with the knowledge and skills necessary to successfully launch a law practice, anticipating that the lawyers will do so in under-served communities.[70] One of these skills is how to successfully market legal services to clients on low incomes and with modest means, including how to 'unbundle' legal services so that the attorney prepares clients to do some of the work themselves.[71] Incubators thus respond to attorneys' concern about the fiscal viability of rural practice, specifically the fear that too few residents in a sparsely populated, economically depressed area will be able to afford legal assistance. Incubators thus empower lawyers to optimise their chances of success as solo practitioners or in small practices.

While all incubators are different, many underwrite some business costs by offering free legal research software and bar memberships.[72] Ongoing mentorship and support are also typical features of incubators. The first incubator programme was established in New York City in 2002,[73] and the vast majority of the 60 incubators in 32 States, as of mid-2020,[74] are in metropolitan areas.[75] A handful, however, aim to train and support rural lawyers in Arkansas, Iowa, Montana, Nebraska, New Mexico, North Dakota and Vermont.[76] Although most rural incubators are too new to evaluate their success, early reports provide some reason for optimism.

The Arkansas Rural Practice Incubator Project, for example, an 18-month programme housed at the University of Arkansas at Little Rock Bowen School of

[67] Pruitt et al (n 5).

[68] ibid.

[69] Senate Bill 461 (Wisconsin State Legislature, 2019) at https://docs.legis.wisconsin.gov/2019/proposals/sb461; Pruitt et al (n 5).

[70] D Young, 'Musings from an Incubator Director: Do Legal Incubators *Really* Work?' (ABA for Law Students, 3 October 2019) at www.abaforlawstudents.com/2019/10/03/do-legal-incubators-really-work/.

[71] 'Incubator Guide' (California Commission on Access to Justice, October 2014) at www.calbar.ca.gov/Portals/0/documents/accessJustice/2014%20Incubator%20Guide.pdf.

[72] ibid.

[73] 'Lawyer Incubator Directory' (American Bar Association, 2020) at www.americanbar.org/groups/delivery_legal_services/initiatives_awards/program_main/program_directory/.

[74] ibid.

[75] ibid.

[76] ibid; 'Greening the Desert' (n 47).

Law, was founded in 2018 with five participants. Though the programme is based in the State's largest city and State capital, it targets for service the impoverished and rural Mississippi Delta region. Among the first five participants, each has remained involved in rural practice since finishing their term with the incubator. Their practices vary significantly, however, with only one working full time in private practice. In addition to some civil work for clients, the others wear myriad hats, for example running other businesses or serving as a part-time prosecutor. These other roles ease pressure on law practice finances, and may also come with employment benefits that accompany government jobs.

All of the programme's initial participants were from rural areas and came to law school with aspirations to return home. Only one applicant sought to participate in the incubator's second cohort, and two, both from rural areas, applied for the third cohort. Acknowledging the significance of budgetary pressures on these rural entrepreneurs, the incubator recently decreased the cohort size and doubled the one-time stipend for participants from $3,000 to $6,000.

## C. Succession Planning

Other programmes are designed to foster relationships similar to those facilitated by incubators, but the focus is more explicitly on assisting aging rural attorneys to pass their practices on to the next generation. The State Bar of Georgia's Succession Planning Pilot Program, for example, 'connects retiring solo practitioners with new law graduates, facilitating the eventual succession in the management, and potentially ownership, of the practice'.[77] Another programme with similar aims, this one created by the Colorado Attorney Mentoring Program and the Colorado Bar Association's Modern Law Practice Initiative, connects rural lawyers with recent law graduates. Colorado's Rural Virtual Practice Program is incubator-like, with a curriculum focused on developing business strategies. Participants experience rural practice by connecting with their mentor, both virtually and through in-person visits.[78] The relationship allows the mentee to become known in the rural community, while the mentor assesses whether to include the mentee in succession plans.

Iowa founded one of the first such match-making programmes in 2012, when Phil Garland, chair of the Iowa State Bar Association's Rural Practice Committee, began to connect law students with aging solo practitioners and rural firms for summer placements.[79] Garland met his own successor, Carrie Rodriguez, through

[77] Pruitt et al (n 5).

[78] J Karp, 'No Country for Old Lawyers: Rural US Faces A Legal Desert' *Law 360* (27 January 2019) at www.law360.com/articles/1121543/no-country-for-old-lawyers-rural-u-s-faces-a-legal-desert.

[79] S McCammon, 'For Jobs, Some Young Lawyers Are Keepin' It Rural' (National Public Radio, 16 July 2012) at www.npr.org/2012/07/16/156863177/for-jobs-some-young-lawyers-are-keepin-it-rural.

this programme. Critically, Garland decided not to require Rodriguez to buy out his practice; he plans simply to give her his 'book of business' when he retires.[80] Many aging practitioners, however, are unwilling to forgo such compensation when transitioning to retirement, thus leaving in place another fiscal barrier to the young lawyer who might otherwise find rural practice to be viable.

Like the Iowa programme that facilitates summer placements by law students, several summer externship programmes provide opportunities for law students to be immersed in rural life. One University of Nebraska programme brings students to rural areas for 'speed date' interviews with local attorneys;[81] and another, the Rural Practice Initiative, places law students with solo or small rural practitioners for five weeks during the summer.[82] Similar programmes exist in Kansas,[83] Maine,[84] North Dakota, Ohio,[85] Oregon,[86] South Dakota, Vermont[87] and Wisconsin,[88] while Georgia[89] and New Mexico[90] appear to be moving towards them too. Law schools sometimes pay the students a stipend to supplement their compensation from the employer.[91] The Illinois State Bar Association's Rural Practice Institute and the Fellowship Program is the newest addition to this list.[92] The Program seeks to use clearinghouses to pair both law students and recent graduates with established rural lawyers.[93] Program participants receive a $5,000 relocation and expense stipend, and young attorneys receive an additional $5,000 upon the completion of their first year as a rural practitioner. National programmes also exist, including Equal Justice Works and Legal Services Corporation's Rural Summer Legal Corps, which supports 35 law students in rural summer externships each year.[94]

[80] Karp (n 78).

[81] Laird (n 26).

[82] HA Wandler, 'Spreading Justice to Rural Montana: Rurality's Impacts on Supply and Demand for Legal Services in Montana' (2015) 76(2) *Montana Law Review* 225.

[83] 'Greening the Desert' (n 47); Washburn University School of Law, 'Rural Law', at www.washburnlaw.edu/practicalexperience/rural/index.html.

[84] Pruitt et al (n 5); L Woodbury, 'Tackling the Rural Law Crisis' *Maine Law Magazine* (Winter 2018–19) at https://mainelaw.maine.edu/wp-content/uploads/sites/1/rural-law-magazine.pdf.

[85] 'Greening the Desert' (n 47).

[86] 'Courts Need to Enhance Access to Justice in Rural America' (Conference of State Court Administrators, 2018) at https://.cosca.ncsc.org/__data/assets/pdf_file/0026/23399/policy-paper-1-28-2019.pdf.

[87] NK Gallagher, 'Maine School Moves to Reverse Shortage of Rural Lawyers' *Portland Press Herald* (22 October 2017) at www.pressherald.com/2017/10/22/maine-school-moves-to-reverse-shortage-of-rural-lawyers/#.

[88] Wandler (n 82).

[89] Pruitt et al (n 5).

[90] CA Clark, 'State Supreme Court Endorses Proposals to Help New Mexicans Obtain Civil Legal Services' *Los Alamos Daily Post* (26 January 2020) at www.ladailypost.com/state-supreme-court-endorses-proposals-to-help-new-mexicans-obtain-civil-legal-services/.

[91] Wandler (n 82).

[92] E Finkel, 'ISBA's Rural Practice Initiative Encourages Law Students, Recent Graduates to Settle Down in a Small Town' *Illinois Bar Journal* (February 2021) at www.isba.org/ibj/2021/02/smalltownlaw.

[93] DR Thies and LJ Wood, 'ISBA Launches Rural Practice Fellowship Program as a Component of Rural Practice Institute' (Illinois State Bar Association, January 2021) at www.isba.org/committees/lawrelatededucation/newsletter/2021/01/isbalaunchesruralpracticefellowship.

[94] 'Rural Summer Legal Corps' at www.equaljusticeworks.org/law-students/part-time-summer/rural-summer-legal-corps/.

These programmes have been successful in placing law students in rural areas after graduation, at least for the short term. The Rural Justice Program, a funded summer programme in North Dakota, reports that 'at least eight of the couple dozen scholarship recipients since 2015 who have graduated, including those who received support for rural placements, are working in rural parts of the state'.[95] Half of the summer externs from the first year of South Dakota's Program committed to the Rural Attorney Recruitment Program,[96] and at least one student from Maine's Program accepted a post-graduation position with a rural firm.[97] While private firm placement is the primary focus of these programmes, the State Bar Association of North Dakota facilitates rural exposure by funding law student externships with rural judges.[98] We return to a further discussion of the role of law schools in alleviating the rural attorney shortage in section IV.E.

## D. Channelling Urban Resources to Rural Areas

When too few attorneys live in a rural area to meet the needs of residents, justice-system stakeholders have sometimes responded with technology-based interventions. Telephonic and videoconferencing technologies have allowed rural residents to connect with attorneys outside of their community, though rural broadband deficits continue to undermine these efforts. As the Covid-19 pandemic has driven both courts and attorneys to invest in technology, the post-pandemic landscape may see more remote work by urban lawyers for rural clients.

The Arizona State Bar, for example, has a client-matching service that functions independently of the client's location.[99] These sorts of interactions may be better suited to some needs than to others. A Canadian study found 'that the geographic reach of lawyers is not … strictly confined to their immediate locale but instead extends over different ranges of geographic space, depending on the service being delivered and the characteristics of lawyers and their clients'.[100] In other words, for some types of routine legal work, it is more important to have a local lawyer. For more specialised work, it is reasonable to expect the work to be done by specialists typically found in metropolitan areas, and technology is critical to facilitating that representation.

The Covid-19 pandemic has created incentives for attorneys, courts and other justice-system stakeholders to make massive investments in technology. Those investments may prove critical to better serving rural clients whose spatial isolation creates material barriers to their access to justice. On the other hand,

[95] Simpson (n 39).

[96] Pruitt et al (n 5).

[97] Woodbury (n 84).

[98] Laird (n 26).

[99] 'Courts Need to Enhance Access to Justice in Rural America' (n 86).

[100] J Baxter and A Yoon, 'No Lawyer for a Hundred Miles?: Mapping the New Geography of Access of Justice in Canada' (2015) 52(1) *Osgoode Hall Law Journal* 9, 48.

the rural-urban justice gap may be aggravated rather than ameliorated if courts continue to use 'virtual' appearances and other tech-facilitated interactions even after the pandemic ends. This is because the lack of reliable broadband will effectively deny access to many rural residents, even as technology facilitates easier access for others.[101]

Further, while it is tempting to expect technology to alleviate legal deserts and related rural A2J challenges, technology should not be treated as a panacea to solve either.[102] Having lawyers residing and working in rural areas, functioning as integral parts of the community, should remain the goal. Nevertheless, temporarily mobilising lawyers to work in rural communities – either via technology or in person – can be part of the solution, and a few good models exist. The Bay Area Rural Justice Collaborative is a group of legal services non-profits and law firms that bring free legal clinics to exurban and isolated communities on the far periphery of the San Francisco metropolitan area.[103] The Government Law Center at Albany Law School formed the Rural Law Initiative, which provides legal assistance to small businesses and start-ups in rural upstate New York.[104] Another way to channel the surfeit of urban legal capital to rural legal deserts is to create incentives for urban lawyers to provide pro bono assistance there. Ohio[105] and Tennessee[106] are two States that do so by awarding continuing legal education (CLE) credit for such work.

We have already discussed the strategy of getting law students into rural communities for the purposes of rural practitioners' succession planning, but even shorter forays by law students and lawyers into rural areas can yield significant impact. California,[107] Nebraska,[108] New York,[109] South Carolina[110] and Wisconsin[111] all have programmes that bus attorneys and law students into rural areas for pro bono clinics. These trips provide brief opportunities to engage with and experience rural life. So-called alternative spring breaks to rural areas similarly give students a brief but meaningful glimpse of rural communities, while also helping meet those communities' legal needs.[112] The Greater Wisconsin Initiative

[101] D Newman, J Mant and F Gordon, 'Vulnerability, Legal Need and Technology in England and Wales' (2021) 21(3) *International Journal of Discrimination and the Law* 230.

[102] Statz et al (n 18).

[103] 'Rural Justice Initiative' at www.onejustice.org/probonojustice/rural-justice-initiative/.

[104] T Perlman, 'The Rural Law Initiative' (Albany Law School Government Law Center, 16 April 2019) at www.albanylaw.edu/community-impact/news/government-law-centers-rural-law-initiative-releases-first-its-kind-new.

[105] 'Courts Need to Enhance Access to Justice in Rural America' (n 86).

[106] JE Cabral et al, 'Using Technology to Enhance Access to Justice' (2012) 26(1) *Harvard Journal of Law & Technology* 241.

[107] Pruitt et al (n 5); 'Rural Justice Initiative' (n 103).

[108] Laird (n 26).

[109] ibid.

[110] M Fitts, 'Rolling Office Will Help USC Bring Legal Services to SC's Remote Areas' *The Post and Courier* (21 October 2019) at www.postandcourier.com/columbia/rolling-office-will-help-usc-bring-legal-services-to-scs-remote-areas/article_3c008da4-f11e-11e9-8817-bfbf737b325a.html.

[111] Pruitt et al (n 5).

[112] 'Courts Need to Enhance Access to Justice in Rural America' (n 86); Pruitt et al (n 5).

Bus Tour programme has been particularly successful, with one-third of participants subsequently securing legal positions in non-urban parts of the State.[113] Many of these initiatives are joint efforts among law schools,[114] bar associations[115] and non-profits,[116] a fact that underscores the value of building coalitions among stakeholders with the shared goal of ameliorating the rural lawyer shortage and associated rural justice challenges.

## E. Expanding the Pipeline to Rural Practice

Beyond these programmes that provide exposure to rural practice as a means to increase the pool of candidates interested in it, other programmes look deeper into the prospective rural attorney pipeline, to college (undergraduate) and even high school students. In this section, we discuss some of these programmes, with special attention paid to initiatives within legal education.

### *i. The Role of Legal Education*

As already suggested by the discussion of rural opportunities for law students, co-curricular activities in law school, particularly experiential opportunities such as clinics, externships and internships, can play important roles in exposing students to rural career trajectories and rural clients. Penn State, for example, has a Rural Economic Development Clinic that focuses primarily on serving agricultural, food and energy clients on business matters.[117] Stanford Law School's Organizations and Transactions Clinic performs similar work in the greater San Francisco Bay Area. The University of Minnesota Law School's Rural Immigrant Access Clinic assists non-citizens in rural areas.[118] Other programmes may offer interactions with rural inhabitants and the issues facing them and their communities, including UC Irvine's Community and Economic Development Clinic and the UC Davis Law School's Tribal Justice Project and Water Justice Clinic.[119]

Student groups that promote rural practice have been formed at a handful of law schools. The University of Arkansas Little Rock Bowen School of Law and Maine Law are the first in the nation to form chapters of the Finch Society, an organisation through which students can connect with rural and small-town

[113] Karp (n 78).
[114] Pruitt et al (n 5).
[115] Laird (n 26); Pruitt et al (n 5).
[116] Perlman (n 104).
[117] 'Rural Economic Development Clinic' at www.pennstatelaw.psu.edu/practice-skills/clinics/rural-economic-development-clinic.
[118] F Mina, 'Law School Opens Clinic for Rural Immigrants' *The Minnesota Daily* (11 February 2019) at https://mndaily.com/233777/news/aclinic/.
[119] Pruitt et al (n 5).

practitioners and learn about rural practice.[120] These organisations also advocate for the interests of rural attorneys. Maine Law's Finch Society, for example, drafted the bill that proposed tax credits for rural practising attorneys.[121]

While this survey of rural and rural-adjacent programmes shows some promise, law schools could do more to draw attention to rural issues and validate rural practice. While many schools sporadically offer food and agricultural law courses, only a few schools, such as UC Davis School of Law,[122] the University of South Carolina, University of Michigan Law[123] and Harvard,[124] have classes dedicated to rural justice systems and issues.[125] Validation can also come in other forms, such as featuring alumni doing rural work in monthly news updates and alumni profiles, and inviting them back to campus to share their experiences with students.

Beyond including rural issues in the curriculum, law schools can bring flexibility and creativity to the delivery of legal education.[126] Notably, the Covid-19 pandemic potentially catalysed a new era of legal education as law schools were compelled to grapple with the transition to online education. This forced experiment with remote learning may lead the legal academy to be more open to such enterprises in the future. Indeed, even before Covid-19 struck, a handful of law schools offered combined on-campus/online programs to deliver legal education to rural residents who otherwise might be deterred from undertaking legal studies because of the time, expense and other opportunity costs associated with moving to a law school.[127] Until it was shuttered during the pandemic, Seattle University had a unique program that allowed its students to attend their third year of law school in Alaska, the only State without a law school.[128] Among the 170 students who have participated in that program over the years, 60 per cent returned to Alaska to work.[129]

### ii. *After Law School*

The law student debt crisis – primarily a function of steep rises in law school tuition over the past two decades – undoubtedly contributes to the rural lawyer shortage.

[120] ibid.

[121] ibid.

[122] Pruitt et al (n 5).

[123] E Prifogle, 'Law in Rural America Seminar' at www.emilyprifogle.com/law-in-rural-america.html.

[124] 'Harvard Law School Course Catalog' at https://helios.law.harvard.edu/CourseCatalogs/hls-course-catalog-2019-2020.pdf.

[125] 'California's Attorney Deserts: Access to Justice Implications of the Rural Lawyer Shortage' (California Commission on Access to Justice, July 2019) at www.calbar.ca.gov/Portals/0/documents/accessJustice/Attorney-Desert-Policy-Brief.pdf.

[126] Pruitt et al (n 5).

[127] 'The ABA-Approved Online Hybrid JD Program from the University of Dayton' at https://onlinelaw.udayton.edu/online-jd/; 'Blended Learning at Mitchell Hamline Law', https://mitchellhamline.edu/academics/j-d-enrollment-options/blended-learning-at-mitchell-hamline/.

[128] 'What's the Latest on the School of Law's Plan to Open a Satellite Campus in Alaska' *The Newsroom* (14 July 2014) at www.seattleu.edu/newsroom/stories/archive/whats-the-latest-on-the-school-of-laws-plan-to-open-a-satellite-campus-in-alaska.html.

[129] ibid.

In 2018, the average law school graduate had about $145,000 in student debt.[130] For graduates of some schools, the average is currently closer to $200,000.[131] With the exception of the University of California at Berkeley, annual tuition at every law school ranked in the top 10 by *US News and World Report* was more than $60,000, with Columbia University the highest at $76,088.[132] Indeed, the schools with the greatest average student debt are three of these top 10 schools, debt that may be compounded by the higher costs of living in the cities where the top-ranked law schools typically are located.

Student debt trends aggravate concerns about the financial viability of rural practice, but loan repayment programmes can alleviate financial concerns and reduce barriers for new lawyers. Traditional Loan Repayment Assistance Programs (LRAPs) forgive student debt if the attorney commits to a certain period of qualifying work, typically public interest work or employment in the public sector, depending on the programme. Excluded from 'qualifying work' as defined by most programmes is private sector work, including that in a rural area.[133]

Law schools frequently have their own LRAPs, but only a handful apply to rural private practice. Among them, Yale Law School's programme is income-based, regardless of whether the job is in the public or private sector.[134] Stanford Law School's LRAP will also cover private or solo work, but only if 'at least fifty percent involves providing legal services on a pro bono, reduced, or court-awarded fee basis'.[135] Harvard Law School's programme covers some private firm opportunities 'outside of major cities'.[136] Only the University of Michigan Law School's loan forgiveness programme explicitly references rural practice.[137] Michigan Law explains that it wishes to encourage students to pursue the job of their choice, including 'working for a small law firm in a lightly populated area'.[138]

Since 2015, the State of Nebraska has funded an LRAP for those who agree to practise for at least three years in 'public legal service' or in a 'designated legal professional shortage area'. Kansas will similarly make loan payments of $15,000

[130] 'Trends in Graduate Student Loan Debt' (National Center for Education Statistics Blog, 2 August 2018) at www.nces.ed.gov/blogs/nces/post/trends-in-graduate-student-loan-debt.

[131] 'Law Schools Where Graduates Have the Most Debt' *US News and World Report* (2022) at www.usnews.com/best-graduate-schools/top-law-schools/grad-debt-rankings?_sort=indebt-desc debt.

[132] '2023 Best Law Schools' *US News and World Report* (2022) at www.usnews.com/best-graduate-schools/top-law-schools/law-rankings.

[133] H Haksgaard, 'Rural Practice as Public Interest Work' (2019) 71(2) *Maine Law Review* 209, 210 (arguing that federal loan forgiveness programmes should be expanded to cover rural lawyers because '[r]ural lawyers provide public interest lawyering through pro bono cases, mixed practices, community service, and even through providing fee-paid services in rural communities').

[134] ibid.

[135] 'Miles and Nancy Rubin Loan Repayment Assistance Program' (Stanford Law School, October 2017) at www.law.stanford.edu/wp-content/uploads/2015/03/LRAP-2018-Program-Terms-1.pdf.

[136] Haksgaard (n 133).

[137] 'Income Based Debt Management FAQs' https://michigan.law.umich.edu/resource-center/income-based-debt-management-faqs.

[138] ibid.

over five years to professionals, including attorneys, who live and provide services in a designated 'Rural Opportunity Zone', which encompasses dozens of the State's counties.[139] Loan forgiveness programmes for rural lawyers have been considered, but not funded, in several other States, including North Dakota,[140] Wisconsin,[141] New York[142] and Georgia.[143]

### *iii. Before Law School*

While studies have shown that law students who grew up in rural areas are more willing to consider rural practice post-graduation,[144] only one initiative addresses the pipeline to rural practice by seeking to tap the nascent human capital within rural communities. Nebraska's Rural Law Opportunities Program (RLOP) helps rural students make it to and through college and law school, with the expectation that they will return to rural places to practise.[145] Beginning in 2016, three regional public universities in Nebraska began recruiting youth from the State's rural reaches to pursue legal careers. Each year since, five high school students have been awarded free college tuition to a regional university. If they maintain a 3.5 GPA and otherwise meet requirements, the students are guaranteed admission to the University of Nebraska College of Law.[146]

The RLOP seeks to emulate a similar programme at the University of Nebraska Medical School, which boasts a rural return rate of 60 per cent. Before the RLOP, 17-20 graduates (about 15 per cent) of the University of Nebraska College of Law gained employment in rural areas each year. The law school is aiming to channel an additional 10 students per year into rural careers,[147] a goal driven by fact that 11 per cent of Nebraska counties have no lawyers.[148]

So far, 91 students have participated in the RLOP programmes at the three regional universities, and three of those students have gone on to graduate from law school at the University of Nebraska, the first in 2021 and two others in 2022.

[139] 'Rural Opportunity Zones', Kansas Department of Commerce at www.kansascommerce.gov/program/taxes-and-financing/rural-opportunity-zones-roz/.

[140] Pruitt et al (n 5).

[141] Senate Bill 461 (n 69).

[142] *Report and Recommendations of the Task Force on Rural Justice* (New York State Bar Association's Task Force on Rural Justice, April 2020) at www.nysba.org/app/uploads/2020/03/Report-and-Recommendations-of-the-Task-Force-on-Rural-Justice-as-of-3.18.2020.pdf.

[143] Pruitt et al (n 5).

[144] Pruitt et al (n 19); Pruitt et al (n 5).

[145] L Reed, 'Nebraska Law Tackles State's Rural Legal Needs' *Nebraska Today* (26 October 2016) at https://news.unl.edu/newsrooms/today/article/nebraska-law-tackles-states-rural-legal-needs/.

[146] Simpson (n 39).

[147] N Hytrek, 'New Program Encourages Lawyer Practice in Rural Nebraska' *Sioux City Journal* (18 September 2020) at www.siouxcityjournal.com/news/local/new-program-encourages-lawyers-to-practice-in-rural-nebraska/article_ca1df9d7-3a9c-5057-828d-8af4e2d9b594.html.

[148] Davis (n 10); C Chavis, 'The Past, Present, and Future of Rural Northern New England: A Study of the Demographics Crisis and How It Affects the Rural Lawyer Shortage' (2019) 71(2) *Maine Law Review* 273.

To date, none of the three law graduates is practising in a rural place. The programme appears to be picking up steam and is approaching its goal of 15 new law students each year. As of the fall of 2022, 14 are enrolled in the University of Nebraska College of Law.[149]

## V. Conclusion

In spite of increasing attention to the rural lawyer shortage and associated A2J challenges over the last decade, few rural communities and their residents have reason to expect that their justice system landscape is likely to improve soon. Only a handful of States have been willing to spend money to alleviate a problem that has been a predictable consequence of the past century's rural depopulation trend. South Dakota put its money where its mouth is nearly a decade ago, and its early investments are paying dividends for a number of rural communities. Nebraska, its neighbour to the south, has directed investments more toward the pipeline to the profession, and the outcome of those front-end investments is not yet clear.

Most States' responses have been much less bold. Some programmes tinker around the edges with incentives that may entice a few lawyers to a few rural communities. Others facilitate the diversion of urban legal services, which are plentiful, to rural clients and needs. The latter may be accomplished by increasingly high-tech digital means or by the decidedly low-tech means of bus trips – literally transporting lawyers and law students into rural areas to staff short-term legal clinics. A few State bars have invested in succession planning for aging lawyers, sometimes with law school collaborators. Attorney incubators play a similar role in the relatively few rural places they serve. These, along with other efforts within legal education, aim to give lawyers and law students short-term exposure to rural practice. At best, though, these efforts constitute a mere patchwork that leaves the vast majority of rural communities under-served and some entirely unserved.

One reason for the relative lack of significant action and expenditure to ameliorate rural attorney deserts may be the desire to back only evidence-based solutions. Such solutions cannot be identified, however, without complete and nuanced data, which are still largely lacking. We know where attorney deserts are as of 2019, thanks to the ABA's recent work, but we do not know, for example, how severe the problem associated with an aging profession is in any given State or region. We also do not know what impact Covid-19 has had on rural practitioners. Some have presumably been driven out of business during the economic interruptions associated with the pandemic, while others have probably chosen not to make the investments in technology that became necessary to liaise with clients and courts. Thus, a census and mapping of the profession that updates the ABA's 2020 'Profile of the Legal Profession' will be needed sooner rather than later. That census would

[149] Email from Anthony B Schutz, Director, Rural Law Opportunities Program, University of Nebraska College of Law, 16 October 2022, to Lisa R Pruitt.

ideally track not only age, but also the type of substantive work each attorney does, such as estate planning, family law and criminal law. It would also note whether the attorney is available to accept clients or is, instead, in a role such as prosecutor, judge or in-house counsel that precludes such representation.

We also do not have a good sense of the economics or substantive composition of the typical rural practice – if there is such a thing as 'typical'. Do rural lawyers tend to do a mix of civil and criminal work? How many work part time for a government entity, for example as prosecutor, public defender or judge? What proportion of the income of a typical rural practice comes from court-appointed work?[150] Answers to these questions and others could inform policy interventions. It is thus incumbent on the ABA and other high-level stakeholders, along with scholars, to investigate these issues and continue to develop a clearer picture of the economics of rural practice.

With more information about rural lawyers' practices, including that regarding sources of income in rural communities, stakeholders can better develop initiatives most likely to draw lawyers to rural areas and to help them succeed once there.[151] Policymakers should also continue to evaluate the impact of existing initiatives, including the broader economic impacts of having more lawyers in previously under-served rural communities. Complementary private sector initiatives, such as lower-cost malpractice insurance for solo practitioners earning below a certain income cap, could also help.

Metro-based policymakers will be setting themselves up for failure, however, if they do not also address the gaps in their understanding of rural A2J challenges and how these are experienced on the ground.[152] As the authors of a recent article parsing the difference between 'access' to rural courts on the one hand and to 'justice', on the other, commented, well-funded efforts will likely not succeed if metro-based advocates 'fail to incorporate the lived expertise of pro se litigants, meaningfully acknowledge rural individuals' unique and complex socio-spatial needs, or focus on experiences of justice as much as they do access'.[153]

The rural attorney shortage will not be alleviated without collaboration among a range of institutions, including the judiciary, State bars, legislatures and legal educators (which is a theme that will be returned to in chapter 11 of this book). Other sectors can also be part of the solution, as we have seen in South Dakota, where a wide range of community stakeholders got in on the action of ensuring that new rural attorneys succeed. Further, stakeholders across the nation should remember that there is likely not a 'one size fits all' solution for the rural lawyer shortage. Rather, the most successful interventions will be tailored to meet the needs of individual States and the under-served areas within them.

[150] H Haksgaard, 'Court-Appointment Compensation and Rural Access to Justice' (2020) 14(1) *University of St Thomas Journal of Law and Public Policy* 88.

[151] 'California's Attorney Deserts' (n 125).

[152] Statz et al (n 18) 335.

[153] ibid.

# 3

# Alcohol Laws, Rural Communities and Access to Justice in Kenya

JOSEPH K RONO AND EMMANUEL K BUNEI

## I. Introduction

Alcohol use and abuse remain two of the most recent global problems increasingly being regulated because of their negative social, economic and health implications. In Kenya, many attempts have been made to regulate alcohol use and abuse.[1] Some of the Acts of Parliament that have been introduced in the country include the Chang'aa[2] Prohibition Act 1970, the Alcohol Drinks Control Act 2010 and the Chang'aa Acts of 2013 and 2021. Generally, these statutes have sought to regulate trading and drinking hours, altering how, where and when traditional alcohol can be brewed and sold, among other controls. For example, the Alcohol Drinks Control Act 2010 was enacted to regulate how, where and when alcohol may be consumed.

Though these laws are today beginning to yield positive results after their enactment more than 10 years ago, Kenya still continues to witness cases of unemployment, delayed and unstable marriages, injuries, sickness, and even death and other risks related to the use and abuse of alcohol (both legal and illegal).[3] There have also been varying impacts on the lives and livelihoods of rural and urban communities, which is reflected in the prevalence of data and the trends of alcohol consumption and abuse set out in this chapter. For example, alcohol abuse has been found to be most prevalent in remote rural areas and poorer urban neighbourhoods, where people are facing weighty economic and financial difficulties, which lead to their use and abuse of alcohol to cope with their problems.

[1] Changáa Prohibition Act 1980 (Kenya); Alcoholic Control Act 2010 (Kenya); National Alcohol and Drug Abuse Policy 2018 (Kenya) at https://nacada.go.ke/sites/default/files/2019-10/The%20National%20Alcohol%20and%20Drug%20Abuse%20Policy-%20September%202018_0.pdf (accessed 24 January 2021).

[2] *Changaa* or *chang'aa* is a spirit-like clear drink with a high alcohol content, made by fermenting a mixture of corn/sorghum/millet and sugar for distillation.

[3] RS Mkuu et al, 'Unrecorded alcohol in East Africa: A case study of Kenya' (2019) 63 *International Journal of Drug Policy* 12, doi.org/10.1016/j.drugpo.2018.07.017.

Indeed, the sale and consumption of illegal alcohol have increased as rogue traders seek to exploit consumers, especially in rural and poor urban areas where consumers are unable to afford expensive legal alcohol. Thus, abuse of alcohol in Kenya is disturbingly high and linked to a variety of serious consequences. Yet legal regulation of alcohol in Kenya has encountered cultural, administrative and law enforcement resistance, which has been more visible in rural areas.[4] Overall, this has brought to the fore the need to better understand the lived experiences of rural communities and their access to justice prior to and after legal regulation of alcohol use and abuse.[5]

The chapter is structured as follows. Section II discusses Kenya's criminalisation of alcoholism, while section III is devoted to an overview of alcoholism. Section IV looks at the cultural support for alcohol use in Kenya. The prevalence and present trajectory of alcoholism are discussed in section V. The discussion then moves on in section VI to the cultural ramifications of the outlawing of alcohol use in Kenya. Section VII provides concluding remarks, emphasising that developing countries like Kenya should be more innovative in the ways they make laws and policies touching on cultures and traditions, especially in rural settings. The chapter strongly advocates the employment of diverse methodologies, such as supporting rural populations to obey the law through capacity building and providing alternatives to criminalised cultural practices. Because alcohol use has long been a component of rural communities' social life and practices, criminalising it must be done with caution to prevent illegal, silent and clandestine consumption.

## II. Criminalisation of Alcoholism in Kenya

Traditionally, most societies in Africa – and Kenya specifically – had their means of regulating alcohol production and consumption to curb social harm.[6] For example, alcohol consumption was strictly restricted to adult males and only a certain amount of alcohol was to be consumed, abusers being publicly condemned. Accordingly, consumption of alcoholic brews was limited to their use in connection with socio-cultural practices and beliefs.[7] However, during the colonial period, the traditional way of drinking became entangled with European culture and modern lifestyles. The Eurocentric perspective, in particular, changed the purpose and manner of using alcohol. Early successful African elites followed

[4] EH Kipchumba, 'Challenges Facing the Implementation of Kenya's Alcoholic Drinks Control Act 2010' (2019) 1 *African Journal of Alcohol and Drug Abuse* 23 at www.nacada.go.ke/sites/default/files/AJADA/AJADA%201%20ammended/JP4.%20AJADA%20Volume%20I%20-%20Challenges%20Facing%20The%20Implementation%20Of%20Kenya%E2%80%99s.pdf (accessed 24 January 2021).

[5] National Alcohol and Drug Abuse Policy 2018 (Kenya) (n 1).

[6] Kipchumba (n 4).

[7] JS Mbiti, *African Religions and Philosophy* (Heinemann, 1990); JWE Muregi, 'Combating Illicit Brews in Kenya: An analysis of the legal and institutional frame' (Honours thesis, Strathmore University, 2017).

western culture, norms and values, including which types of alcohol to drink, how much, when and with whom. As a result, drinking among African elites came to be associated more with modernity and, in particular, the modern lifestyles and habits of the colonial masters.

The legal regulation of alcohol in Kenya can be traced back to the early years of the colonial period around 1900. To ensure an adequate labour supply and protect the African native populations from harm, the colonial Government legally regulated alcohol production, distribution and consumption for both local traditional alcoholic brews and imported alcohol.[8] In the Kenya colony, the Traditional Liquor Act was passed to control local community alcoholic brews by curbing their production, consumption and sale.[9] In 1902, the Village Headmen Ordinance was enacted to control native alcohol.[10] Consequently, restrictions were placed on the production of all traditional brews in the country, except for use in ceremonial functions. However, during the state of emergency in 1952, this exception was temporarily withdrawn. As a result, people brewed and consumed alcohol clandestinely.

After Kenya's independence, the colonial laws were adopted and remained in force until 1971, when the Traditional Liquor Licensing Act was announced. However, the Act failed to control traditional brews and adulteration of liquor, especially by methanol, which by 1980 had spread throughout the country.[11] As a result, in 1980, the Chang'aa Prohibition Act was passed to combat the harmful effects of traditional illicit brews.[12] Again, brewing and drinking, specifically of *Chang'aa*, went underground, and adulteration of alcohol accelerated and became more entrenched. Nevertheless, the Act was operational until 2010 when the current alcohol control policy, the Alcoholic Drinks Control Act, was introduced (otherwise known as the 'Mututho laws' after the member of parliament who introduced the bill). The Act was passed to repeal the Chang'aa Prohibition Act of 1980.[13]

The Alcoholic Drinks Control Act 2010 was introduced by the Government as a legal framework to counter all hitherto unresolved problems relating to the regulation of alcohol promotions, and the licensing and provision of treatment to and rehabilitation of addicts.[14] So far, there have been major challenges to the statute's implementation.[15] They include greater alcohol adulteration, corruption

[8] Kipchumba (n 4).
[9] Traditional Liquor Act 1971 (Kenya).
[10] Village Headmen Ordinance 1902 (East Africa).
[11] Kipchumba (n 4).
[12] R Jenkins et al, 'Alcohol consumption and hazardous drinking in western Kenya: A household survey in a health and demographic surveillance site' (2015) 15 *BMC Psychiatry* 230, doi.org/10.1186/s12888-015-0603-x.
[13] J Mututho, 'Alcohol in Kenya: Historical background' (2014) 68th World Congress of IOGT International at Cha Am, Thailand, at www. iogt.org/wp-content/uploads/2014; R Takahashi et al, 'Correlates of alcohol consumption in rural western Kenya: A cross-sectional study' (2017) 17 *BMC Psychiatry* 175, doi.org/10.1186/s12888-017-1344-9.
[14] Kipchumba (n 4).
[15] ibid.

in the promotion and distribution of alcohol, trading in counterfeit alcohol brands and the widespread consumption of illegal brews. Others problems include the lack of political will and inadequate human resources to formulate and implement effective alcohol laws, respectively. As a result, the number of actual arrests, prosecutions and sentences for alcohol offences has been limited. Despite the presence of the legislation in Kenya, the problems linked to alcohol abuse are still widespread and the illegal alcohol trade is thriving, with greater proliferation of counterfeit alcoholic brands and liquor outlets operating without proper licences.[16]

In 2010, the Government of Kenya promulgated a new Constitution, which created two tiers of government, one at the national level and the other at the level of the 47 counties. The two levels of government were allocated distinct functions. Among the many service functions that were devolved to the newly established administrative units were liquor licensing and drug control, under the National Drug Control Authority (NACADA). Prior to 2010, this function was coordinated by liquor licensing courts whose main role was limited to liquor licensing. In 2010, the enactment of the Alcoholic Drinks Control Act allowed NACADA to coordinate all components related to alcohol control. Yet other critical components, such as the provision of regulations to cover the promotion and advertising of alcohol, treatment and rehabilitation services and quality control were barely addressed in the Act.[17] Moreover, the laws aimed at controlling the production, sale and consumption of alcoholic beverages unsuccessfully regulated the industry since they focused on trivial details, applying exorbitant punitive fines that were beyond the means of most brewers.

In 2013, while NACADA was still assisting county governments in building their capacities in preparation for taking up the liquor licensing function, the national Government suddenly transferred all the liquor functions to the county governments due to political pressure from them. As a result, a model county alcoholic drinks control bill, which NACADA was developing, was swiftly adopted in each of the 47 county assemblies before the bill was adequately completed. Given the county governments' lack of an essential legal framework and the capacity to effectively take over this function, coordination of liquor licensing across the counties proved chaotic. Due to this disjunction, an upsurge in alcohol outlets in most rural counties of the country emerged, most of the outlets generally flouting key provisions relating to alcohol control, including the extensive selling of adulterated alcohol outside of retail hours, even to minors.[18]

Accordingly, the devolution of alcohol control functions to county governments became disorganised and resulted in unintended consequences.[19] In fact, in the transitional period, 98 Kenyans were hospitalised and over 100 died as a result of consuming alcohol adulterated with methanol. By May 2014, the effect of consumption of adulterated alcohol on morbidity and mortality rates in various

[16] Kipchumba (n 4); Muregi (n 7); Takahashi et al (n 13).

[17] NACADA, *Alcohol Control and Devolution in Kenya* (2015) at www.movendi.ngo/blog/2015/08/25/alcohol-control-and-devolution-3-lessons-from-kenyas-experience/ (accessed 24 January 2021).

[18] ibid.

[19] ibid.

parts of the country was disastrous. For example, in a period of only six days in May 2014, a total of 493 deaths linked to alcohol were reported in the 13 rural counties of Embu, Kiambu, Makueni, Kitui, Nakuru, Murang'a, Nyeri, Nyandarua, Kirinyaga, Machakos, Trans-Zoia, Uasin Gishu and Kajiado.[20]

The Government's legalisation of *chang'aa* in 2010 was intended to take away the business of home-brewing from establishments where toxic chemicals were added to the brew to make it more potent.[21] Under the Alcoholic Control Act 2010, *chang'aa* was to be manufactured, distributed and sold in glass bottles, and retailers were to display health warning signs.[22] In addition, sales through automatic vending machines and to individuals under the age of 18 were prohibited. Moreover, the Act stipulated that anyone making or selling adulterated *chang'aa* risked penalties of 5 million shillings or five years in jail, or both.[23] Yet most traditional brews, especially *chang'aa*, are considered legal only if producers possess official licences to brew them.[24] Instead of focusing on the quality of *chang'aa*, the Alcoholic Control Act 2010 emphasised the licensing of its production and trading.

While some progressive alcohol control laws have reduced Kenya's alcohol consumption from 17 litres per capita per year before 2010 to 3.4 litres per capita at the present time, unfortunately, some home brews barely meet the required standards stipulated in the law, which are vital for consumers.[25] Furthermore, illegal and unscrupulous traditional and capitalist brewers compromise their values and the law to adulterate alcohol products to make them more intoxicating, which is more appealing to customers. Moreover, in rural areas, control of traditional brews, especially *Busaa*,[26] has largely been left in the hands of local chiefs and administration police, some of whom accept bribes from local brewers to compromise quality standards while generating more income. Therefore, illegal alcohol and brews continue to be a major source of income for some poorer households in rural areas because they are less expensive but stronger.[27] Despite the progressive laws on alcohol control in Kenya, illegal alcohol, particularly *chang'aa* and *busaa*, continues to be popular in most rural regions.

## III. An Overview of Alcoholism

Globally, the growing burden of disorders associated with the use of substances cannot be overemphasised.[28] In 2015, about a quarter of a billion people used

[20] ibid.
[21] National Alcohol and Drug Abuse Policy 2018 (Kenya) (n 1).
[22] Alcoholic Control Act 2010 (Kenya) (n 1).
[23] ibid.
[24] ibid.
[25] 'Kenya: Home delivery fuels alcohol harm' *Movendi International* (6 May 2020) at www.movendi.ngo/news/2020/05/06/kenya-home-delivery-fuels-alcohol-harm/ (accessed 11 January 2021).
[26] *Busaa* is a malt liquor made by fermenting corn flour and sorghum/millet.
[27] Kipchumba (n 4).
[28] Takahashi et al (n 13).

drugs at least once.[29] Even more worrying is the fact that about 29.5 million of those drug users suffer from drug use disorders, experience drug dependence and require treatment. This includes taking the substance in larger amounts for longer than is meant, and finding it difficult to reduce or stop its use. Other drawbacks include spending a lot of time sourcing, using or recovering from use of substances. Yet often users give up important social, occupational or recreational activities for substance use.[30] Together, these factors tend to increase the development of withdrawal symptoms, which can often be relieved only by taking more substances.[31] Worse still, disorders associated with combining alcohol and other drugs paint a more dramatic picture that requires urgent alcohol treatment programmes and investment in human resources to deal with addictions.[32]

Certainly, alcohol abuse and its related addictions and greater harm can cause complex problems for users, their families, friends and other close people to them. In fact, alcohol consumption is the world's third-largest risk factor for disease, disability and injuries.[33] The World Health Organization (WHO) estimates that the global burden of disease attributable to alcohol and illicit drug use amounts to 5.4 per cent of the total burden of disease.[34] Globally, alcohol consumption contributes to 3.3 million deaths and 5.1 per cent of Disability Adjusted Life Years, and its use is linked to more than 200 diseases and injury conditions.[35]

Kenya is currently one of the most alcoholic nations in Africa,[36] and several studies have highlighted the serious nature of alcohol use and abuse in the country.[37] Indeed, the people of Kenya hold positive attitudes towards consumption of both packaged liquor (72 per cent) and traditional brews (69 per cent).[38]

[29] United Nations Office of Drug Control, *World Drug Report* (2017) at www.unodc.org/wdr2017/field/Booklet_1_EXSUM.pdf (accessed 27 January 2022); National Alcohol and Drug Abuse Policy 2018 (Kenya) (n 1).

[30] National Alcohol and Drug Abuse Policy 2018 (Kenya) (n 1).

[31] V Bagnardi et al, 'Flexible Meta-Regression Functions for Modeling Aggregate Dose-Response Data, with an Application to Alcohol and Mortality' (2004) 159(11) *American Journal of Epidemiology* 1077, doi.org/10.1093/aje/kwh142; Kipchumba (n 4).

[32] A Kendagor et al, 'Prevalence and determinants of heavy episodic drinking among adults in Kenya: Analysis of the stepwise survey' (2018) 18 *BMC Public Health* 1216, doi.org/10.1186/s12889-018-6057-6; JB Musungu and PK Kosgei, 'Production and consumption of non-standardized alcohol in Kenya: With whom does the buck stop'? (2015) 3(10) *Global Journal of Arts, Humanities and Social Sciences* 8 at www.eajournals.org/wp-content/uploads/Production-and-Consumption-of-Non-Standardised-Alcohol-in-Kenya.pdf (accessed 24 February 2020); National Alcohol and Drug Abuse Policy 2018 (Kenya) (n 1).

[33] Bagnardi et al (n 31); WHO, *Global Status Report on Alcohol and Health* (2011) at www.drugsandalcohol.ie/14675/ (accessed 24 January 2021).

[34] National Alcohol and Drug Abuse Policy 2018 (Kenya) (n 1).

[35] Kendagor et al (n 32).

[36] J Luesby, 'Let's talk about Kenya's alcoholism' *Business Daily* (Nairobi, 7 July 2021) at www.businessdailyafrica.com/bd/opinion-analysis/columnists/let-s-talk-about-kenya-s-alcoholism--3464038 (accessed 24 August 2021).

[37] Kendagor et al (n 32).

[38] Republic of Kenya, *The National Protocol for Treatment of Substance Use Disorders in Kenya* (2017) at www.afro.who.int/sites/default/files/2017-09/The%20National%20Protocol%20for%20treatments%2014%2007%202017.pdf (accessed 20 January 2021).

Data on alcohol use in Kenya indicate that more than half of alcohol users are aged 10–19 years.[39]

In 2018, Kenya was ranked among the top countries worldwide for years of life lost due to alcohol.[40] The report showed that while 76 per cent of the adult population abstain from drinking alcohol, each year more than 2,000 road traffic deaths are due to alcohol.[41] Indeed, alcohol consumption in Kenya is worryingly high, with home deliveries making access to liquor much easier.[42]

Across Kenya, rates of alcohol addiction are high, with the city of Nairobi having the highest rate (8.4 per cent). In practice, 2.4 per cent of alcohol users are dependent on the substance[43] and 7 per cent of Kenyan men have an alcohol use disorder.[44] In Nairobi, women who had partners who also drink alcohol were more likely to experience short- and long-term violence, with partners of heavy drinkers reporting more domestic violence than those of moderate drinkers.[45] Commonly, injuries and deaths from consumption of home-made alcohol in Kenya are reported in the media.[46] Among primary school pupils, prevalence stands at 38.2 per cent. Consumption of formal (recorded) alcohol that includes beer, liquor and wines accounts for 56 per cent of alcohol use, while illegal alcohol such as *chang'aa*, *busaa* and other types accounts for 44 per cent.[47] In 1998, 23.4 per cent of patients involved in motor vehicle accidents in Eldoret municipality were positively intoxicated, with blood alcohol concentrations of 12.2 per cent.[48] Yet in both rural and slum urban Kenya, alcoholism is hidden and victims are silent.[49] Accordingly, reliable data on alcoholism and its impact on rural and slum urban communities are incomplete.[50] To date, there is no convincing evidence that criminalising illegal alcohol prevents wider consumption of alcohol or its related harms.[51] Moreover, punishing someone to deter others from alcohol use also appears problematic.[52] While criminalising the production of harmful alcohol may seem more ethically

[39] Kendagor et al (n 32); National Alcohol and Drug Abuse Policy 2018 (Kenya) (n 1).

[40] WHO (n 33).

[41] ibid.

[42] 'Kenya: Home delivery fuels alcohol harm' (n 25).

[43] 'Kenya: Alcohol Law Works' *Movendi International* (7 May 2019) at https://movendi.ngo/news/2019/05/07/kenya-alcohol-law-works/ (accessed 24 January 2021).

[44] 'Kenya: Home delivery fuels alcohol harm' (n 25).

[45] P Gichangi et al, *Domestic Violence in Kenya. Report of a baseline survey among women in Nairobi, Kenya* (2002) (Federation of women lawyers, Nairobi, Kenya) at http://erepository.uonbi.ac.ke:8080/xmlui/handle/123456789/46305 (accessed 10 January 2021).

[46] WHO (n 33); Reuters, 'Global brewers push local beers to quench African palates' (2016). At www.reuters.com/article/us-africa-beer-idUSKCN0ZV1PA (accessed 24 January 2021).

[47] 'Kenya: Alcohol Law Works' (n 43).

[48] O Wilson 'Alcohol-related road traffic injuries in Eldoret, Kenya' (1998) 75(12) *East Africa Medical Journal* 708.

[49] Kendagor et al (n 32); National Alcohol and Drug Abuse Policy 2018 (Kenya) (n 1).

[50] Takahashi et al (n 13).

[51] A Holland, 'An ethical analysis of UK drug policy as an example of a criminal justice approach to drugs: a commentary on short film *Putting UK Drug Policy into Focus*' (2020) 17(97) *Harm Reduction Journal*, doi.org/10.1186/s12954-020-00434-8.

[52] Muregi (n 7); Holland (n 51).

tenable, nonetheless, it has not reduced the supply of illegal alcohol nor contributed to effective regulation of illegal alcohol in the market,[53] especially in rural areas where alcoholism remains clandestine.

## IV. Cultural Support for Alcohol Use in Kenya

Most drinkers of alcohol in Kenya today are taking advantage of the traditional African rural culture of alcohol consumption to drink and abuse alcohol. Alcohol is traditionally used in African culture to entertain, celebrate, fulfil religious rites, practices and beliefs; strengthen personal, family and social relationships;[54] and of course drinkers drink to get 'high'. Current alcohol users and abusers are plunging into various alcohol distribution outlets to take advantage of weak alcohol laws and widespread drinking opportunities, including illegal alcohol.

Traditionally, alcohol was less contaminated, and was prepared and drunk in moderation among friends, relatives, neighbours, those respected and a few select close peers, usually elderly men.[55] Often alcohol was drunk after working hours or on specific occasions in stated locations. Alcohol addiction was erratic and widely condemned.[56] Generally, everyone dreaded being labelled an 'alcoholic', and the demand for alcohol was restrained as drinkers did not just drink to get 'high' but for a purpose, often to socialise or when discussing important matters.[57] Thus, alcohol abuse was minimal, and yet currently the contamination and abuse of alcohol have become more extensive and hazardous.

Indeed, communities in Western Kenya and Eastern Uganda share both similar ethnic and cultural practices and lifestyles, including consumption of traditional brews, especially *chang'aa* and *busaa*, which are common in the two regions. Whereas *chang'aa* is more popular among men, women prefer *busaa*, probably due to latter's lower alcohol content and sweeter taste.[58] While alcohol content for *chang'aa* has been estimated to range from 15.3 per cent to 34 per cent, for *busaa* it ranges from 3.9 per cent to 5.4 per cent.[59] While in rural areas traditional brews are usually brewed, distributed, sold and drunk within neighbourhoods around people's homes, in urban areas brews are prepared, distributed, sold and drunk outside the formal bars and shops.[60] While profit considerations motivate modern

[53] Holland (n 51).

[54] Mbiti (n 9); JK Rono and E Nyaga, 'Impact of use and abuse of alcohol on human resource development in Kenya: A case of Moi University students' (2002) 2(2) *Journal of Education and Human Resources* 158.

[55] Mbiti (n 9); Muregi (n 7).

[56] Mbiti (n 9).

[57] ibid; Muregi (n 7).

[58] RK Papas et al, 'Estimating alcohol content of traditional brew in western Kenya using culturally relevant methods: The case for cost over volume' (2010) 14(4) *AIDS Behavior* 836, doi.org/10.1007/s10461-008-9492-z.

[59] ibid.

[60] Takahashi et al (n 13).

brewers and distillers, demand for more affordable, intoxicating and accessible alcohol motivates the consumers of alcohol.

Although beer is currently unaffordable for most locals in rural Eastern Kenya, customers are generally men, which reflects similar studies in East Africa.[61] In patriarchal communities, alcohol intake among men is more associated with masculinity, and with dependence and lesser financial empowerment among women.[62] In general, men tend to have easier access to money than women; and among rural women, alcohol intake is inconsistent with feminine expectations[63] and therefore less tolerated. More women than men in rural areas tend to drink at home, which is more comfortable for them, as compared to men who often drink in public places.[64] Though there are differences in drinking behaviours between men and women, empirical evidence on socio-demographic and cultural differences in alcohol consumption between rural and urban areas is incomplete.

The law in Kenya has not outlawed alcohol use for cultural practices, and brewers and alcohol entrepreneurs use these cultural practices in most rural regions of the country, such as child namings, circumcision ceremonies, weddings, burials and so on, as a cover-up to defeat alcohol laws.[65] The clandestine brewing, distributing, trading and drinking of illegal alcohol thrives in most rural regions of Kenya.[66]

## V. Prevalence and Current Trends of Alcoholism in Rural Kenya

In rural sub-Saharan Africa, alcohol consumption is widespread.[67] The lack of attention to rural trends can be seen across several sections of this chapter. Although alcohol-related problems are emerging as major health issues in Africa,[68] only a few surveys on alcoholism have been conducted in rural settings in sub-Saharan Africa.[69]

Whereas the effects of alcohol consumption are emerging, information on why, where, how and when alcohol is abused in rural Kenya, and by whom, is scarce.

[61] CJ Othieno et al, 'Risky HIV sexual behaviour and depression among University of Nairobi students' (2015) 14 *Annals of General Psychiatry* 16, doi.org/10.1186/s12991-015-0054-2.

[62] SD Rathod et al, 'Epidemiological features of alcohol use in rural India: A population-based cross-sectional study' (2015) 5(12) *BMJ Open* e009802, doi.org/10.1136/bmjopen-2015-009802.

[63] S Teferra et al, 'Hazardous alcohol use and associated factors in a rural Ethiopian district: A cross-sectional community survey' (2016) 16 *BMC Public Health* 218, doi.org/10.1186/s12889-016-2911-6.

[64] Takahashi et al (n 13).

[65] Mbiti (n 9); Muregi (n 7); Papas et al (n 58); National Alcohol and Drug Abuse Policy 2018 (Kenya) (n 1).

[66] Takahashi et al (n 13); Papas et al (n 58).

[67] Takahashi et al (n 13).

[68] C Ferreira-Borges et al, 'The impact of alcohol consumption on African people in 2012: An analysis of burden of disease' (2016) 21(1) *Tropical Medical International Health* 52, doi.org/10.1111/tmi.12618.

[69] Teferra et al (n 63).

Jenkins and others found in rural western Kenya that hazardous alcohol consumption was higher among men, unmarried and self-employed people, and people from households with the lowest and highest incomes.[70] These findings suggest that there is a need for more targeted public-health education among youths at risk and rural residents, who have less access to resources and opportunities.

In 2011, the national prevalence rate of people aged between 15–64 years was 13 per cent;[71] in some regions, the number and frequency of deaths resulting from consumption of adulterated alcoholic drinks had reached alarming levels. For example, rural regions of central Kenya reported the highest alcohol abuse consumption levels in the country, ranging from a high of 51.5 per cent in Nyandarua County to a high of 75.4 per cent in Kirinyaga. In April 2010, 12 people lost their lives in the capital of Kenya, Nairobi. In July 2010, five people in rural Kiambu county lost their lives; while 23 died in August 2010 in Nairobi's Kibera slum; five died in Laikipia, another rural county; and 140 died and tens were blinded in Mukuru kwa Njenga slum in Nairobi.[72] This is because in those regions, the drinking of alcohol occurs silently and in secrecy; and the alcohol that is available is more adulterated, easily available and affordable.[73] Yet in 2007, the estimated lifetime prevalence rate for alcohol in Kenya was 39 per cent.

Kenya is the third-largest consumer of alcohol in Africa, with 43 per cent of alcohol consumed being commercial beer.[74] As of 2017, the national prevalence rate of alcohol consumption was 12.2 per cent. While the national prevalence statistics are scarce, a few studies in Kenya have reported prevalence rates to be higher in rural areas.[75] The types of alcohol most commonly consumed were bottled beer (64.8 per cent) and local brews.[76] Mkuu and others found that 67 per cent of unrecorded alcohol is consumed in rural areas.[77] Kendagor and others found that young males, especially those with less education, married and who use tobacco, were more likely to report heavier alcohol use.[78]

In 2016, NACADA's national survey on alcohol and drug abuse among secondary school students in Kenya revealed that alcohol was the most abused drug (9.3 per cent), followed by prescription drugs (6.8 per cent), Khat/*miraa* (5.9 per cent), tobacco (5.2 per cent), cannabis/*bhang* (3.7 per cent), inhalants (0.8 per cent), heroin (0.4 per cent) and cocaine (0.4 per cent).[79] Khat is a plant

[70] Jenkins et al (n 12).
[71] NACADA, *Alcohol Use in Central Province of Kenya. A baseline survey on magnitude, causes and effects from the perspective of community members and individual users* (Policy Brief No 4/2011).
[72] ibid.
[73] ibid.
[74] ibid.
[75] Jenkins et al (n 12); Takahashi et al (n 13).
[76] Bagnardi et al (n 31).
[77] Mkuu et al (n 5).
[78] Kendagor et al (n 32).
[79] NACADA, *National Survey on Alcohol and Drug Abuse Among Secondary School Students in Kenya* (2016) at https://nacada.go.ke/sites/default/files/2019-10/Report%20on%20National%20ADA%20Survey%20among%20Secondary%20School%20Students_2016_2.pdf (accessed 24 January 2021).

whose leaves and stem are chewed to induce euphoria, lower the need for food and sleep, and treat depression, fatigue, obesity, stomach ulcers and male infertility. But it also decreases sexual desires and increases aggression.[80] Cannabis, also known as marijuana, is a psychoactive drug used for both recreational and medicinal purposes, generally to get 'high' by smoking, vaporising, within food or as an extract. But it has mental and physical effects, including relaxation, altering the state of mind and sense of time, difficulty concentrating, increased appetite, anxiety, hallucinations and psychosis, among others.[81] In practice, in Kenya, high school students get exposed to alcohol and other illegal drugs, mostly Khat and cannabis, between the ages of 13 and 19 years.[82]

Furthermore, consumption of illegal and methanol-adulterated alcohol is extensive in rural parts of Kenya.[83] Methanol is a product of poorly adulterated alcoholic beverages, and its toxic effects are a common occurrence in many parts of the developing world, especially among those of lower socioeconomic status.[84] Sometimes it is used to fortify illicit spirits and home-made brews.[85] But some unscrupulous dealers sometimes package methanol as ethanol.[86] In 2014, in rural Central Kenya, consumption of illicit brews laced with methanol led to the death of 60 persons and 70 hospitalisations. Other cases of methanol poisoning were reported in Nandi and Uasin Gishu Counties.[87] Unfortunately, the majority of those affected were youths and poor persons from rural areas and slums in urban areas. Other negative signs linked to alcoholism in Kenya include increased heart and respiratory rates, hypertension and altered mental status, and blurred vision, coma, death and so on.[88]

Though many efforts have been made to reduce and prevent alcoholism in Kenya, policies aimed at the effective regulation and control of alcohol use and abuse are rather erratic.[89] Therefore, understanding levels of alcohol use and abuse in rural areas, and how rural communities experience changes in laws and regulations about alcohol use and abuse, is crucial for the promotion of safety and quality of life. So far, not much is known about the extent of alcohol use and abuse in rural Kenya and how rural residents respond to alcohol legislation. The next section discusses how social norms existing among many communities impede the successful implementation of alcohol use and abuse regulations in Kenya.

[80] RxList, *Khat health benefits, side effects, uses, dose and precautions* (2021) at www.rxlist.com/khat/supplements.htm (accessed 31 January 2022).

[81] National Alcohol and Drug Abuse Policy 2018 (Kenya) (n 1); Republic of Kenya (n 38); RxList (n 80).

[82] www.wikipedia.org/wiki/Cannabis_(drug) (accessed 24 January 2021).

[83] Ferreira-Borges et al (n 68).

[84] SE Collins, 'Associations between socioeconomic factors and alcohol outcomes' (2016) 38(1) *Alcohol Research: Current Reviews* 83.

[85] National Alcohol and Drug Abuse Policy 2018 (Kenya) (n 1).

[86] Republic of Kenya (n 38).

[87] NACADA, *Summary report of morbidity and mortality caused by alcohol consumption in various parts of the country as 11 May* 2014 (NACADA Board of Directors, 2014).

[88] National Alcohol and Drug Abuse Policy 2018 (Kenya) (n 1).

[89] ibid.

## VI. Cultural Consequences of Criminalisation of Alcohol Use in Kenya

For a significant proportion of the population in Kenya, alcoholism has become part of everyday life and culture. On a daily basis, drinkers hang around neighbourhoods with the aim of getting some sponsors or small cheap contracts to buy alcohol. Hence, the high level of alcohol abuse in the country has cut off a huge proportion of the labour force, particularly males in rural areas and poor urban neighbourhoods,[90] from engaging in meaningful development efforts.

Culturally, drinking tends to run through families and appears to be shared among friends, relatives, neighbours and communities. Unemployment and poverty enhance the chronic scarcity of material resources in households, which heightens alcohol use and abuse, which leads to an increase in addictions and violence.[91] Yet greater demand for alcohol swells the business of brewing, marketing and selling alcohol. Hence, both modern local brewers and capitalists compete for more profits by targeting the largest number of customers. Modern brewers then compete to produce more competitive drinks, which are often more adulterated, affordable, accessible and intoxicating. Although such businesses are illegal and morally unreasonable, they endure because certain unscrupulous entrepreneurs and capitalists often use cultural practices to justify drinking and bribe corrupt law enforcement officials to defeat the law.

Consequently, heavy episodic alcohol use in Kenya is staggering and the consequences are disastrous.[92] So far, little is known about the consequences of the failed attempts to regulate alcohol use and abuse, especially among younger drinkers. Alcohol abuse harms the physical and mental health of people, weakens the immune system, and is linked to road traffic accidents, injuries and deaths. In addition, it fuels violence, such as domestic violence and gender-based violence, and increases the already heavy burden on healthcare systems, the emergency services and law enforcement.[93] Further, alcoholism has been associated with a variety of mental disorders, and yet the country's mental-health workforce remains 'grossly understaffed', with only one psychiatrist for every half million Kenyans, and less than 1 per cent of the country's health services delivering any mental health component at all.[94] In addition, socially, alcohol has disrupted families; and economically, alcohol has wasted valuable resources, including personal and family finances and other properties.[95] In addition to increasing domestic violence, in particular gender-based violence and neglect of responsibilities, alcohol abuse

[90] Luesby (n 36).
[91] Rono and Nyaga (n 54).
[92] Kendagor (n 32); WHO, *Global status report on alcohol and health* (2018) at www.who.int/publications/i/item/9789241565639.
[93] 'Kenya: Alcohol Law Works' (n 43); WHO (n 92).
[94] Luesby (n 36).
[95] Kipchumba (n 5).

has been linked to higher poverty levels, particularly those relating to scarcity of material resources in households. Yet the rights of victims are often ignored.

Generally, alcoholism tends to set up pathways for hopelessness, which are reinforced by increased addictions.[96] Alcoholic youths who are experiencing unemployment and poverty also tend to pile up crises and risks. These include adverse life events, psychological distress, less helpful friends, and limited social support networks and satisfaction. Consequently, their need for more and more alcohol is amplified, which complicates their drinking habits and lifestyles. Indeed, such youths are more prone to hazardous alcohol use.[97]

Since alcohol is a depressant, the more alcohol one drinks, the more one becomes miserable and the worse the addiction, and the greater the hopelessness and the demand for more intoxicating liquor. Despite straining relationships and exposing addicts to accumulation of other risks, including physical or psychological problems, alcohol addicts continue to crave more substances, which complicates their addiction. Yet rehabilitating addicts is often a long-term and culturally complex problem. For alcoholics, alcohol is a 'must', and the sudden discontinuance of its use and the associated withdrawal symptoms can be difficult to manage in diverse cultural and social settings, even for governments. Since addiction dominates, it becomes indispensable and renders the habitual supply of alcohol crucial.

Yet consumers of alcohol and addicts have the right to healthy and safe drinks, to orderly and stable marriages, and the right to be included in development activities free from the harms resulting from adulterated alcohol. Moreover, they have the right to be treated fairly and to access just laws and fair treatment following arrest, trial and even in prison if sentenced. But law enforcers often stumble regarding the rights of alcohol consumers and addicts, who often become the victims of bribes, police abuse and violence on arrest. Moreover, sometimes brewers distil, distribute and sell adulterated and illegal alcohol without being arrested, since some rogue police officers accept bribes, abet offences or fail to enforce the law. When arrested, alcohol users and entrepreneurs easily defeat the law by bribing law enforcement officers, especially chiefs and the police. As a result, few offences reach the courts and eventual trial.[98]

Moreover, it is often not the financially stronger alcohol users and entrepreneurs who get arrested but rather the financially weaker alcohol drinkers and entrepreneurs who are unable to bribe their way out of the law, who report more arrests, prosecutions, sentencing and imprisonment.[99] While in prison, the convicted alcohol users and entrepreneurs often experience poor prison conditions that deny them their basic rights, including healthy food, clean water, sanitation and environment, proper medication and training. In addition, the lack of political will to pass and implement effective alcohol laws on the part of the national and regional

[96] 'Kenya: Alcohol Law Works' (n 43); WHO (n 92).
[97] Rono and Nyaga (n 54).
[98] Kipchumba (n 4).
[99] NACADA (n 17).

governments provides opportunities for greater use of illegal alcohol and limited punishments for alcohol abuse.[100] As a result, illegal alcohol is widely available, with greater levels of addition and devastating consequences for the victims, their families and the economy.[101] For the victims, access to justice is complicated by a number of factors, including cultural practices, violation of rights, evasion of the law and the lack of political will. As far as brewers and rogue police officers are concerned, the existence of bribes and weak laws compromise their access to justice and their punishment respectively. Yet the limited punishment of illegal alcohol users, rogue alcohol entrepreneurs and law enforcers has scarcely any effect on the prevalence of underground brewing, distribution, trading and drinking of illegal alcohol.

## VII. Conclusions

This chapter explores the impact of changes to regulations on alcohol use on lives and livelihoods in rural Kenyan communities. It also explores the dynamics that accompany the rural communities' access to justice in relation to the criminalisation of cultural practices associated with alcohol use. Understanding how rural communities experience changes to alcohol laws and regulations about alcohol use is crucial to the development of effective laws and laws that promote management of public health and for safeguarding livelihoods. The chapter contributes to the emerging field of rural criminology by providing a critique showing the consequences of criminalising cultural practices, such as the legal regulation of alcohol use in rural Kenya.

Many attempts to legally regulate alcohol use and abuse in Kenya have been unable to eradicate adulteration or effectively regulate the brewing, distribution and trading of illegal alcohol, or control drinking. While Kenya has a national alcohol policy, criminalisation of cultural practices such as alcohol use has had profoundly different impacts on the life experiences of drinkers of alcohol in rural communities. Hitherto, key players in the criminal justice system and in government, both at the national and at the county levels, have received lukewarm support in formulating and enforcing effective alcohol laws. Yet the use and abuse of alcohol in rural Kenya is disturbingly high, with severe consequences. Therefore, there is a need to formulate and implement effective alcohol laws to control alcohol adulteration, distillation, distribution and sale; drinking hours; and fair and just law enforcement for all. Specifically, there is a need:

(a) to reduce alcohol harm among young people, families and other productive citizens. The Government needs to strengthen the national alcohol and drug abuse policy, enhance political commitment to formulating and

[100] NACADA (n 87).
[101] NACADA (n 17); National Alcohol and Drug Abuse Policy 2018 (Kenya) (n 1).

implementing effective alcohol laws, and eradicate corruption at all levels of alcohol production, distribution and sale;

(b) to limit access to illegal alcohol during periods of crisis, in pursuit of which counties should strengthen alcohol policy measures and existing alcohol laws to reduce consumption of illegal alcohol and its harmful consequences;

(c) to have an effective national system for treatment of alcohol use disorders, which requires a coordinated and integrated response by many actors to deliver policies and interventions based on scientific evidence in diverse cultural and rural settings. This can be achieved by targeting diverse groups of people at most risk of illegal alcohol use and abuse;

(d) to provide effective treatment services for alcoholics. The public health system must coordinate with social care services and other community services to ensure that treatment is available, accessible, affordable, evidence-based and diversified. Moreover, such services must match the needs of each alcoholic, be available in all similar rural settings and accessible at most hours. In addition, the environmental treatment should be more friendly, culturally sensitive and focus on the specific needs of each alcoholic;

(e) to reverse alcohol abuse. Interventions should target social networks of consumers of alcohol, change drinkers' attitudes towards illegal alcohol and brews, and tackle the issue of the availability of illegal alcohol and traditional brews. Given the resource constraints in tackling the problem of alcoholism in rural settings, innovative community-based approaches using locally available resources to mitigate the problem of alcoholism should be piloted and implemented in similar rural cultural contexts. Moreover, the poor economic status in rural settings should be addressed, and alternative sources of income for brewers of illegal alcohol and traditional brewers and sellers should be created.

# 4

# Accessibility to Justice for Rural Livestock Farmers in Selected Provinces of South Africa

## *Rural Communities and the Justice System*

WITNESS MALULEKE

## I. Introduction

Despite the increasing trend of urbanisation throughout Africa, the majority of the continent's population still lives in rural areas, and will continue to do so for the near future. It is nevertheless still often the case that, for people living in poor rural areas lacking basic facilities, towns and particularly large cities are seen as 'heavens of opportunity', where jobs, education, health care and *access to justice* can be obtained.[1] Approximately 70 per cent of people found in the Southern African Development Community (SADC) depend on agriculture for food, income and employment, while livestock farming contributes 30 to 80 per cent of the agricultural Gross Domestic Product (GDP) in Africa; this conforms to the delivery of agriculture-led growth and socio-economic transformations as envisioned in the Malabo Declaration on Africa's Accelerated Agricultural Growth and Transformation,[2] emphasising shared prosperity and improved livelihoods.[3] In South Africa, 80 per cent of the land is mainly suitable for extensive livestock farming.[4] It is also recognised that agriculture is one of the cornerstones of the

[1] T Binns, A Dixon and E Nel, *Africa: Diversity and Development* (Routledge, 2012).

[2] Malabo Declaration on Accelerated Agricultural Growth and Transformation for Shared Prosperity and Improved Livelihoods (26–27 June 2014) at www.resakss.org/sites/default/files/Malabo%20Declaration%20on%20Agriculture_2014_11%2026-.pdf (accessed 10 October 2022).

[3] B Ben, JC Moreki, B Wame, T Kebadire and K Lesaba, 'A survey of livestock theft at Mogonono village in Kweneng District of Botswana' (2018) 3(4) *Journal of Animal Science and Veterinary Medicine* 94.

[4] Department of Agriculture, Fisheries and Forestry, *Trends in the Agricultural Sector* (Department of Agriculture Fisheries and Forestry, Pretoria, 2012).

South African economy.[5] Thus, different crimes committed within rural agricultural communities need to be researched and not neglected, as this sector positively contributes to the family sustainability of livestock farmers.[6] Stock theft remains particularly problematic; this is not a new crime and is considered as old as farming itself.[7]

In dealing with the significant problem of stock theft, it is clear that customary or traditional courts have several considerable advantages over formal modern courts, such as their geographical convenience, informality, simplicity, lower cost, and an absence of backlogged cases that ensures that matters are disposed of speedily.[8] However, there are also serious concerns about customary courts, such as: the lack of formal training of the presiding officers; the exclusion of legal representation before such courts, in spite of the long prison/correctional centre sentences they are allowed to impose; and the fact that informal nature of the proceedings may not offer accused persons the best opportunities to defend themselves. On the other hand, judges in customary courts may readily appreciate the traditional markings on livestock and have a good general understanding of the cultural and social context of this crime.[9] Consequently, this chapter was guided by two of the framing questions underpinning this collection, namely: How do people experience the institutions of justice in rural areas, and how does this rural experience differ from an urban experience?

The chapter addresses these questions by considering rural livestock farmers' access to justice, as offered by the South African magistrates' courts and traditional courts. The magistrates' court has the power to hear any alleged crime except rape; it can impose fines not exceeding R60,000 and/or sentence an offender to imprisonment for a maximum of three years.[10] The traditional court, on the other hand, refers to a customary institution or structure, which is constituted and functions in terms of customary law and custom, for the purpose of resolving disputes.[11] The nature of these courts differs in rural areas as compared to the application and administration of justice by the system available in urban areas. Moreover, the impact of crime in rural areas has required considerable changes to existing laws,

[5] WJ Clack, 'The extent of stock theft in South Africa' (2013) 26(2) *Acta Criminologica: Southern African Journal of Criminology* 77.

[6] ibid.

[7] ibid.

[8] BJ Dambe and CM Fombad, 'The Stock Theft Act and Customary Courts in Botswana: Justice sacrificed on the altar of expediency' (2020) 52(1) *The Journal of Legal Pluralism and Unofficial Law* 1.

[9] ibid.

[10] K Booyens, 'The South African Criminal Justice System' in C Bezuidenhout (ed), *A Southern African Perspective on Fundamental Criminology*, 2nd edn (Pearson South Africa (Pty) Ltd, 2020).

[11] Traditional Courts Bill 2016 (South Africa), *Government Gazette* No 40487 of 9 December, Republic of South Africa: Pretoria.

legislative frameworks and policies, further contributing to the difference between options for justice available in rural areas, when compared with South African urban areas.

All South African provinces, especially the rural segments, are said to be affected by the crime of stock theft, which is regarded as a property-priority crime in many provinces, such as Limpopo (LIM) and KwaZulu-Natal (KZN) Provinces.[12] This crime is becoming globally and increasingly transnationally organised, and is presently complex in nature. Stock theft consists of the stealing of stock or produce belonging to another person.[13] This scourge ranges from stealing individual animals for the pot to doing it on an organised scale.[14] The author has observed that despite the seriousness of this problem, little research has been done to determine the methods used by South African courts to control it and their effectiveness in dealing with this crime. Research investigating the functioning of South African courts to respond to prevailing criminality associated with stock theft remains a critical issue and requires major academic support. Thus, the rural smallholder and small-scale commercial farmers, also known as 'family livestock farms', are highly contested in both political and academic circles.[15]

Notably, cattle, sheep and goats worth more than R1.2 billion were stolen in South Africa during the 2018/19 financial year.[16] It is also revealed that this figure applied only to the value of the animals stolen and did not take into account additional costs, such as the judicial processes, recovery costs, farmer costs and policing, among others. Approximately 30,000 head of livestock were reported stolen during this period.[17] The value of the cattle that were stolen was approximately R900 million, plus about R200 million worth of sheep and R100 million of goats. The majority of the losses that were reported to the police occurred in KZN Province, where the most cattle were stolen; followed by the Eastern Cape, where the target was generally sheep; and thereafter the Free State, where both cattle and sheep were targeted by thieves. Of the many challenges facing South African livestock farmers in general, stock theft is still one of the biggest problems affecting this sector;[18] it is also considered a more serious threat in regions

[12] W Maluleke, 'The Use of Deoxyribonucleic Acid in Combating Stock Theft in South Africa', unpublished Doctoral Thesis (Tshwane University of Technology, 2016).

[13] Institute of Security Studies Crime Hub, *The Definitions of Crimes Used to Compile the Crime Statistics/Stock Theft* (Institute of Security Studies, Brooklyn, 2013).

[14] K Geldenhuys, 'Stock theft and what owners can do to protect their stock' *Servamus – Community Based Safety and Security Magazine* (November 2010) 38.

[15] D Chikazunga and G Paradza, *Can Smallholder Farmers Find a Home in South Africa's Food-System? Lessons from Limpopo Province* (Plaas, Institute for Poverty, Land and Agrarian Studies, 2012).

[16] S Dean, 'Stock theft – over R1,2 billion in livestock theft reported in 2018/2019' *Farmer's Weekly* (17 January 2020) 24.

[17] ibid.

[18] W Maluleke, 'Perspectives on Stock Theft Prevention in the Giyani Policing Area of Limpopo Province', unpublished *Magister Technologiae* (Tshwane University of Technology, 2014).

bordering other countries, such as the Eastern Cape, Free State, KZN, North West and Mpumalanga Provinces.[19]

Chelin has noted that only 20 per cent of stock theft cases are reported across South Africa, suggesting that the actual figure for this crime is unknown.[20] Comparatively, approximately 85 per cent of stock theft is not reported in the United States, with the figure being about 87 per cent in the United Kingdom.[21] In South Africa, most stock thefts are committed as a result of greed by organised syndicates; it has been reported that of the almost 30,000 cases of stock theft recorded in the 2018/19 financial year, approximately 87 per cent involved some form of organised crime as opposed to being crimes of need committed by poverty-stricken individuals trying to survive.[22]

In the selected areas of LIM and KZN Provinces, livestock farmers have recourse to the magistrates' court and traditional court respectively for stock theft. Many farmers have put their trust in the 'traditional prosecution system' with regard to addressing this crime. The rural experiences of access to justice suggests that the trust shown is indicated by the number of stock theft cases dealt with or referred to the traditional court, rather than transferring them to the local magistrates' court. It also cannot be argued that the traditional justice system serves the purpose of the latter court and is recognised by the Constitution of the Republic of South Africa, 1996. Chapter 12 of the 1996 Constitution recognises the significance of customary law; and in section 212(1) the value of the role played by traditional leaders, particularly in matters affecting local communities, is highlighted,[23] stock theft being one of the scourges affecting the emerging and communal rural farmers. This chapter thus explores rural experiences of access to justice, focusing on the available justice systems on offer – the magistrates' courts versus the traditional courts. These courts are often said to be working in isolation, with different benefits, depending on the which court is selected. The current lack of any relationship between these courts, and their related ineffectiveness, runs alongside the associated impact of the laws, legislative frameworks and policies on the lives of rural livestock farmers, when compared with their urban counterparts, in terms of access to justice.

[19] W Maluleke, 'Proposing a new Deoxyribonucleic Acid technology conceptual framework in combating stock theft in South Africa: Empirical evidence' (2020) 48(4) *Journal of the Social Sciences* 2693.

[20] R Chelin, 'Organised crime moves in on South Africa's livestock industry' *Daily Maverick and ICSS Today* (19 November 2019) at https://issafrica.org/iss-today/organised-crime-moves-in-on-south-africas-livestock-industry (accessed 24 February 2021).

[21] ibid.

[22] ibid.

[23] The Constitution of the Republic of South Africa as adopted by the Constitutional Assembly on 8 May 1996 and as amended on 11 October 1996 (B34B-96).

# II. An Overview of Rural Experiences of Access to Justice in South Africa

## A. Rural Experiences of Access to Justice Compared to Urban Standards

There is no doubt that people living in rural areas should be able to enjoy free and easy access to justice for the protection of their rights.[24] Nevertheless, as this chapter will show, the reality is that they are 'dying or forgotten'.[25] Automation, globalisation, technology and urbanisation are some of culprits making livelihoods from agriculture, natural resource extraction and manufacturing obsolete, further fuelling social problems and causing distributive injustice through collective political gains. Achieving legal goals based on their impact rests on compliance; this is clearly a central aim of the administration of the Criminal Justice System (CJS), using breaches of 'Criminal Law, to uphold laws, punishments and criminal behaviours'.[26] Moreover, the related impacts are complex and complicated, coupled with various consequences. What determines court decisions, either by the magistrates or by traditional courts, remains a pressing challenge. Furthermore, interesting theories exist, providing insight into the processes of the South African magistrates' courts and traditional courts in rural settings.[27]

Improving access to justice has increasingly been recognised as a critical dimension of inclusive growth and a means for tackling inequality. The inability to access legal and justice services in rural areas can be both a cause and a result of disadvantage and poverty.[28] Clearly understanding 'Critical Theory' can provide clarity as regards accessibility to justice in the rural setting, as it integrates the value of social justice, which requires institutional and organisational arrangements to be amended,[29] which can be accomplished by actively engaging in reclaiming, appropriating, sustaining and advancing the inherent human rights of equity and fairness in social, economic, educational and personal dimensions, into the practice of research for reform.[30]

[24] A Lapkin, 'The problems of access to justice in rural areas (on the example of Ukraine)' (2019) 68 *SHS Web of Conferences* 1.

[25] AM Eisenberg, 'Distributive justice and rural America' (2020) 61 *Boston College Law Review* 189.

[26] WA Bogart, 'Compliance with Law – Deterrence and its Alternatives' in WA Bogart, *Consequences: The Impact of Law and Its Complexity* (University of Toronto Press, 2002) 53.

[27] WA Bogart, 'Introduction' in Bogart, *Consequences: The Impact of Law and Its Complexity* (n 26) 3.

[28] Organisation for Economic Co-operation and Development, 'Equal Access to Justice: OECD Expert roundtable background notes' (7 October 2015) at www.oecd.org/gov/Equal-Access-Justice-Roundtable-background-note.pdf (accessed 19 February 2021).

[29] D Hlalele, 'Social Justice and Rural Education in South Africa' (2012) 30(1) *Perspectives in Education* 111.

[30] KP Goldfarb and J Grinberg, 'Leadership for social justice: Authentic participation in the case of a community centre in Caracas, Venezuela' (2002) 12 *Journal of School Leadership* 157.

Much of what has been reported about rural communities' efforts to access justice has focused on initiatives in practice in urban areas. As a result, little is known about community justice in rural areas.[31] In South Africa, it is nevertheless clear that rural areas' honour is built on shared values and morals, which differ from those in urban areas. In rural areas, community justice exists when values are honoured and the communities' rules are upheld; the current justice system, on the other hand, stresses the interdiction and sanctioning of rule violations and ignores the necessity for rewarding compliance with the rules and fostering the diversity of cultures in ways that can lead to a fulfilling life. Rural justice thrives when those differences are acknowledged and celebrated. The process of building rural justice will succeed when opportunities are created to fully explore shared values and the desired related outcomes.[32] Therefore, opportunities should be created for methods of participation in rural justice.[33]

The local CJS operating in *rural areas* has been overlooked and under-resourced. Many rural areas have fewer social services, and this leads to the need to travel longer distances for service appointments, a small pool of CJS practitioners, and probably outdated technology and infrastructure. Remote South African Police Service Stock Theft Units (SAPS STUs) offices are found in South Africa. Other services, such as the opening of cases and effecting arrests, still require victims to access local police stations in the inner cities. Local and regional courts are often situated in townships, making access to courts for rural communities undoubtedly limited.[34] To address crime successfully in rural areas, one needs to understand the complexity of the environment, to respond to crime when it happens and to prevent future incidents. However, this is currently not possible, due to the perception, right or wrong, that as a result of failures in the policing and justice systems, criminals have a good chance of getting away with their crimes, which creates a sense of lawlessness.[35] Rural legal pluralism, on the other hand, reflects communal cultures, values, politics and history, and enables post-colonial countries to continue preserving their traditional and cultural practices and values while resolving conflicts.[36]

Residents in the urban areas are said to enjoy the privilege of easy access to and the benefit of institutions of the justice system, from the lower courts – namely, the regional and magistrates' courts – to the higher courts, the Supreme Court of

[31] WJ Dickey and P McGarry, *Community Justice in Rural America: Four Examples and Four Futures* (United States Department of Justice, 2001).

[32] M Colchester, *Justice in the Forest: Rural livelihoods and forest law enforcement* (The Centre for International Forestry Research: Bogor, Indonesia, 2006).

[33] Dickey and McGarry (n 31).

[34] Maluleke (n 18).

[35] U van der Westhuijzen, 'Rural safety: perception vs reality' *Farmer's Weekly* (18 July 2021) at www.farmersweekly.co.za/opinion/by-invitation/rural-safety-perception-vs-reality/ (accessed 19 January 2022).

[36] L Sadiki, 'Towards an African Criminology' in Bezuidenhout (ed) (n 10) 640.

Appeal and the Constitutional Court, with well-resourced infrastructure, many staff and financial resources.[37] Rural people also generally have less access to education, health and other essential services, besides the distribution of land; for rural people living in poverty, secure access to land and its natural resources, and to justice, is thus vital for their empowerment, food security and ability to improve their financial situation. Furthermore, since they are often faced with disproportionate levels of seasonal and informal employment, unsafe working conditions, limited access to markets, lack of access to basic services, and exclusion based on gender, ethnicity and other factors, it is essential for rural people to have access to social protection.[38]

In support of this submission, the Access to Justice (A2J) initiatives united empirical data and analysed policies to argue that the prevailing A2J initiatives are flawed at three primary levels, namely:[39]

(a) failure to meaningfully recognise the limits of rural infrastructural capacity and the complex barriers low-income rural residents in particular navigate;
(b) a presumption that anyone in a crisis situation, let alone someone facing these barriers, can effectively be their own attorney; and
(c) a professional understanding of justice that is critically at odds with rural individuals' own expectations.

The study highlighted broader tensions that emerge when dominant narratives around 'access' are held up against the lived experience of those who daily encounter rural attorney shortages and other structural inequities. As the chapter demonstrates, this profound mismatch of expectations is hugely consequential, resulting in forms of 'access' that are experienced in rural areas as barriers to justice.[40] Therefore, in this author's opinion, the challenges noted by the cited researchers seemed to be threatening the efficacy of rural administration of justice. This calls for urgent intervention, as rural development can be reset to achieve sustainable development by making rural development the centre of attention, instead of relegating it to the side-lines as an appendage to urban development. More attention should be paid to the following matters:

- Ending the rural–urban divide through the adoption of the *in situ* urbanisation model.
- Ending inequality within rural areas.
- Achieving rural development while preserving the environment.[41]

[37] Booyens (n 10).

[38] United Nations Department of Economic and Social Affairs, 'World Social Report 2021: Reconsidering Rural Development' at https://knowledge.unccd.int/publications/world-social-report-2021-reconsidering-rural-development (accessed 19 January 2022.

[39] M Statz, R Friday and J Bredeson, '"They had access, but they didn't get justice": Why prevailing access to justice initiatives fail rural Americans' (2021) XXVIII(3) *Georgetown Journal on Poverty Law and Policy* 321.

[40] ibid.

[41] United Nations Department of Economic and Social Affairs (n 38).

The 'rural' and 'urban' areas have thus often been seen as quite separate, but in reality there are many complex interrelationships between them. However, in improving rural environments, rural authorities face a daunting task and have a pressing future agenda, not least, facing seemingly insurmountable problems regarding providing access to justice.[42]

## B. The Impact of Policy Changes on Access to Justice in Rural and Urban Areas

Although rural-based studies have been relatively ignored in research and policy, the issues of stock theft, consumption and distribution of illegal drugs, and lack of justice in rural areas are considered, amongst others, some of most pressing problems facing rural police and the rural environment, presenting special problems that cannot be addressed by urban solutions.[43] Therefore, the CJS should be made non-threatening to victims, continuing to provide special training for the personnel working within the system, including the local police, prosecutors and judges, as well as other members of the Justice, Crime Prevention and Security (JCPS) cluster: the SAPS, the Department of Justice and Constitutional Development (DoJ & CD), which includes the National Prosecuting Authority (NPA), the Department of Correctional Services (DCS), the Department of Home Affairs (DHA), the South African National Defence Force (SANDF), and the Defence and Military Veterans and State Security Agency (SSA). The SAPS, DoJ & CD and DCS comprise the core of the CJS.[44] In addition, ensuring access to justice for rural citizens is key to realising existing basic rights and related protections, addressing inequalities and generating change contributing to sustainable economic growth and reducing poverty. Access to justice in rural areas means that relevant authorities respect existing laws and regulations, and everyone understand their rights, together with their ability and power to claim those rights and to seek remedies when they are infringed.[45]

Moreover, CJS agencies in rural settings are reported to be struggling to meet requirements emanating from new policies or mandates and limited resources. Therefore, CJS members are straining the already limited existing resources and facilities. Rural areas are also experiencing population growth and increased rural

[42] Binns, Dixon and Nel (n 1).

[43] CR Mann, L Pettiway, L and RS Weisheit, 'Drugs and the Community' in *Critical Criminal Justice Issues Task Force Reports from the American Society of Criminology to Attorney General Janet Reno* (United States Department of Justice Office of Justice Programs, National Institute of Justice, 1997) 49.

[44] E Erez et al, 'Violence against women: Overview' in *Critical Criminal Justice Issues Task Force Reports* (1997) (n 43) 61.

[45] Food and Agriculture Organisation, *Rural Women and Access to Justice: FAO's contribution to a Committee on the Elimination of Discrimination against Women (CEDAW) half-day general discussion on access to justice* (Food and Agriculture Organisation, 2013).

diversity, adding to the challenges that CJS agencies face linked with understanding the administration of justice in different rural areas and limited workforces. In contrast, urban courts have a higher degree of formality and bureaucratisation compared to rural areas, based on protective orders. Documented variations between urban and rural areas in terms of case administration, processing and sentencing show considerable differences.[46] Nevertheless, it can be useful for researchers and practitioners interested in engaging with rural justice to consider their own 'lived experiences' and related practical ethics,[47] with the application of the 'Capability Approach', which recognises the achievement of freedom and justice.[48]

Certain groups of individuals may be vulnerable and treated differently by their fellow citizens and actors within the CJS, such as local police officers, judges, prosecutors, defence lawyers and corrections officers.[49] This treatment is often in contravention of international human rights standards. For example, prior to 1994, the apartheid regime in South Africa, under the guise of parliamentary supremacy, used the law in such a manner that it was experienced by the people as a legal instrument of racial oppression and systematic discrimination, and the justice system as a whole was not viewed as accessible by most South Africans and was not considered to be legitimate.[50] The author submits that the role of the South African judicial system in advancing access to justice over the past 26 years disguise the broader roles played by the various players within the justice system, such as the courts, the judiciary, the NPA, the DoJ & CD, the above-mentioned JCPS cluster and other social partners, all of which made and continue to make an immense contribution to improving access to justice and its quality for South African citizens, with the following caveats in mind:

- There is still a long way before rural justice can be accessed equally by all.
- Issues of cost and a lack of knowledge present barriers to the fulfilment of the constitutional guarantee of access to justice.
- Backlogs and a lack of capacity in the courts present a serious challenge to the fulfilment of access to justice.
- It is also affirmed that rural justice is a very serious issue that requires consideration by all stakeholders.[51]

[46] ibid.

[47] M Patrick et al, 'Planetary Health Justice: feminist approaches to building in rural Kenya' (2020) 1(1) *Buildings and Cities* 308.

[48] A Sen, *Development as Freedom* (Oxford University Press, 1999).

[49] United Nations Office on Drugs and Crime, *Criminal Justice Reform in Post-Conflict States: A guide for practitioners* (United Nations, 2011).

[50] South African Presidency, *Twenty-Year Review South Africa – 1994–2014, background paper: Judiciary* (The Presidency Office: Pretoria, 2020).

[51] ibid.

Therefore, in the author's opinion, policies should vary significantly across geographic areas and in establishing priorities. However, many policies are developed via an 'umbrella approach', mainly merging the needs of people in both urban and rural areas. Although from a general observation of policy development in the country, politicians, as law makers, are developing policies in a fashion that attempts to afford everyone access to justice, local populations nonetheless still suffer from far greater disparities in the justice system than do urban populations. The author thinks that these disparities are caused not only by fundamental differences in social status across segments of the population, but also by inequities in economic status. Community-wide problems like poverty, unemployment, poor education and poor public transportation also contribute to inequities of justice. The author further suggests that until we develop infrastructure in rural areas, and the social policies needed to achieve equality in justice between urban and rural areas, justice is likely to appear to be done on paper in rural areas but not achieved in practice.

## C. The Legal Impacts on the Lives of Rural Livestock Farmers

Long before the Code of Hammurabi set the law for ancient Mesopotamia, people relied on cooperative agreement, under threat of force at times, focusing on rules that would enable social and economic activities to be ordered.[52] With the evolution of societies – from close-knit kinship groups to larger and more diverse communities, the rural areas included, with more complex activities – the need for more formal rules increased. In many developing regions like South Africa's rural areas, laws remain unimplemented or they are implemented selectively; sometimes they are impossible to implement at all.[53] The legal problems are often experienced in various parts of society, with negative results on the lives of individuals in both rural and urban areas, including stress-related illness, physical ill-health, relationship breakdown, lack of educational knowledge for selecting available options, bullying, harassment, the need to move home, and loss of income or financial strain, with considerable adverse consequences and effects on a broad range of circumstances, thus leading to a substantial impact on the everyday lives of individuals.[54]

The existing laws are regarded as systems of rules established to guide individuals to embrace existing 'Acts, By-laws, Ordinances, Codes and Decrees' to formalise

[52] World Bank, 'Chapter 3: The role of law' in *World Development Report 2017* at https://openknowledge.worldbank.org/bitstream/handle/10986/25880/9781464809507_Ch03.pdf?sequence=35&isAllowed=y (accessed 19 February 2021).

[53] ibid.

[54] D Macourt, 'Youth and the law: the impact of legal problems on young people' in *Updating Justice No 38* (Law and Justice Foundation: New South Wales, 2014).

societal agreements and public policies that are often implemented through formal laws;[55] moreover, policies and laws are also referred to as symbolic and instruments of law and regulations influencing individuals' daily applications of law based on CJS protections.[56] The emergence of rural laws, policies and regulations has helped to shape people's experiences in line with the legal consciousness and perceptions about applied laws by lay rural persons, as well as by legal actors in practice.[57] Certainly, the Stock Theft Act (No 57 of 1959) imposes a severe sentence that has adverse consequences for an accused, so the shortcomings of traditional courts should not be treated lightly. The cases in question should be handled with the utmost diligence, with legal representation for the accused being recognised.[58] The presiding officers should be required to have formal training in the administration of justice in terms of experience in handling stock theft offences; failing that, the cases at issue should be removed from the jurisdiction of the customary courts and reserved for courts competent, in terms of personnel and procedure, to deliver proper justice, while acknowledging that customary courts will continue to play an important role in the speedy administration of justice in African rural areas.[59]

Analysis reveals that it is seldom the practice that laws in rural area are codified. Most rural areas follow the norms and practices of their forefathers, which are expected to be implemented by the community leaders, including the Chiefs, Kings, Queens and *Indunas* heading those respective communities. As regards the concept of the rule of law in rural areas, there are two different viewpoints in academic circles. The paradigm shift in law has meant that the rule of law needs to be codified, not to substitute for the rural laws but to ensure that rural law conforms to the 1996 Constitution and makes full use of legal means to manage rural activities. This presents a predicament as regards the practice of law. The traditional leaders are viewed as the ultimate arbiters in the resolution of communal social problems: they are the executors of laws in their rural areas. The new paradigm shift requires that villagers' rights must not be violated in any way; power should not be greater than existing laws.

## III. Magistrates' and Traditional Court Approaches to Stock Theft Cases: Comparative Views

The South African law courts and the SAPS STUs are part of the South African CJS that aims to maintain order in society by preventing and controlling crime and

[55] T van dijk and R Beunen, 'Laws, People and Land Use: A sociological perspective on the relation between laws and land use' (2009) 17(12) *European Planning Studies* 1979.

[56] Macourt (n 54).

[57] Stanford Law School, *Law in Everyday Life. Stanford Program in Law and Society*, Fifth Conference for Junior Researchers, Stanford Law School, Stanford, CA, 11–12 May 2018.

[58] South Africa. 2011. Stock Theft Act (No 57 of 1957), Juta Law, 46 (34535), Sep 30:1–2.

[59] Dambe and Fombad (n 8) 14.

criminal conduct.[60] Section 165 of the 1996 Constitution provides that the judicial authority of the 'Republic' be vested in the courts. Section 165 also protects the independence, impartiality, dignity, accessibility and effectiveness of the courts to the extent that an order or decision issued by a court binds all persons to whom and organs of state to which it applies. South Africa is a constitutional state with a separation of powers between the legal and executive authorities. All must pass muster with the Constitutional Court, which is the ultimate court of appeal on legislative matters. The South African legal system is based on Roman Dutch law.[61]

In terms of section 165(1) of the 1996 Constitution, the judicial authority of the Republic of South Africa vests authority in the courts established by the Constitution and any other law. Section 165(2) of the 1996 Constitution requires the judiciary to be independent and impartial and subject only to the Constitution and the law. In terms of section 34 of the Constitution, 1996, every person shall have the right to have justiciable disputes settled by a court of law or, where appropriate, another independent, impartial forum. It is therefore the constitutional right of every person to seek relief from the courts.[62] However, what the law provides and what happens in practice is quite different: in cases brought before the courts (the DoJ & CD), upstanding and trustworthy livestock farmers have been portrayed as potentially guilty of stock theft. They were found guilty in the public eye during court proceedings. It should, however, be emphasised that it is not the community that delivers a verdict. Declaring someone guilty in the public arena is easy, but in terms of section 35(3) of the Constitution, 1996, every accused person has the right to a fair trial, which includes the rights to be presumed innocent until proved guilty, to remain silent and to testify during the proceedings.

Based on the presentations in court of the legal representatives of the accused, it was apparent that their duty was to find weaknesses in the evidence brought by witnesses. Such evidence is then deemed inadmissible before the court. Often, the witnesses and victims fail to offer evidence that could irrefutably prove the allegations. What often frustrates witnesses during stock theft cases is the lack and limited rendering of solid evidence, with heavy reliance on investigations conducted by the SAPS STUs, which cover matters including the colour of the stock, injuries, wounds, and the shape and size of horns and spots, basing their conclusion on the fact that 'if something belongs to you, it is easy to identify it'. This is not enough for the livestock owners as victims to prove their cases before the court, let alone win the case. What also emerged during the court proceedings was the level of education of the livestock owners as witnesses and victims of this crime.

[60] M Van Heerden, 'Parole board administrative action: an encroachment on the judicial decisions of the courts of law of South Africa' (2011) 24(2) *Acta Criminologica: Southern African Journal of Criminology* at https://hdl.handle.net/10520/EJC29068.

[61] 'Key sectors – Overviews of some of South Africa's key economic sectors' in *South African Business [Online]* 2012/2013 at https://webkiosk.globalafricanetwork.com/south-african-business-2022/66292608/40 (accessed 10 October 2022).

[62] KD Chetty and MA Fouche, 'The South African Judiciary' in MA Fouche (ed), *Legal Principles of Contracts and Commercial Law*, rev 6th edn (LexisNexis, 2007).

One of the victims, who lost 17 herds of cattle at that time, had a formal education only up to Grade 2. Witnesses are sometimes treated with disdain, partly on account of their level of education.

In cases that involve forensic evidence, it can be conclusively proved that the crime was committed. In such instances, experts' findings were submitted as evidence, and the investigators acknowledged the potential importance of such evidence. In addition, the prosecution presented such evidence before the court with more confidence. Despite the denials of the accused, such evidence can prove otherwise and hefty sentences are guaranteed. However, the defence lawyers are equally competent, and are prepared to protect ruthless stock thieves. Overall, the performance of the magistrates' court in the provinces is disastrous; they are known for their disposal of stock theft cases. The efficiency of the magistrates' courts in handling stock theft cases is thus questionable, owing to their inadequate understanding of the traditional markings, including their colours, that local people are accustomed to use for identifying livestock. Thus, the majority of rural residents argued that customary courts would be best suited to handle stock theft cases, because the *Tihosi* and *Indunas* – Kings – who preside over such cases, understand and have detailed knowledge of this crime.

They further argued that some leeway should be given to livestock owners to choose whether their cases should be tried by customary courts or magistrates' courts, to avoid manipulation of the entire system, since the magistrates' courts are not well versed in matters of stock theft and are reported to be corrupt. Alleged perpetrators engage the Government in lengthy and expensive cases, wasting taxpayers' money; they also employ sophisticated defence lawyers who win cases on technical grounds; they further deploy sophisticated legal jargon to the dismay of victims and witnesses, who may be uneducated rural dwellers. The alleged perpetrators can afford to hire shrewd lawyers and advocates, who end up getting them off. The complexity of the magistrates' court procedures, and the involvement of well-prepared defence lawyers and alleged corrupt CJS officials, prevents justice from prevailing. The livestock farmers acknowledged the inadequacies with which these courts are faced while dealing with stock theft cases. Therefore, these courts should be provided with assessors who have detailed knowledge of this crime. The victims should also know procedures to follow on appeal.

## IV. Conclusions

This chapter shows that the rural experiences of access to justice in recent years clearly favour the work of the traditional court to dispose of stock theft cases speedily with financial recompense for the victims of the crime. Nevertheless, the magistrates' courts still remain important. This chapter has also draw attention to a wide range of issues relating to access to justice for rural livestock farmers. It was established that they are often reluctant to report this crime and testify against potential thieves in court. As result of the latter, officials for both the courts in contention encounter difficulties in establishing ownership of unbranded livestock and possession of illegal stolen, relocated or even slaughtered livestock. The impact of this crime on these livestock farmers (poorly resourced and small-scale farmers) is severe. It is further highlighted that these farmers do not trust the functioning and performance of the local DoJ & CD, believing that to attend court proceedings can be costly and the proceedings take a long time to complete, the crime being 'laundered' through illegitimate means linked to high levels of corruption in accessibility to justice. Thus, their only hope lies in the operations of the local traditional court. It was also discovered that a cloud of no confidence hangs over the police as far as the farmers and community members affected are concerned, with increasing levels of stock theft being reported, in the absence of combined adequate and accessible justice systems.

In order to achieve positive rural access to justice and sustainable livelihoods throughout South Africa, it is imperative that a balance be established and clearly understood between the court systems identified: the limitations and strengths of each court should be effectively utilised in developing strategies embracing rural and urban differences. Only then will tangible improvements in the lives of the rural livestock farmers be witnessed. It is inevitable that future interventions will be guided by an urgent need to improve the provision of justice to South African rural people, including placing more emphasis on diversification of the options available in rural and urban areas, while empowering marginalised individuals and groups in both settings. The importance of tapping into African knowledge systems and practices, with the use of the traditional court in dealing with stock theft, should be deemed relevant to the prevention, control, combating and investigation of stock theft in South Africa.

Finding effective and lasting solutions to stock theft requires collective involvement and responses from more than just the farming community and the local SAPS. All community organisations and all spheres of government, including municipalities, provincial government structures and national departments – including the Department of Environmental Affairs, the Department of Agriculture, Land Reform and Rural Development (DALRRD), the Department of Agriculture, Forestry and Fisheries (DAFF), the Department of Forestry, Fisheries and the Environment (DFFE) and the Department of Social Development (DSD) – must work together. Other stakeholders to be included are Faith-Based Organisations (FBOs), private security companies, farm watches and local businesses. In summary, a concerted effort is needed to harness access to justice for rural people. More importantly, the legal voices and concerns of rural populations must be part of the process that aims to improve their lives. An important priority is to ensure that rural and urban access to justice planning structures and processes are appropriate to meet both present and future needs. Such should be recognised and incorporated into working justice models, while revising the planned strategies based on laws, legislation and policies introduced during the colonial period in South Africa.

# 5

# Why Doesn't a Mother Whose Son was Murdered Seek Justice?

## *A Critical Approach to the Relationship between Socio-Cultural Structure and Access to Justice in Rural Communities by Reconstructing the Sabahattin Ali's* Kağnı (The Oxcart) *Short Story*

MURAT MADENÜS

## I. Introduction

The fact that crime is an urban phenomenon is a social reality that we construct in our minds. Official crime statistics and studies based on these statistics reinforce this construction process. For this reason, crime and justice in rural areas are not among the subjects of mainstream criminology. However, there is a sui generis crime phenomenon in rural areas.[1] But this is not a phenomenon that can be easily researched even if it is desired. Rural communities, due to their closed cultural structure, do not easily accept the researcher within their private borders.[2] Literary works dealing with daily life in rural communities allow researchers to transcend these borders. To these ends, in this chapter I will reconstruct the situation of access to justice in a village in Türkiye in the 1930s by using Turkish social realist author Sabahattin Ali's short story *The Oxcart*[3] as a sociological source.

Rules of law are products of the cultures of societies.[4] However, much more important than this is that the functioning of these rules is based on the cultures

[1] See especially, JF Donnermeyer and W DeKeseredy, *Rural Criminology* (Routledge, 2014) 6, 26 for 'Myths about rural crime'.

[2] W Clack, 'The Extent of Stock Theft in South Africa' (2013) 26(2) *Acta Criminologica: African Journal of Criminology & Victimology* 77.

[3] S Ali, *Kağnı, Ses, Esirler*, 6th edn (Yapı Kredi Yayınları, 2010) 9, 12.

[4] The effect of culture on law is a subject that has been discussed since the first sociologists. See, eg, M Weber, *Economy and Society* (University of California Press, 1978) 641, 900.

of societies. Therefore, no matter how ideal the rules are on paper, they take on their actual social reality within the culture in which they are applied. As Lisa Moore will later explore in chapter 10 of this volume, location matters in how it shapes people's lives. This situation is more evident in rural communities with their own unique cultures than in modern urban societies with heterogeneous cultural structures. Because of their homogeneous and closed cultural structure, it is generally not possible for official legal rules to translate into practice in harmony with theory in rural communities. People's relations with the law are mostly determined by their status in the cultural structure that dominates the community, and as a result of this, law has a different impact on the lives of people who are members of the same rural community. While some people may have the power to easily avoid the restrictions and sanctions of the legal rules that run contrary to their own interests, and to legitimise their own illegal actions, others may refrain from seeking justice due to secondary victimisations that they will have to endure. It is not possible for us to understand these different experiences of justice in rural communities from a theoretical legal perspective. In order to understand these experiences, we need to adopt a 'criminological imagination'[5] and critically consider the socio-cultural structure that dominates the community.[6] However, as in many countries, studies on crime and justice in rural communities and data that can be used in new studies are very scarce in Türkiye too.[7]

Türkiye is a country in which until recently the rural population was higher than the urban population, and which still has a significant rural population.[8] This situation has created a rural crime phenomenon that needs to be taken seriously in Türkiye, from past to present.[9] So much so that there has been a law enforcement agency – Turkish General Command of Gendarmerie – that has been responsible for the safety and security of rural areas in Türkiye since 1839.[10] But there has been hardly any criminology study about rural areas in Türkiye. The main reason for this is that Turkish rural sociology was imported from the rural sociology of the United States (US).

[5] For the adaptation of CW Mills' concept of 'sociological imagination' to criminology, see especially E Carrabine et al, *Criminology: A Sociological Introduction*, 2nd edn (Routledge, 2009) 5, 6.

[6] See especially Donnermeyer and DeKeseredy (n 1) for a critical approach to rural crime.

[7] This is a general situation about crime in rural areas. See, eg, J Jones, 'The Neglected Problem of Farm Crime: An Exploratory Study' (2010) 9(1) *Safer Communities* 36.

[8] United Nations, Department of Economic and Social Affairs, Population Division, *World Urbanisation Prospects: The 2018 Revision* (United Nations, 2019).

[9] For a narration of the crimes that took place in the villages during the Ottoman Empire in the 19th century, see especially T Uzer, *Makedonya Eşkiyalık Tarihi ve Son Osmanlı Yönetimi* (Türk Tarih Kurumu, 1987) 46.

[10] A Sönmez, 'Transition of Domestic Security in the Ottoman Empire: From Zaptieh Organization to Gendarme' (2012) *International Congress of Asian and North African Studies* (10–15 September 2007) 2855 at www.ayk.gov.tr/wp-content/uploads/2015/01/SÖNMEZ-Ali-OSMANLI-DEVLETİ'NDE-İÇ-GÜVENLİĞİN-DÖNÜŞÜMÜ-ZAPTİYE-TEŞKİLATI'NDAN-JANDARMA'YA.pdf.

Sociology is one of the sciences that most feeds criminology.[11] Sociology studies in Türkiye started early, and the first chair of sociology in Türkiye was established in 1914.[12] In Turkish sociology, which was influenced by the French school in its first period, the village was seen as the home of the basic values of society, but it was not considered as a research topic on its own.[13] Towards the end of the 1930s, Turkish sociology's contact with US sociology began and continued increasingly following the Second World War. Rural sociology, which emerged in the US at the beginning of the twentieth century, was imported into Turkish sociology as part of this process.[14] As a result, the approach of US rural sociology, which does not deal with the phenomenon of rural crime,[15] has also been transferred to Turkish rural sociology. Consequently, although Türkiye has a historical and social reality, rural crime has never become an important subject of study in Turkish rural sociology. In the same period, rural crime occurred as a part of rural daily life in the works of many artists who talked about society in different ways. Literature has been at the forefront of this.

The first works to mention the village in Turkish literature are found in the last quarter of the nineteenth century.[16] However, social realistic village literature, which takes a critical approach to dealing with the relations of daily life in the village and the social structure that produces these relations, has developed since 1950. Social realist authors frequently included crime in the village, the reasons that led to crime, and the interaction between the parties to the crime and the functioning of justice in their works. They produced their works with the assumption that the negativities relating to these issues stemmed from the socio-cultural and socio-economic structure that dominates the community.[17] One of the pioneers of this movement is Sabahattin Ali.[18] Ali, who has published works in the genres of poetry, short stories and novels, frequently included the social problems experienced in Anatolian villages in the 1930s and 1940s in his stories. Thanks to the fact that he chooses to view his subjects from a realistic perspective and has critical creativity, Ali's works remain up-to-date despite the passing years. These features make the literary works of Sabahattin Ali and other social realist

[11] JF Donnermeyer, 'Introduction to the *International Handbook of Rural Criminology*' in JF Donnermeyer (ed), *The Routledge International Handbook of Rural Criminology* (Routledge, 2016) 3.

[12] B Gökçe, 'Türkiye'de Sosyolojinin Gelişimi' in *Türkiye'de Sosyal Bilimlerin Gelişmesi ve Dil ve Tarih-Coğrafya Fakültesi Sempozyumu Bildiriler* (Ankara Üniversitesi Basımevi, 1998).

[13] S Sağlam, 'Implementations and Discussions Regarding the Villages in Turkey and Their Reflections on Turkish Sociology' (2016) 53 *Sosyoloji Konferansları* 221.

[14] U Planck, 'Village Sociology in Turkey' in *Problems of the Development of Agriculture and Information on the State of Rural Sociology in Various Countries* (Warsaw, 10th Polish Conference of Rural Sociologists, 1971).

[15] For the US approach to rural sociology that excludes rural crime, see especially Donnermeyer and DeKeseredy (n 1) 34; Donnermeyer (n 11) 3.

[16] R Kaplan, *Cumhuriyet Dönemi Türk Edebiyatında Köy* (Akçağ Yayınları, 1997) 1, 64.

[17] Hİ Ünser, 'Approach to Village Reality of the Institute Graduate Writers (1950–1960)' (2021) 61(2) *Journal of Turkish Language and Literature* 709.

[18] C Rathbun, *The Village in the Turkish Novel and Short Story 1920–1955* (Mouton, 1972) 45.

authors important sources for understanding crime and justice in rural Türkiye. But whether fiction can be used to compile sociological and criminological data is a controversial issue.

What I am talking about here is not the content of a field like sociology of literature, which deals with the conditions of the period in which the work was created and the relationship between the author and society. What I mean is the use of fiction as data to be analysed directly by the researcher.[19] I am on the side of those advocating the appropriateness of use in this debate. I am absolutely not against the use of quantitative methods in the social sciences. However, I am of the opinion that the extreme positivist perspective, which fetishises numbers and statistics, has a lot of deficiencies in understanding and interpreting social life. On the other hand, I am of the opinion that qualitative methods that base their reliability solely on collecting data from real people are also insufficient in constructing social reality. These inadequacies are frequently encountered in the studies about crime and justice in rural areas.

Many crimes that occur in rural communities are born and die within the community.[20] These crimes are not reflected in official statistics, and researchers who construct their studies on official statistics accept the statistical illusion that there is no crime in rural areas. Therefore, when acting from this point of view, the issue of access to justice in rural communities does not even come to the fore. Qualitative researchers, on the other hand, accept the situations reflected by their interviewees as a social reality.[21] However, an interview is also a social interaction. The interviewees, who are also members of the rural community, reconstruct their communities and their positions within the communities as they would like them to be envisioned in the researcher's mind. Researchers also build their studies on these realities, as they are reflected to them. It should therefore be questioned how reliable the projected reality can be.

On the other hand, the freedom and capacity of artists to create releases them from the manipulation of these illusions. The phenomenon that the official average ignores, the deep meaning that cannot be discerned in the shallowness of superficial discourse, takes its place in the works of these artists. The voices of the disadvantaged, not accepted as normal, become audible in fiction.[22] If we turn to

[19] For examples of using fictional reality as data sources in sociology and criminology, see especially J Frauley, *Criminology, Deviance, and the Silver Screen: The Fictional Reality and The Criminological Imagination* (Palgrave Macmillan, 2010); MH Jacobsen (ed), *The Poetics of Crime: Understanding and Researching Crime and Deviance Through Creative Sources* (Ashgate Publishing, 2014) pt II, 'Crime in Fiction', 95–170; M Longo, *Fiction and Social Reality: Literature and Narrative as Sociological Resources* (Ashgate Publishing, 2015).

[20] See, eg, E Barclay, JF Donnermeyer and PC Jobes, 'The Dark Side of Gemeinschaft: Criminality within Rural Communities' (2004) 6 *Crime Prevention and Community Safety* 7.

[21] For qualitative data sources and methods of analysing data by qualitative researchers, see JW Creswell, *Qualitative Inquiry and Research Design: Choosing Among Five Approaches* (SAGE Publications, 2012) 145, 212.

[22] For a simple narration of the ability of artists to create reality in fiction, see especially V Ruggiero, *Crime in Literature: Sociology of Deviance and Fiction* (Verso, 2003) 1, 8.

our subject – fiction written by authors who have sociological imagination,[23] to adopt Mills's words, or the ability to tell about society,[24] using Becker's definition – the crime and justice phenomenon in the backyard of the rural area is made visible. In this context, in this chapter I benefit from opportunities offered by literature. I use Sabahattin Ali's short story *The Oxcart*, in Ruggeiro's words, 'as a tool for the communication of sociological meaning and the elaboration of criminological analysis'.[25] I analyse the story as a case study and try to understand and interpret a part of access to justice in the rural communities of Türkiye.

## II. A Murder in the Village

Ali reveals the pattern of a murder in the village with his one-sentence introduction: 'Because of a cropland problem, Savruks' Hüseyin shot Mehmet the Yellow in Arkbaşı.'[26]

Let us start with the cause of the murder. Savruks' Hüseyin commits the murder because of a cropland conflict. Cropland is indispensable for villagers' agricultural production. Although the characteristic feature of the new hegemony class that has emerged with globalisation has been to get rid of dependence on the land,[27] the possession of land has always been the main determinant of socioeconomic status in Turkish villages. Therefore, land conflicts are prevalent in Türkiye and have an important place among rural crimes. In such events, the status of the actors and their interactions with each other contribute to our understanding of the community structure.

The perpetrator is Savruks' Hüseyin. He is the son of an *agha*, that is, a wealthy and influential person with extensive land. The name of Hüseyin's family, which precedes his given name, represents multiplicity, unity and power. The deceased is Mehmet the Yellow. He does not have anybody other than his elderly mother and his surname is not reputable enough to be placed before his given name. 'The Yellow' is Mehmet's nickname, and he is probably called that because of his appearance: it represents loneliness and powerlessness.

In a village murder, the perpetrator, the deceased, and all the other villagers definitely know each other. Thanks to this density of acquaintanceship,[28] the members of the community know each other's status, the norms that dominate

[23] For the concept of 'sociological imagination', see CW Mills, *The Sociological Imagination* (Oxford University Press, 2000).

[24] For examples of different tools for telling about society, see HS Becker, *Telling About Society* (University of Chicago Press, 2007).

[25] Ruggiero (n 22) 1.

[26] Ali (n 3) 9 (author's own translation).

[27] Z Bauman, *Globalisation: The Human Consequences* (Polity Press, 1998) 9, 11.

[28] For the concept of density of acquaintanceship and its effect on rural communities, see especially WR Freudenburg, 'The Density of Acquaintanceship: An Overlooked Variable in Community Research?' (1986) 92(1) *American Journal of Sociology* 27.

the community and the functioning of the norms, and thus can build and present their own selves to others in line with their goals.[29] They do all of this within the boundaries of the reality of daily life that they have built with the influence of the socio-cultural structure within which they live from the moment they are born.[30] Similarly also in Ali's story, the villagers interpret the situation that emerged after the murder within the boundaries of the realities of their own daily life and act in line with their own benefits.

## A. First Reactions of the Villagers

Expressing the murder in one sentence, Ali begins to describe the villagers' first reactions after the murder: 'The occupants of a thirty-house village crawled all over each other. They were surprised. Everybody was waiting for the arrival of the gendarmes in fear.'[31]

Murder is an irreparable crime. The occurrence of such a crime in the village causes chaos. The villagers are astonished at first; but astonishment soon gives way to fear. In Türkiye the safety and security of villages are ensured by the gendarmerie who, having military discipline, are different from the police. Villagers both love and respect the gendarmerie while also being wary of them. At the time of the story, the 1930s, the arrival of the gendarmerie in the village after such a serious crime would cause anxiety and fear. But, having overcome their initial astonishment, the villagers begin to think, considering the characteristics of the place in which they live:

> However, the gendarmerie station was six hours away from here; they would not stop by for as long as fifteen days unless somebody from the village brought the news of the murder. This was the last thing that came to the mind of the villagers.[32]

In the past, villages were located far from cities and each other; and, despite the opportunities provided by technology,[33] they continue to be relatively distant places today. Being at a distance adds the feature of the village's being closed off. It is not possible for an outsider to be aware of what is happening in the village unless news comes from inside. The villagers in our story also realise this reality and start to think about this reality. They remember that, at the time of the story, when there were almost no motor vehicles and patrols were made on foot or sometimes on horseback, even the closest gendarmerie station is hours away and most of the

[29] See especially E Goffman, *Presentation of Self in Everyday Life* (University of Edinburgh, 1956) for a broader sociological perspective.

[30] See especially PL Berger and T Luckman, *The Social Construction of Reality: A Treatise in the Sociology of Knowledge* (Penguin Books, 1991) for a broader sociological perspective.

[31] Ali (n 3) 9 (author's own translation).

[32] Ali (n 3) 9 (author's own translation).

[33] See, eg, D Newman, J Mant and F Gordon, 'Vulnerability, Legal Need and Technology in England and Wales' (2021) 21(3) *International Journal of Discrimination and the Law* 230.

time the gendarmerie will not visit the village for days. From this moment on, they begin to act under the influence of the socio-cultural structure produced by the social reality of the village.

## B. Blocking of Access to Justice of a Mother whose Son has been Murdered and Her Acceptance of the Situation

As already mentioned, villages are generally isolated places, and this causes them to produce their own unique culture. Therefore, although formal legal norms should be valid, in practice 'actual operating rules'[34] prevail, even following a murder in these isolated communities.

Murder is a crime that should be investigated directly, without any need for a formal complaint. The legal norm dictates this. However, for an investigation to begin, the state must be aware of the crime. In a village this is not always and immediately possible, especially in the past, and so actual operating rules that force the residents to act according to the parties' status in the community come into play:

> [A]fter that, the elders of the village gathered around Hüseyin's father, Mevlüt Agha, in the coffeehouse. Mehmet the Yellow had no one except his elderly mother. They confronted her; started to persuade her not to complain.[35]

Ali's telling of the story indicates that the rules are made by the elite of the village. These are the influential men of the village, such as the *agha*, the headman, the *imam* and the respected elders. Ali emphasises that these people, who are also the architects of the order that is claimed to prevent crime in rural communities, even if they are also guilty, can side with the strong, whose friendship they believe will be beneficial and whose enmity will bring harm. Ali then explains why the old woman should not complain, from the mouth of the elite:

> Hey crone, what will you gain from it if you complain? Who would go and testify that Mevlüt Agha's son shot a man? Even if someone does, if you go to the town once or twice in a month and abandon your field for four or five days each time, who will plant it; who will take care of your job for you? The town is a two-day journey. If you go, they might say witnesses did not come, and you will have to go again next week. Your trial would probably get postponed. You might confuse the dates and you will! The gendarmerie will take you away. Even if you want to, you can't get rid of all these burdens and you would perish.[36]

Let us now consider these justifications, which are the products of the socio-cultural structure of the community, one by one.

[34] HS Becker, *Outsiders: Studies in the Sociology of Deviance* (The Free Press, 1997) 17.
[35] Ali (n 3) 9 (author's own translation).
[36] Ali (n 3) 9 (author's own translation).

Whether the main determinant of social life is economy or culture has not been decided since Marx and Weber.[37] Regardless, class division based on the economy turns equality before the law into a utopian concept. This situation manifests itself in a rural-specific situation in terms of disadvantaged groups, and the old woman in our story is a member of these groups.

Courthouses tend to be located in provincial and district centres. However, as a result of rational modern calculations such as workload and cost, courthouses are sometimes not established even in some districts. Therefore, the courthouse is far away for economically disadvantaged villagers. In the past, when transportation was not as easily available as it is today, it could take days for villagers to make a single trip to the courthouse. Although transport facilities have been improved, rural and urban methods of transport are incomparable and it is still quite burdensome for villagers to have their judicial proceedings situated in a distant venue.

On the other hand, in a community where the powerful can impose their own rules, witnesses whose information is taken into account in the pursuit of justice seldom take the side of justice without further consideration. This is because they fear the enmity of the powerful. Besides, witnesses usually do not want to be exposed to the burdens that victims have to endure. Some of them may accept the witness summons and go to court for the first time, but the protracted process will interrupt their work. The Turkish proverb, 'If you don't have a job, be a witness, if you have a lot of money, be a guarantor', describes the burden of being a witness. Therefore, witnesses try to get out of it at the first opportunity. The absence of witnesses causes the judicial process to be further prolonged. Therefore, poor victims in particular may not want to continue proceedings. However, it is not easy to terminate the process once started, and those who know this can easily use it against poor villagers, as seen in our story.

Another social fact that turns into a weapon the powerful can use against the poor is religion. According to the village elite in our story, the death of Mehmet the Yellow is a matter of destiny, the will of Allah. The old woman's appeal to justice is nothing more than opposition to the will of Allah using man-made law. According to the *imam*, what the old woman should do is submit to her destiny:

> So, it was an accident. Allah the Almighty has so willed, will you oppose Allah's order with a court of law? No matter what you do, your son won't come back. Let's get this thing over with.[38]

With these words, Ali depicts religion as one of the most effective determinants of the rural community structure. Ali critically considers the impact of religion on the rural community, and he is not alone in this thought. Mahmut Makal, the author of *A Village in Anatolia*, one of the first social realist novels in Turkish literature, used the words 'our villagers were created to serve religion' in his notes

[37] See, eg, M Gould, 'Marx and Weber and the Logic of Historical Explanation: The Rise of Machine Capitalism' (2016) 16 *Journal of Classical Sociology* 321.

[38] Ali (n 3) 9 (author's own translation).

based on ethnographic observations, and then stated that the villagers actually do not act according to religion but attribute a religious character to their traditional actions.[39] Analysing the development of secularism in Türkiye, Berkes conceptualises this attitude as the 'force of tradition, which tends to promote the domination of religion'.[40] The force of tradition shapes the structure of the community and creates its sanctified elite.

Each rural community has its own unique structure of belief and functioning. This structure and its functioning are determined and abused by the elite of the rural community and produce functions appropriate to the rural community to which the structure belongs. Functions always produce the order of the community, but the order does not produce positive functions for everyone.[41] The elite can easily turn religion into an 'apparatus'[42] that allows them to protect their daily interests. For this they use the most irresistible concept of religion, 'destiny'. By including actions that are the product of human will and harming the weak within the concept of 'destiny', they can turn them into an order that the divine creator wants and which cannot be prevented.

However, besides the irresistible protection afforded by destiny, there is also a price to harmful behaviour, and the price determined by the elite serves to neutralise the damaging behaviour of the powerful. The elite in our story also offer to pay the price of the harm to persuade the victim with a threatening approach:

> Mehmet the Yellow was of no use to you anyway. He used to hang out at weddings, waste the money that you gained from the crops and give it to women. Mevlüt Agha says he will always get your back from now on. What do you say?
>
> …
>
> Isn't it, huh? Say it, huh! Have you been convinced? Say it now![43]

By these words Ali reveals how the elite use social functioning to neutralise their unlawfulness and to force the victim to accept that neutralisation. Neutralisation techniques are a mechanism by which people produce justifications to show that they are not really responsible for their crimes.[44] The powerful have more opportunity to make this mechanism work. Ali indicates that depreciating those they harm, declaring their existence bad are among the methods that elites frequently use for neutralisation. Ali next shows how successful the neutralisation was and how suddenly everything returned to normal:

> The people in the coffeehouse slowly left. The old woman walked and sat by her son's bedside. With one hand she began to repel the flies, and with the other she was wiping

[39] M Makal, *A Village in Anatolia*, tr W Deedes (Vallentine, Mitchell, 1954).

[40] N Berkes, *The Development of Secularism in Turkey* (Routledge, 1998) 6.

[41] RK Merton, *Social Theory and Social Structure* (Free Press of Glencoe, 1949) 40.

[42] See especially L Althusser, *On the Reproduction of Capitalism: Ideology and Ideological State Apparatuses* (Verso, 2014) for the concept of 'ideological state apparatus' that I am inspired by.

[43] Ali (n 3) 9–10 (author's own translation).

[44] See especially GM Sykes and D Matza, 'Techniques of Neutralisation: A Theory of Delinquency' (1957) 22(6) *American Sociological Review* 664, 670.

> her eyes, which were small as chickpeas because of age and sickness. She looked like she was waiting for a patient's last minutes. She was waving her hand slowly, repelling the flies. An old man, shouting in a low voice, sent the children home. Others also dispersed slowly. A few young men got the body and took it home. By evening, everything was back to normal. The deceased was washed and buried as calmly as if he had died of natural causes after a long illness. Mevlüt Agha sent two milk goats, a bag of flour and a bag of sugar to Mehmet the Yellow's mother before the azan.[45]

In order to understand how this happens, it is necessary to consider the processes of individual lives within the community. Persons belonging to different classes of an unequal socio-economic structure construct the realities of their daily life under the influence of this structure. This causes them to have a different consciousness,[46] and as a result they perceive the same event in different ways and act according to their social status. After the murder in our story, the *agha* whose son killed an old, lonely and poor woman's son decides that he can easily cover up the murder. The elite of the village believe that it will be beneficial for them to side with the powerful even if it is illegal, while the rest of the village think that keeping silent is the best option. In such a situation, the poor and lonely old woman decides that acceptance rather than the pursuit of justice will cause her less harm. As a result, the socio-cultural rules actually operating, which are produced by the unequal socio-economic structure, normalise the murder and a mother whose son was murdered agrees not to seek justice.

## C. Spread of News of the Murder Outside the Community and Intervention of the State

It is a paradox that a rural crime may easily be hidden or may equally be exposed. It is pretty easy to hide because only a few people living in an isolated community may be aware of the crime. On the other hand, it is also very easy for the crime to become public knowledge outside the community if almost all the members of the community are aware of it; if even one of them carries the news outside the community, it will be enough for news of the crime to spread. The earlier part of the story is an example of the first situation, while what follows is an example of the second situation.

The perception that rural communities consist only of relatives and neighbours helping each other is a rural idyll we construct in our minds.[47] People living in rural communities can experience lots of conflict with each other. Each side in a conflict will look for opportunities to cause difficulties for the other. The unlawful

[45] Ali (n 3) 10 (author's own translation). The *azan* is the Muslim call to prayer.

[46] See, eg, R Eyerman, 'False Consciousness and Ideology in Marxist Theory' (1981) 24 *Acta Sociologica* 43, 56 for a Marxist interpretation.

[47] See, eg, J Jones, 'Looking Beyond the "Rural Idyll": Some Recent Trends in Rural Crime' (2012) 89 *Centre for Crime and Justice Studies* 8, 9; P Somerville, R Smith and G McElwee, 'The Dark Side of the Rural Idyll: Stories of Illegal/Illicit Economic Activity in the UK Countryside' (2015) 39 *Journal of Rural Studies* 1.

act of one of them can present just such a chance to the other. The murder in our story becomes public knowledge after a person who is in conflict with Hüseyin is made aware of the crime: 'Mehmet the Poor, who is a shoemaker in the town and at loggerheads with the Savruks' Hüseyin, immediately informed the government about the murder he heard from the villagers'.[48] After that, the state starts to intervene:

> At first the prosecutor wanted to come by himself, accompanied only by the doctor. But later, he did not dare to travel on horseback for days in the heat of August. Instead, he sent two shrewd gendarmes, telling them to investigate the case. The doctor, being more cautious, sternly instructed the gendarmes to remove the body and bring it back to town if there had been a murder.[49]

The state investigates the murder through its prosecutor and law enforcement officers. As a public official, the doctor also plays an important role in the investigation. These public officials are generally well-educated urbanites from different regions, appointed by the central Government; they may view a job in the rural area as drudgery, an example of this being given in our story. From this moment on, Ali describes what happened after the intervention of the gendarmes:

> It was about a month later, two cavalry gendarmes came to the village. They dismounted in front of the coffeehouse. When he saw them, the headman's heart leapt, because they were not the gendarmes from the local station, they were probably coming from the province. One of the gendarmes immediately took out a pen and paper at the coffeehouse, and started to take statements from everyone, starting with the headman. The other gendarme was walking up and down in the village square.[50]

The assigning of gendarmes from another region indicates the existence of an important event. As an example of this, the situation in our story is a serious indication that the state has stepped in to ensure the justice it has promised. With the intervention of the gendarmes the rules operating in practice disappear and the rules of the state begin to work. This means that official rules of law will begin to apply. From this moment on, the question we need to answer is whether the rules of the state operating in a socially unequal structure can offer justice to the old woman in addition to punishing the criminals.

## D. Secondary Victimisation

Victims do not report a large number of the crimes to which they are exposed for different reasons.[51] They generally take this decision at the end of a rational thinking process. Before reporting the crime, victims think about the possible

[48] Ali (n 3) 11 (author's own translation).
[49] ibid (author's own translation).
[50] ibid (author's own translation).
[51] See, eg, JV Kesteren and JV Dijk, 'Key Victimological Findings from the International Crime Survey' in SG Shoham, P Knepper and M Kett (eds), *International Handbook of Victimology* (CRC Press, 2010) 161.

repercussions of reporting. If they believe that the cost of reporting outweighs the benefit they think they will get from justice, they may prefer not to report the crime.[52] The community structure and the victim's position in the community affect the outcome of the comparison. Mehmet the Yellow's mother evaluates the situation and does not report the murder even though her own son was killed. Even when the state intervenes, this situation does not change:

> Mehmet the Yellow's mother did not say anything in her statement. Only: 'I'm not a claimant about anyone!' she said. She even responded to the query 'Did your son die of natural causes or was he shot?' with the same sentence. The pain of her son's loss had not yet left her, but falling into the hands of the government was much more terrible to her than her son's death. Thirty years ago, one of the villagers had a bag of bulgur stolen in the town's market and called her as a witness. She was thinking about her shuttling to court for six full months and the neglect of her fields at that time. However, she was also younger at that time …
>
> Then, Mehmet would not come back, also it would not be beneficial to make an enemy of Mevlüt Agha, then she would starve to death in the village. So she always denied it.[53]

Ali's words from the old woman's mouth provide important sociological data on reporting crime, the initiator of access to justice in rural communities. While much more common at the time the story takes place, most people in rural communities still make a living from farming. Farming is more than a job, it is a lifestyle. It requires tasks that need to be done daily, even hourly, and farmers can never neglect their duties. Although at the time of the story it was more common, small family businesses still constitute the majority compared to large industrial farms, and many of the small farmers are not financially able to employ non-family workers. Hence farmers spend all their time fulfilling the requirements of farming. One farmer describes this situation as being 'worse than prison'.[54] Being involved in a judicial process of such intensity keeps the farmer from his work for a considerable time. The impact of this on poor farmers is much more devastating and therefore they do not report many crimes; if they have to be involved in the judicial process they often suffer secondary victimisation.

Although it may seem absurd at first, the victim's identification of the perpetrator is another factor that prevents the reporting of crime in rural communities.[55] A victim who thinks that his neighbour has committed the crime may worry about being accused of slander if he makes a complaint without concrete evidence;[56]

[52] See, eg, W Skogan, 'Reporting Crime to Police: The Status of World Research' (1984) 21(2) *Journal of Research on Crime and Delinquency* 113.

[53] Ali (n 3) 11 (author's own translation).

[54] M Madenüs, 'Agricultural Crime Fact in Rural Communities: The Denizli Bozkurt Sample' (unpublished PhD dissertation, Gazi University, Ankara, 2021) 212.

[55] See, eg, KM Anderson and M McCall, *Farm Crime in Australia* (Australian Institute of Criminology, 2005).

[56] See, eg, E Barclay, 'The Determinants of Reporting Farm Crime in Australia' (2003) 27(2) *International Journal of Comparative and Applied Criminal Justice* 31.

or, as is seen in Ali's story, victims may think they would suffer further harm if they were to complain about a member of the elite.

However, murder is a crime investigated on behalf of the public and therefore a complaint is not required. The reasoning behind this practice is not to allow an act that creates disorder in society and causes serious harm to society to go unpunished; it is thus intended to prevent similar acts. However, if this aim were to push the victim's easy access to justice into the background, the intervention of the state might lead to second victimisation of the victim.

When the actors in the criminal justice system limit themselves only to the fulfilment of their official duties, the law is enforced but the spirit of the law dies. In particular, the full and easy access of disadvantaged individuals to justice needs interpretations by the actors in the criminal justice system that will keep the spirit of law alive. Otherwise, the judicial process may do more harm to the victims than the crimes to which they are exposed.[57] It is much more possible to encounter such examples in rural communities where there are strong socio-cultural barriers to access to justice.

There is an example of this situation in our story. The gendarmes who find the body, identify and catch the criminals are convinced that they have completed their duty. Thus, the prosecutor and the doctor who commissioned them are convinced that they also have fulfilled their duty. However, this does not mean anything to the old woman, and with the task of carrying the body of her own son to the town her secondary victimisation begins:

> Clinging to the side of the oxcart, she walked a little further. Her feet were were getting tangled. She wanted to shout 'Oooh' to the oxen, but her voice stuck in her throat; her hands slipped from the oxcart and she fell to the ground, as, covered in the dust, she got up again and ran … Before she could catch the oxcart, she fell again, her face buried in the fine white and ashen dust of the road.
>
> As the oxcart hit the stones, it slowly moved forward on its own, throwing the wrapped corpse from side to side and making a screeching noise that rose and fell, leaving behind a light cloud of dust under the moonlight and in the silence of the night.[58]

The stark reality that shines through Ali's powerful literary expression is the justification of those who claim that an old, lonely and poor woman's search for justice after her son was killed caused nothing more than new harm to her. Double victimisation.

## III. Conclusion

My analysis shows that literature began to produce ideas very early on about crime and justice in rural areas, which sociology and criminology have only just

[57] See, eg, U Orth, 'Secondary Victimization of Crime Victims by Criminal Proceedings' (2002) 15(4) *Social Justice Research* 313.

[58] Ali (n 3) 12 (author's own translation).

discovered. The artist's ability to think outside the box and the fact that words offer the artist the opportunity to construct a deep meaning has made fictional literary texts much more powerful in telling about society. Literary texts are thus invaluable data sources for sociologists and criminologists.

In my study, Ali's words made me hear the voice of a mother that I would have difficulty hearing as a sociologist, and presented to me the creative narrative, which I was lacking, with a subtle and simple integrity. Many things have changed since Ali told his story, both in Türkiye and in the wider world. However, Ali's narrative reflects both the historical background of access to justice in rural communities and offers universal suggestions about the current state of the issue.

Ali's narration shows that the rural idyll, which has been imprinted on the cultural memories of almost all societies, is an illusion. Contrary to what was promised with the rural idyll, from past to present, there is a crime phenomenon in rural communities that needs to be taken seriously. This fact emerges from the effect of rural characteristics. The murder in Ali's story is an example of this, and such crimes are called rural crimes. Rural crimes are produced by the social organisation of rural communities, while mainstream criminology refers only to its crime-preventing features. This also applies to access to justice in rural communities, which is an important aspect of rural crime.

Access to justice begins with the victim's reporting of the crime to official bodies. The victim's right to report is legal guaranteed and everyone has equal rights in this regard. However, the social organisations of rural communities produced by the rural socio-economic and socio-cultural structure can prevent easy access to justice. The fact that the mother in Ali's story cannot prosecute the person who killed her son shows what kind of illusion legal equality on paper creates.

Poverty, combined with the difficulties of rural geography, has prevented the old woman from accessing justice, and gave the powerful the opportunity to legitimise and neutralise their criminal acts. In a community order that works in this way, especially disadvantaged people's easy access to justice needs the actors in the criminal justice system to adopt interpretations that can keep the spirit of the law alive. The experience of the elderly woman after the intervention of the state is an indication that intervention by the actors in the criminal justice system without such an interpretation can cause secondary victimisation of the victim.

Consequently, understanding the access to justice of especially disadvantaged people in rural communities requires a critical perspective on the cultural structure in these communities and use of a sociological and criminological imagination. This point of view, which also dominates Ali's narrative, shows us that equality before the law and, as a part of it, easy access of all members of rural communities to justice, cannot progress beyond a utopian dream within a socio-cultural structure that is reproduced in communities where socio-economic equality does not exist, regardless of history and place.

# 6

# Rethinking Access to Justice for Indigenous Peoples

FIONA ALLISON AND CHRIS CUNNEEN

## I. Introduction

This chapter focuses on Indigenous peoples and access to justice. It shows that access to justice is particularly limited for Indigenous peoples living in rural and remote areas. Further, the chapter argues that access to justice must be conceptualised to incorporate Indigenous rights, most importantly the right to self-determination. Finally, we make some suggestions about improving access to justice for Indigenous peoples living in rural and remote areas. While the chapter concentrates in particular on First Nations peoples within Australia,[1] we begin by drawing attention to the wider position of Indigenous peoples globally. According to the United Nations, there are over 476 million Indigenous peoples living in more than 90 countries and they comprise over 6 per cent of the world's population.[2] Not surprisingly, there is great diversity in languages, cultures and histories. There is also diversity in the legal, political and, in some cases, constitutional relationships with state entities. However, there are also commonalities. Across both urban and rural regions, Indigenous peoples are significantly more likely to be living in *extreme* poverty compared to non-Indigenous people. In particular the rural demographic is important because over 73 per cent of global Indigenous populations live in rural areas – here they comprise one-third of all people living in extreme poverty.[3] More than 86 per cent of Indigenous peoples globally work in the informal economy, compared to 66 per cent of their

[1] A note on terminology. We use 'First Nations' peoples when referring to Indigenous peoples in Australia, also referred to as Aboriginal and Torres Strait Islander peoples. We use 'Indigenous' peoples in reference to the international context. In some international literature the phrase 'Indigenous and Tribal Peoples' is used. In line with the UN we use 'Indigenous' to cover both.

[2] International Labour Organization, *Implementing the ILO Indigenous and Tribal Peoples Convention 169. Towards an Inclusive, Sustainable and Just Future* (ILO, 2019).

[3] Extreme poverty is defined as living on less than $1.90 per day: ibid.

non-Indigenous counterparts. Health, housing and other social outcomes show similar poorer trajectories.[4]

These issues are not limited to Indigenous peoples living in medium- to low-income countries (the global south). In high-income countries similar social, economic and political disparities are also reproduced. For example, Australia is a wealthy liberal democracy and consistently ranks among the top countries internationally in the United Nations Human Development Index (HDI). However, the HDI ranking for Indigenous people within Australia is similar to that of El Salvador.[5] Like Indigenous peoples elsewhere, First Nations people in Australia are much more likely to live in regional or remote areas than non-Indigenous people (63 per cent compared to 29 per cent).[6] Their economic and social exclusion is evident in a range of areas, including poor access to quality housing and health services, high rates of unemployment, poor educational outcomes, and high rates of criminalisation and incarceration.[7] It is widely recognised that the long-term and ongoing effects of colonisation, land theft and racial discrimination have been causal factors in bringing about and maintaining the current state of affairs.[8]

Over the last decade the authors have been conducting research in First Nations communities across Australia and working alongside First Nations organisations and other community-based and public-funded legal services on access to justice and legal needs – a body of research and writing referred to as the Indigenous Legal Needs Project (ILNP).[9] Much of this work has focused on regional, rural and remote communities, given that this is where First Nations people are more likely to live. The research has identified substantial levels of legal need and substantial problems for First Nations people in accessing justice. The high level of unmet legal need compromises First Nations peoples' capacity to realise their full legal entitlements. Nearly 20 years ago an Australian Senate Inquiry found that in remote communities, access to justice is 'so inadequate that remote Indigenous people cannot be said to have full civil rights'.[10] Our research shows that this statement is still relevant today.[11] Access to justice is important in its own right, but it

[4] United Nations Development Program (UNDP), *Human Development Report 2014* (UNDP, 2014).

[5] United Nations, *State of the World's Indigenous Peoples* (UN Department of Economic and Social Affairs, 2009) 23.

[6] Productivity Commission, *Overcoming Indigenous Disadvantage 2020* (Commonwealth of Australia, 2020) 1.13.

[7] ibid.

[8] L Behrendt et al, *Aboriginal and Torres Strait Islander Legal Relations* (Oxford University Press, 2019).

[9] For a summary see F Allison, M Schwartz and C Cunneen, 'The Civil and Family Law Needs of Indigenous People 40 Years after Sackville: Findings of the Indigenous Legal Needs Project' in A Durbach, B Edgeworth and V Sentas (eds), *Law and Poverty in Australia* (Federation Press, 2017) ch 16.

[10] Senate Legal and Constitutional References Committee, *Legal Aid and Access to Justice* (Australian Parliament, 2004) 5.120.

[11] Allison, Schwartz and Cunneen (n 9); F Allison, M Schwartz and C Cunneen, '"That's discrimination!" Indigenous peoples' experiences of discrimination in the Northern Territory' (2013) 8(5) *Indigenous Law Bulletin* 8; C Cunneen, F Allison and M Schwartz, 'Access to justice for Aboriginal people in the Northern Territory' (2014) 49(2) *Australian Journal of Social Issues* 21; C Cunneen,

is also essential to combating social disadvantage and exclusion, especially when this exclusion compounds vulnerability to experiencing further legal problems. Improved access to justice is one important component in addressing the social and economic marginalisation of First Nations people.

## II. The Concept of Access to Justice in an Indigenous Context

Access to justice is generally understood in the context of addressing the barriers that inhibit individuals who have a legal problem from securing their rights or achieving a satisfactory legal outcome through legal dispute resolution mechanisms. For example, the Human Rights Council UN Expert Mechanism on the Rights of Indigenous Peoples identifies access to justice as 'requiring the ability to seek and obtain remedies for wrongs (human rights breaches) through institutions of justice, formal or informal, and in conformity with human rights standards' and as 'essential for the protection and promotion of all other human rights'.[12] Elsewhere, access to justice is itself identified as a human right, as well as being a means of protecting other (human) rights.[13] Various strategies have been introduced over time to implement this framework, often involving reform of the legal system.[14] Alternative dispute resolution (ADR), for instance, emerged as a response to the formality, delays and cost associated with using courts and tribunals. Government subsidised legal services were also introduced in response to costs associated with accessing legal assistance and representation.[15]

Definitions of access to justice are often framed by and within the dominant legal system, which may result in a failure to reflect the needs and viewpoints of those who are seeking justice, including Indigenous peoples. There have been calls to expand the current definition of access to justice so that it is better informed by those seeking justice.[16] Access to justice, it is argued, ought to be providing

F Allison and M Schwartz, *The Civil and Family Law Needs of Indigenous People in Queensland – A Report of the Australian Indigenous Legal Needs Project* (James Cook University, 2014); F Allison, C Cunneen and M Schwartz, *Indigenous Legal Needs Project: Western Australian Report* (James Cook University, 2014); M Schwartz, C Cunneen and F Allison, *Indigenous Legal Needs Project: Victorian Report* (James Cook University, 2013); F Allison, C Cunneen and M Schwartz, *Indigenous Legal Needs Project: Western Australian Report* (James Cook University, 2014); C Cunneen and M Schwartz, *Civil and Family Law Needs of Aboriginal People* (New South Wales Legal Aid Commission, 2008).

[12] Expert Mechanism on the Rights of Indigenous Peoples Advice No 5: *Access to justice in the promotion and protection of the rights of indigenous peoples*, A/HRC/EMRIP/2013/2, 3, para 3.

[13] UNDP, *Programming for Justice: Access for All* (Bangkok, UNDP, 2005.

[14] A Currie, *Riding the Third Wave: Rethinking Criminal Legal Aid within an Access to Justice Framework* (Research and Statistics Division, Department of Justice, Canada, 2003) 2.

[15] R Sackville, 'Some thoughts on access to justice' (2004) 2 *New Zealand Journal of Public and International Law* 85.

[16] G Paquet, 'The judgement of wider courts' in Department of Justice (ed), *Expanding Horizons: Rethinking Access to Justice in Canada*, Proceedings of a National Symposium (Department of Justice Canada, 2000) 80.

forms of justice that meet 'citizen needs' and can be attained through processes that justice seekers, including members of more marginalised groups, are likely to engage with, participate in or lead. Examples of potential expansions range from policy reform that might avert legal problems from arising in the first instance, to protest movements seeking justice for particular problems or disputes, and political activism for more inclusive democratic representation.[17] An expanded concept of access to justice may shift the concept away from its current predominant focus on individual legal disputes or problems and may not reference formal legal remedies or rights at all.

We are interested in rethinking what access to justice means for Indigenous peoples within post-colonial settings, and particularly in a settler colonial situation such as Australia where First Nations peoples are a minority population who have been largely dispossessed of their land and subjected to ongoing discrimination. Current conceptualisations of access to justice[18] tend to be limited by their focus on non-Indigenous legal remedies and enhancing access to existing legal services and processes that have been largely defined and implemented within western colonial paradigms. For Indigenous peoples, access to justice is enshrined as a specific right in the United Nations Declaration on the Rights of Indigenous Peoples (UNDRIP).[19]

Though a universal human right, Article 40 of the UNDRIP indicates that access to justice in an Indigenous context ought to be informed by Indigenous understandings of justice. The UNDRIP sets out key principles that inform these perspectives and underpin all UNDRIP rights. These are self-determination, participation in decision-making, protection of culture and equality. As such, any reframing of access to justice from an Indigenous standpoint needs to reflect and strengthen these principles. The impact of cultural difference, Indigenous law, and the historical and contemporary experiences of colonisation, including genocide, land theft, the forced removal of children and extensive criminalisation, mean that Indigenous understandings of 'justice' and access to it can have a very different resonance from the dominant view.[20] In Australia, First Nations' perspectives on what constitutes effective access to justice are largely excluded from prevailing conceptualisations and policy recommendations. Even where the

[17] C Parker, *Just Lawyers: Regulation and Access to Justice* (Oxford University Press, 1999) 56.

[18] Allison, Schwartz and Cunneen (n 9) 247–48; National Congress of Australia's First Peoples (Congress), 'Access to Justice in Australia: Aboriginal and Torres Strait Islander Peoples' Experience' in W Littlechild and E Stamatopolou (eds), *Indigenous People's Access to Justice, Including Truth and Reconciliation Processes* (Institute for the Study of Human Rights, Colombia University, 2014).

[19] Art 40 reads as follows. 'Indigenous peoples have the right to access to and prompt decision through just and fair procedures for the resolution of conflicts and disputes with States or other parties, as well as to effective remedies for all infringements of their individual and collective rights. Such a decision shall give due consideration to the customs, traditions, rules, and legal systems of the indigenous peoples concerned and international human rights.' UN General Assembly, *United Nations Declaration on the Rights of Indigenous Peoples*: resolution/adopted by the General Assembly, 2 October 2007, A/RES/61/295.

[20] National Congress of Australia's First Peoples (Congress) (n 18).

concept of access to justice has been more expansive to incorporate, at its widest margins, democratic representation, participation in social movements and civic education for respect of rights, there has been little attention to the specific justice needs of First Nations people, or how their perspectives can broaden our understanding of access to justice. In short, we are interested in identifying what genuine access to justice might look like from a First Nations' viewpoint.

## III. Identifying First Nations Legal Needs in Regional, Rural and Remote Areas

In the first instance it is essential to ascertain the nature and extent of the legal needs of First Nations peoples. Access to justice has broad application to criminal, civil and family law contexts. However, in terms of First Nations, the focus in Australia to date has been largely on reforming the criminal justice system. The Royal Commission into Aboriginal Deaths in Custody (RCADIC) reported in 1991. Since then, State and Territory as well as federal policies, and First Nations' community activism, have predominantly focused on the critical problem of criminalisation and the over-representation of First Nations peoples in youth and adult prisons – a problem that has in many respects deepened since the RCADIC.[21] Until quite recently there was much less discussion of enhancing civil and family law access to justice for First Nations peoples, despite its importance. The ILNP was the first systematic research to spend time in First Nations communities across Australia and talk with communities about their civil and family law problems.[22] The ILNP visited 40 remote, regional and urban Indigenous communities across four States and one Territory: New South Wales (NSW), the Northern Territory (NT), Victoria, Queensland (Qld) and Western Australia (WA). These jurisdictions have approximately 90 per cent of all First Nations peoples in Australia. Data were collected in these communities from nearly 800 Indigenous focus group participants through a questionnaire and through group discussions.[23]

We found substantial levels of unaddressed legal need. In particular, seven priority areas were highlighted: housing (tenancy), discrimination (racial), credit and debt and associated consumer law, social security, child protection, and wills and estates.[24] Almost all of these issues were frequently reported by a

[21] In 2020, First Nation young people accounted for almost 50% of the child prison population and First Nation adults 29% of the adult prison population: Australian Bureau of Statistics (ABS), *Prisoners in Australia 2020* (ABS, 2021); Australian Institute of Health and Welfare (AIHW), *Youth Detention Population in Australia 2020* (AIHW, 2021). First Nations people comprise approximately 2% of the total adult population and approximately 6% of the population aged 10–17 years.

[22] Allison, Schwartz and Cunneen (n 9).

[23] ibid 234–35.

[24] ibid 235.

large proportion of participants in the above questionnaire and group discussions in the communities we visited. Tenancy was by far and away the most common issue for First Nations people in every State – it was reported by around half of participants (depending on both gender and jurisdiction) and largely reflected the shocking condition of housing for First Nations people in Australia. In some individual communities *every* participant reported difficulties in this area. Women in all States were more likely than men to experience tenancy issues. In addition, some four in every 10 people we spoke with had encountered (generally race-based) discrimination in interactions with government and non-government agencies. Credit/debt-related issues concerning bills or loans affected between 18 and 35 per cent of participants, depending on the State. Of those receiving social security benefits, between 23 and 33 per cent had experienced a problem or dispute, most frequently around access to and being cut off from benefits and overpayments, resulting in debt.

Wills were significant as a priority area of unrecognised and unmet legal need. Very few First Nations people have a will (between 6 and 13 per cent of participants across the different States). However, the majority of people expressed a desire for legal help to draw up a will. We found that it is not uncommon for First Nations people to experience a dispute after a death, for example involving the location of burial, and these can arise from the strong cultural connections to specific lands (Country) and kinship relations. One area of legal need that we included as a priority that was consistently highlighted in discussions as causing great hardship and distress was child protection matters.[25] We uncovered enormous concern about the negative immediate *and* inter-generational impacts of child removal on First Nations individuals, families and whole communities, which many people saw as replicating the earlier colonial policies of forcibly removing children.

First Nations peoples rarely engaged with civil and family laws to defend or assert their rights. Overall, the majority of participants reported not having had any assistance with or not having experienced satisfactory resolution of civil and family law disputes or problems. For example, 88 per cent of participants in Victoria and 79 per cent in the NT had not sought legal or other professional help or otherwise tried to resolve an incident of discrimination.[26] In NSW, the NT and Victoria, close to 90 per cent of participants had not accessed assistance for social security-related issues. Reasons for this included lack of awareness of relevant legal rights and remedies, a lack of access to legal help and advice, and a general distrust and avoidance of the legal system – which has arisen from frequent punitive interactions with police, criminal courts and prisons, as well as the inter-generational

[25] Generally, the percentage of participants experiencing a child protection-related problem was not as high as in other priority areas. Between 7% and 25% of people identified a child protection issue, depending on the State. The percentages were higher among women than men.

[26] Schwartz, Cunneen and Allison, *Indigenous Legal Needs Project: Victorian Report* (n 11); Allison, Schwartz and Cunneen, '"That's discrimination!"' (n 11).

experience of the civil, criminal and family law as tools of colonial subjugation and oppression.[27]

Many of the priority legal issues arose from the interaction between First Nations people and government agencies, especially those involving child protection, social security and housing. One reason this occurs is that poverty creates a dependency on welfare services, which leads to far greater scrutiny by government. For example, the prevalence of social security-related issues is relatively high in First Nations communities because of their disproportionate levels of reliance on welfare benefits.[28] Around three-quarters of all ILNP participants reported receiving benefits, inevitably increasing the incidence of social security-related disputes. Most of the housing-related issues concerned public housing tenancies – reflective of the fact that First Nations people are social housing tenants at disproportionate levels, rather than private tenants or owners (or mortgagees) of their own homes. The use of public housing means that tenants are policed to a greater degree for non-compliance with policies, including 'three strikes' policies that lead to eviction if a tenant is found to have engaged in 'disruptive' or 'anti-social behaviour'.[29] We found that changes in public policy over recent years have increased the prevalence of legal problems for First Nations people. The shift in welfare policy to principles of *conditionality*, whereby access to welfare is based on the 'responsibilisation' of citizens through ensuring behavioural change and the meeting of certain obligations, has generated a range of legal problems, particularly in social housing, social security and child protection.[30] These legal issues arise in part because conditionality is governed by increased regulatory processes, such as linking social security and child protection to income management, school attendance and other behavioural requirements. As Wacquant has noted, social welfare has come to be informed by the same values and philosophies as criminal justice: deterrence, surveillance, stigma and graduated sanctions.[31]

## IV. A Local Study: The Barkly Region

More recently, our access to justice work has been extended through an in-depth study of one region, the Barkly local government area of the NT ('the Barkly'). The NT is one of eight States and Territories within the Australian federal system. Some 30 per cent of the NT population are First Nations peoples. Our work was

[27] For a general discussion of these issues, see Behrendt et al (n 8).

[28] Allison, Schwartz and Cunneen (n 9) 235.

[29] Cunneen, Allison and Schwartz, 'Access to justice for Aboriginal people in the Northern Territory' (n 11).

[30] ibid.

[31] L Wacquant, *Punishing the Poor. The Neoliberal Government of Social Insecurity* (Duke University Press, 2009) 288.

conducted at the request of a number of community legal service providers.[32] Approximately 70 per cent of the Barkly's population are First Nations, the majority of whom speak at least one of the 10 larger local Indigenous languages, which include Warumungu, Warlpiri and Alyawarr. English is often a second, third or fourth language. The population of the Barkly comprises fewer than 8,000 people living mostly in small communities, which include some of the most remote settlements in Australia. The Barkly local government area is the second largest in Australia and covers 322,000 square kilometres – which by way of comparison is significantly greater than the size of the United Kingdom. The small population scattered over a vast area poses its own demands on access to justice: the legal (and other) service delivery models developed in regional centres or urbanised communities do not work effectively in this remote environment.

In addition, the statistical profile of the area shows widespread socio-economic exclusion. There are lower levels of formal education; the median income is less than half that of the NT; and unemployment in the Barkly is three and half times higher than across the NT. In some communities close to 90 per cent of the adult population are unemployed. Across the Barkly region nearly 70 per cent of housing is public housing, and in some communities it is 90 per cent.[33] Despite the growing demand by government and others to conduct business online, access to Internet and phone services is highly variable. In many of the smaller communities a significant majority of houses have no Internet connection. These statistics are relevant to issues of access to justice – both in creating legal need and in responding to legal problems or disputes. However, alongside these negative social and economic indicators, there are also positive indicators of social and emotional well-being in the Barkly associated with strong connection to Country, language and culture. All of these negative *and* positive attributes come into play when thinking about legal need, access to and the meaning of justice.

The legal issues we found in the Barkly were broadly similar to those in our ILNP national survey,[34] encompassing housing, discrimination, social security, credit/debt and consumer, criminal, child protection, employment education, neighbour, wills and financial institutions (including superannuation) issues. Housing (tenancy) was by far the most frequently identified legal problem – by more than two-thirds of the people with whom we spoke. However, rather than focus on the nature of these problems, in the remainder of this chapter we look towards responses. Some of the suggestions align with more traditional definitions of access to justice through seeking to reform criminal, civil and family law justice system responses for better or more just delivery of services. Other strategies push

[32] The Northern Territory Legal Aid Commission, the Northern Australia Aboriginal Justice Agency, the Central Australian Women's Legal Service, and the Central Australian Aboriginal Family Legal Unit. See F Allison and C Cunneen, *Access to Justice in the Barkly* (Jumbunna Institute for Indigenous Education and Research, 2020) at www.legalaid.nt.gov.au/access-to-justice-in-the-barkly-2020.

[33] Allison and Cunneen (n 32) 9.

[34] Allison, Schwartz and Cunneen (n 9) 235.

out existing parameters of access to justice a little further through the modifications of and adaptations of existing systems. Finally, a third approach is to look at non-legal strategies to improve justice outcomes.

## V. Improving Indigenous Access to Legal Services in Rural and Remote Areas

Legal services play a crucial role in enhancing Indigenous justice outcomes. They provide a link to what many First Nations people still see as a largely hostile and colonial system of law. Barriers to effective engagement identified in our research can include inflexible and bureaucratic systems, such as form filling, strict appointment systems and increasing requirements for Internet access.[35] These problems are significantly compounded in the Barkly, where there are language and literacy issues, and where the delivery of face-to-face services is limited by vast distances between small populations. Some communities in the Barkly have what are referred to as 'bush courts', where magistrates and lawyers fly into communities for the day (once a month or less frequently) to conduct hearings.[36] However, in general these are confined to criminal matters and only those that can be determined by a magistrate. Other issues of great importance to the community, such as child protection matters, are heard in Tennant Creek, the main town in the Barkly. Families are often unable to attend these hearings because of distance and cost, thus a court may determine a child's removal in the absence of any parental participation in the proceedings. For example, the distance from remote communities such as Alpurrurulam in the eastern Barkly to Tennant Creek in the west is nearly 600 kms and over eight hours' driving on partly unpaved roads, which are also impassable in the wet season.

Legal problems are compounded in rural and remote areas because both community sector and government *non-legal* supports are also very difficult to access or are unavailable, and this is especially the case in very remote areas like the Barkly, where family and children, domestic violence, financial counselling, and disability, mental health and substance abuse support services are either not provided or can be accessed only periodically.[37] Greater collaboration, coordination and shared resources between agencies could provide some improvement to service delivery in remote areas. Other requirements include improvements to the use of First Nations interpreters and better access to information about the law and responses to legal issues. Creative mechanisms for legal information sharing are also required – especially those that do not overly rely on printed material

[35] ibid.

[36] N Siegel, 'Is White Justice Delivery in Black Communities by "Bush Court" a Factor in Aboriginal Over-Representation within our Legal System?' (2002) 28(2) *Monash University Law Review* 268.

[37] Allison and Cunneen (n 32) 140–50.

but utilise other mediums, such as radio, visual art or storytelling. In addition, we found that government agencies (such as social security and child protection) must take more responsibility for ensuring community members can access basic information on legal rights and responsibilities. In our community discussions, First Nations people identified the feeling of hopelessness and at times despair when they have little awareness of even the first steps to take when a problem or dispute arises or where to go for information or assistance.

Another avenue for change is strategic litigation and policy reform by legal services, which can be an effective response to systemic issues and have positive consequences for communities. For example, the community of Santa Teresa was recently successful in a class action against the NT government related to squalid housing conditions and failure to carry out maintenance and repairs.[38] The Australian Lawyers for Remote Aboriginal Rights (ALRAR) acted for the community, having identified that the NT housing was poorly maintained and left many people 'without electricity, hot water, cooking facilities or functioning toilets for weeks, months and even years at a time'.[39] The NT Civil and Administrative Tribunal found that the NT government was legally liable to provide habitable housing in remote communities, and that compensation was owed to community members in Santa Teresa for the NT government's failure to maintain housing at a safe and healthy level.[40] The class action has generated collective responses in other communities within both the NT and Western Australia.

## VI. Expanding the Parameters of Access to Justice Through Modifying Existing Systems

Other strategies have the capacity to push out existing parameters of access to justice through modifications and adaptations to existing systems (as suggested elsewhere in this collection, such as chapter 12 on Syria). Our work in the Barkly highlighted possibilities for the greater use of non-legal actors to improve access to justice. For example, although lacking in many services, most remote communities have community health centres. Our interviews with local community health workers (most of whom are First Nations) showed that they have a keen awareness of the intersections between social, health and justice issues. Many of the community health staff we talked with identified inadequate and overcrowded housing as both health and legal issues, and that overcrowded houses in disrepair lead to other issues concerning domestic violence and child protection, which also cause

[38] The case is at www8.austlii.edu.au/cgi-bin/viewdoc/au/cases/nt/NTCAT/2019/7.html.
[39] See at www.alrar.org.au/santa-theresa-community-housing-claim.
[40] See at www8.austlii.edu.au/cgi-bin/viewdoc/au/cases/nt/NTCAT/2019/7.html.

both health and legal problems. The use of a legal health-check tool by health and other services can help link people to legal assistance by identifying the problems noted above and others, such as outstanding debts, warrants and other government orders. We have seen the development in some parts of Australia of health justice partnerships between Aboriginal community-controlled health services and legal services as a way of rethinking, identifying and expanding legal assistance.[41]

Another example of modifying existing legal processes is the role of local community Elders in the court system. Many States in Australia have specialist criminal courts where First Nations Elders play a role in advising the court on sentencing individual offenders.[42] Although varying in their structure and practices, these are collectively known as 'Indigenous sentencing courts'. At present they are restricted to criminal matters. There has been some use of this approach with Elders in courts through community Law and Justice Groups in the NT. However, there is substantial room for expanding the model into areas of civil and family law relating to, for example, matters of tenancy, debt and child protection. Community members often spoke of the need to improve community self-determination: participation and the direct involvement of local community in the administration of justice is one way of developing this capacity.

## VII. Encompassing Non-Legal Strategies to Improve Justice Outcomes

Our work in the Barkly highlighted the need for non-legal strategies to meet the needs of First Nations people seeking justice and for strategies that are informed by core First Nations principles, including self-determination, respect for culture and participation in decision-making. Community members in the Barkly spoke about the importance of changes *within and by the community* to reduce the occurrence of legal problems and contact with the legal system. Enhancing justice outcomes requires a community development approach that can lead to more collective responses to systemic legal and socio-economic issues. Community development approaches in Indigenous communities involve engaging with Elders and with community to determine priorities and solutions to problems. In the context of access to justice they involve developing community capacity to respond to issues such as domestic violence, financial literacy and basic legal assistance. Some of the specific initiatives in this area include the further development of community-controlled night patrols, who work to provide community

[41] F Allison, *Evaluation of the Law Right Wuchopperen Health Justice Partnership and Law Yarn* (2019) at www.lawright.org.au/wp-content/uploads/2021/09/Final_Independent_evaluation_Wuchopperen_HJP_2019.pdf.

[42] E Marchetti, 'Indigenous Sentencing Courts in Australia' in A Deckert and R Sarre (eds), *The Palgrave Handbook of Australian and New Zealand Criminology, Crime and Justice* (Palgrave Macmillan, 2017).

assistance and maintain social harmony without the involvement of State police and criminal courts, and similarly an expanded role for community-based mediators to respond to conflict within communities. A further suggestion is the skilling of people within the community in basic financial counselling to help improve financial literacy within communities.

From our discussions, it was also clear that community members wanted workable structures through which to voice their concerns about community-wide issues,[43] to exercise cultural authority and to be First Nations community-led. Within the Barkly region there is currently a Cultural Authority Group in Tennant Creek and Local Authority Groups in the smaller communities. These groups comprise First Nations community people and essentially provide advice to the local Barkly Shire Council on local government matters. However, this structure provides an opportunity for further development in identifying and responding to legal issues at a collective level. For example, at one meeting we attended between Barkly Regional Council and the Local Authority Group in Alpurrurulam there was extensive discussion with the regional police commander over the inadequacy of police responses in the area. These meetings can potentially provide the opportunity to discuss a range of systemic criminal, civil and family law problems that impact on the community, and to search for greater systemic solutions.

There was also interest in Tennant Creek in developing a justice reinvestment (JR) initiative. In Australia, JR uses community development approaches that recognise and build on Indigenous self-determination, whilst also reforming criminal justice and other government systems and service delivery.[44] In a number of urban, regional and remote areas, local First Nations communities have introduced JR initiatives aimed in the first instance at reducing incarceration but with a clear vision that other areas that drive criminal justice contact must be addressed, including the design and provision of community services, education, child protection, housing and employment (and the intersection of discrimination with all these areas). The reform of policy and practice is a focus (rather than litigation or other reliance on legal rights or processes). This type of strategy and the use of community development principles and practice, led by First Nations peoples, fits within an appropriately expanded definition of access to justice. It is particularly important in rural and remote Indigenous communities because, as outlined in this chapter, there is a chronic absence of mainstream services.

Justice reinvestment and community development approaches also address two of our key findings from our work on access to justice. First, many First Nations people experience multiple *legal* issues simultaneously, and these can 'snowball' and multiply out of control. In relation to tenancy, for instance, eviction

[43] Including lack of housing repairs and maintenance, various types of debts, problems with exploitation by local traders and by larger commercial interests, inappropriate policing and poor responses by other government agencies.

[44] Information on justice reinvestment implementation in Australia can be found on the Justice Reinvestment Network Australia website at www.justicereinvestment.net.au.

of Indigenous people from public-housing tenancies due to rental arrears leads to homelessness. This then feeds into issues of overcrowding, debt and further tenancy problems (such as the non-payment of higher utility bills, and eviction) in those households that try to accommodate the homeless. Second, there are interconnecting links between unaddressed civil and family law needs and criminalisation. Lack of recognition of civil law rights to housing, education and employment, for example, disenfranchises First Nations peoples on multiple levels, which in turn leads to higher rates of contact for First Nations peoples with the criminal justice system. In turn, criminalisation compounds problems with, for example, housing, debt and child protection.[45] Thus improving Indigenous capacity to access civil and family law justice is likely to build resilience in individuals and communities, to reduce criminalisation and to contribute to increased levels of Indigenous social inclusion. The formal separations between civil, family and criminal law are often an artificial distinction that has little connection to the complex problems people face. These issues are important for all First Nations people, irrespective of whether they live in urban, rural or remote communities. However, these problems are profoundly exacerbated in rural and remote areas because of the absence of services – to a point noted at the beginning of this chapter that basic civil rights are impinged.

## VIII. Conclusion

This chapter represents some of our preliminary thoughts on developing First Nations responses to access to justice – it is not meant to be prescriptive but rather reflective of the community-based empirical work that we have undertaken over recent years in a variety of First Nations communities in Australia, particularly in regional, rural and remote areas. First Nations people share some similar problems in accessing justice with other people living in poverty and situations of precarity, such as refugees, asylum seekers, the homeless, and people living with mental illness and disability. However, there is also no doubt that geographic remoteness creates particular problems for service delivery, and First Nations people are much more likely than non-Indigenous people to be living both in poverty and in rural and remote areas.

There are also substantial differences in access to justice for First Nations people compared to other people, based on Australia's history of colonisation and the use of law as a tool of oppression: the criminal law to suppress resistance, civil law to create racially discriminatory regimes of extensive segregation, forced labour and alienation of land, and family law through child welfare laws that forcibly removed generations of children. Any strategy designed to improve First Nations access to

[45] Allison, Schwartz and Cunneen (n 9) 246–47.

justice can only succeed if it accounts for this historical experience – an experience that informs contemporary views that see the law as an alien system which is the opposite of one that provides remedies for wrongs and delivers justice.

We have argued here that there are some changes that can be made to reform the system; that the legal system can be changed within to ensure better access and justice outcomes. The use of class actions to force change is one example. We have also argued that the legal system can be modified in particular ways for better outcomes, and health justice partnerships have been one specific development that has particular application for rural and remote First Nations communities. Finally, we have argued for the importance of non-legal strategies to achieve justice outcomes. These can involve First Nations-developed and -led interventions like night patrols and community mediators. They can involve structures of decision-making that are culturally specific and legitimate to First Nations communities, such as Local Authority Groups and Law and Justice Groups in the NT. They can involve various community development approaches, such as JR. These latter approaches recognise the necessity to locate solutions to the social exclusion of First Nations people *outside* the law and also to think through how justice might be defined within a wholly First Nations domain.

Human rights and specifically Indigenous rights are applicable to Indigenous peoples irrespective of whether they live in urban, rural or remote locations. However, as we have argued in this chapter, these rights, and in particular self-determination and the ability to access justice mechanisms, are especially pertinent to Indigenous peoples living in rural and remote areas. All of the approaches identified for improving access to justice in this chapter are consistent with the core principles that underpin the UNDRIP, in particular self-determination, participation in decision-making and protection of culture. They lead us to think about how on a broader level our conceptualisation of access to justice can incorporate the Indigenous domain as one that respects Indigenous law, culture, knowledge and methodology. We began this chapter by contextualising the discussion of First Nations peoples in Australia within the broader parameters of Indigenous peoples internationally. When we recognise that Indigenous peoples globally are heavily concentrated among the poorest of the poor, and especially in rural areas, and are among the most politically marginalised and socially excluded, then the task of understanding justice and ensuring its access is made all the more urgent. This requires also recognising and building on the many strengths in First Nations communities, and the effective solutions they are able to bring to the problems they face.

# 7

# Barriers to Access to Justice for Members of the Traveller Community: Rediscrimination within the Equality System

FIONA DONSON AND SAMANTHA MORGAN-WILLIAMS

## I. Introduction

The complex legal needs of the Irish Traveller Community, and the entrenched societal exclusion of its members, mean that they are largely removed from access to legal services. This mirrors the exclusion faced by rural communities seeking legal services and representation. An examination of the barriers to justice experienced by the Traveller Community reveals parallels between rural access to justice and minority group access to justice. Although the Irish Traveller Community has significant unmet legal needs across both civil and criminal fields,[1] this chapter will map these barriers in relation to the non-discrimination and equality system, in particular the challenges of accessing justice in complaints concerning discrimination in the provision of goods and services. In doing so, this chapter presents the systematic causes of this unmet legal need and considers the broader implications of this upon the inability of many Travellers to access justice.

## II. Context and Approach

Ireland is often conceptualised as a small country with one main urban hub. While the country is changing, with increased urbanisation in towns and cities across Ireland, the institutions of justice have not adapted to meet that reality. A historic centralisation of legal services, in and around Dublin, has created and exacerbated

[1] Including housing, social welfare, health and education.

a legal desert[2] within which Travellers find themselves when seeking to respond to discrimination. Consequently, many must rely on free legal advice and (specialist) law centres. Further issues arise within the system itself – where the current barriers placed before potential Traveller litigants results in 'rediscrimination'.

This chapter will outline the manner in which the barriers faced by Travellers in accessing justice mirror those experienced by rural communities removed from legal service provision, as considered throughout in this volume. In mapping Traveller exclusion from legal services, the chapter considers the factors that have created a significant unmet legal need, including jurisdictional and administrative barriers. These are approached from the perspective of the Traveller victim, using testimony from recent focus groups.[3] What emerges is a picture that shows that the lived experience of the Traveller Community, whether urban or rural, is one in which legal services are simply out of reach. This arises as a result of both geographical and non-geographical barriers – location having little bearing on whether a Traveller can find legal representation. The experiences set out in this chapter reveal that Travellers are unable to access justice and that the system appears indifferent to this, not least because problem is systemic.

## III. Travellers – From Rural Roots to Marginalised Present

Irish Travellers are an indigenous, ethnic minority with a unique and long-established shared history and tradition.[4] The Irish Traveller Movement notes

[2] For further consideration of legal deserts and justice gaps, see M Statz, Hon R Friday and J Bredeson, '"They Had Access, But They Didn't Get Justice": Why Prevailing Access to Justice Initiatives Fail Rural Americans' (2021) 28(3) *Georgetown Journal on Poverty Law and Policy* 321; Legal Services Corporation, *The Justice Gap: Measuring the Unmet Civil Legal Needs of Low-income Americans* (2017) at www.lsc.gov/sites/default/files/images/TheJusticeGap-FullReport.pdf; LR Pruitt et al, 'Legal Deserts: A Multi-State Perspective on Rural Access to Justice' (2018) 13(1) *Harvard Law & Policy Review* 15; K Stancombe, 'Stretched to Serve in "legal deserts"' (2020) *The Indiana Lawyer* at www.theindianalawyer.com/articles/stretched-to-serve-in-legal-deserts.

[3] The Cork Traveller Women's Network (CTWN) and Traveller Equality and Justice Project (TEJP) completed a number of focus groups as part of a project funded by an Irish Research Council New Foundations grant. The focus groups were completed in December 2019 and January 2020 and focused on mapping Traveller experiences of the equality system through lived experience. The CTWN conducted the focus groups with their women's groups to ensure a 'safe space', and support was available for those taking part. The three focus groups gathered data on Traveller experiences of discrimination via discussion of core issues. Participants were 30 Traveller women (over 18) who were members of the CTWN. See S Morgan-Williams and F Donson, *Barriers to Justice for Irish Travellers Seeking to Challenge Discrimination* (Traveller Equality & Justice Project, 2022) at www.ucc.ie/en/media/projectsandcentres/tejp/IRCNFReportFinal2022(1).pdf.

[4] For a comprehensive discussion on this, see D Watson, O Kenny and F McGinnity, *A Social Portrait of Travellers in Ireland* (Economic and Social Research Institute (ESRI), 2017); see also NC McElwee, A Jackson and C Grant, 'Towards a Sociological Understanding of Irish Travellers: Introducing a People' (2003) 4(1) *Irish Journal of Applied Social Studies* 103; G Gmelch, *The Irish Tinkers: The Urbanisation of an Itinerant People* (Waveland Press, 1985); M MacGreil, *Prejudice and Tolerance in Ireland* (The Research Section: College of Industrial Relations, 1977).

that Travellers are recognised by historical sources to have been a part of Irish society for centuries.[5] Although a small group in Ireland, accounting for less than 1 per cent of the population,[6] Travellers stand out as a group that experiences extreme disadvantage in terms of employment, housing and health. The All Ireland Traveller Health Survey (2010) found that 61 per cent of Travellers experienced discrimination being served in a pub, restaurant or shop; 56 per cent reported discrimination getting accommodation and 55 per cent reported discrimination in seeking work. Unfortunately, little has changed since 2010, with the Watson et al finding in 2017 that Travellers are 22 times more likely than White Irish to experience discrimination in accessing private services. Such inequality is not confined to service provision but is widespread and indiscriminate, impacting upon all areas of life for the Community. The ingrained and often systemic levels of discrimination faced by Irish Travellers have been described by advocates as 'the last acceptable form of racism',[7] and by Travellers as 'a negative, but normal part of the Traveller life'.[8]

Reflecting on the high levels of social inequality and discrimination, the 2017 ESRI Report noted the unfavourable situation facing the Traveller Community, recognising the multi-faceted issues worsened by racism and discrimination:

> It is clear that Travellers are a group disadvantaged in several respects: in terms of educational attainment, employment, housing and health. They have an unusual age distribution, with a relatively large number of children and a smaller number of older adults. They have experienced exceptionally high levels of discrimination compared to other groups in Ireland.[9]

This is evident in the manner which many Travellers both view and access vital services, and how they respond to such acts of discrimination. A report conducted by the Traveller Movement (UK) notes that although most Travellers experience discrimination on a daily basis, 77 per cent of those surveyed stated that they had not sought help in response to such incidents, noting that it is

[5] Some Travellers prefer to use the term *Mincéir* or *Mincéirí* (pl), which is the Cant and original word used to describe Travellers. Travellers are also known as '*an lucht siúil*', meaning 'the walking people' in Irish.

[6] The 2016 Census found 30,987 Irish Travellers representing 0.7% of the general population. Central Statistics Office, *Census of Population 2016 – Profile 8 Irish Travellers, Ethnicity and Religion* (2017) at www.cso.ie/en/releasesandpublications/ep/p-cp8iter/p8iter/p8itd/. See also All Ireland Traveller Health Study, *All Ireland Traveller Health Study. Our Geels*, Technical Report 1 (2010) Table 189 available at https://assets.gov.ie/18860/acc3cfe37d1e4b67a53f7da58eacc725.pdf.

[7] Marc Willers, KC quoted in Traveller Times, 'Marc Willers QC Calls Time On 'The Last Acceptable Racism'' (2016) at https://www.travellerstimes.org.uk/features/marc-willers-qc-calls-time-last-acceptable-racism.

[8] The Traveller Movement, '*The last acceptable form of racism? The pervasive discrimination and prejudice experienced by Gypsy, Roma and Traveller communities*, (2017) at http://travellermovement.org.uk/wp-content/uploads/TMreport1JFINAL.pdf.

[9] Watson, Kenny and McGinnity (n 4) 43.

'a fact of [Traveller] life'.[10] Although this study took place amongst Irish Travellers based in the UK, perceptions that discrimination is 'shameful' and embarrassing are rife throughout the Traveller Community.[11]

This shame and the internalised impact of discrimination in employment and in accessing goods and services are compounded by the inability of many Travellers to access legal representation in order to respond and challenge this through the relevant legal avenues. Access to justice is a crucial right upon which vindication of all other human rights depend. This inability to access legal advice means that Traveller victims of discrimination experience 'rediscrimination'. This occurs by virtue of their exclusion from basic service provision, which is then compounded by barriers to securing legal representation by which they can challenge the initial act of discrimination.

## A. The Irish Traveller Community

Traditionally rooted in rural life, Travellers have since the mid-twentieth century been subject to urbanisation and sedentarisation.[12] As Donahue et al note, although urbanisation was something that was happening more broadly within the state, the Traveller experience of this was an altogether less voluntary and more traumatic experience.[13] The Commission on Itinerancy Report,[14] published in 1963, led to the adoption of a settlement policy to rectify the 'problem' posed by nomadic Travellers. Within 40 years Travellers had gone from nomadic to settled.[15]

The impact of this policy in terms of rural/urban location of Travellers is of course hard to fully pin down. However, it is clear that forced settlement resulted in the Traveller Community's becoming more focused in urban or, perhaps more accurately described, industrial areas of the country. The 2016 Census results found that 'Travellers were more urbanised than the general population with nearly 8 in 10 (78.6 per cent) living in cities or towns (1,500 or more), compared with 62.4 per cent of the total population.'[16]

[10] The Traveller Movement (n 8).

[11] Morgan-Williams and Donson (n 3) 26–27.

[12] M Donahue, R McVeigh and M Ward, *Misli, Crush, Misli: Irish Travellers and Nomadism* (Irish Traveller Movement & Traveller Movement (Northern Ireland), 2016) at http://itmtrav.ie/wp-content/uploads/2016/11/MISLI-CRUSH-MISLI-Irish-Travellers-and-Nomadism.pdf, 9.

[13] ibid.

[14] Commission on Itinerancy, *Report of the Commission on Itinerancy* (The Stationery Office Dublin, 1963).

[15] Donahue, McVeigh and Ward (n 12) 7 reported that statistics from 2001 indicated only 5% of Travellers were nomadic, while a further 15% lived on roadsides. More recent data are not available.

[16] 2016 Census (n 6).

**Figure 7.1** Travellers and total population by area 2016

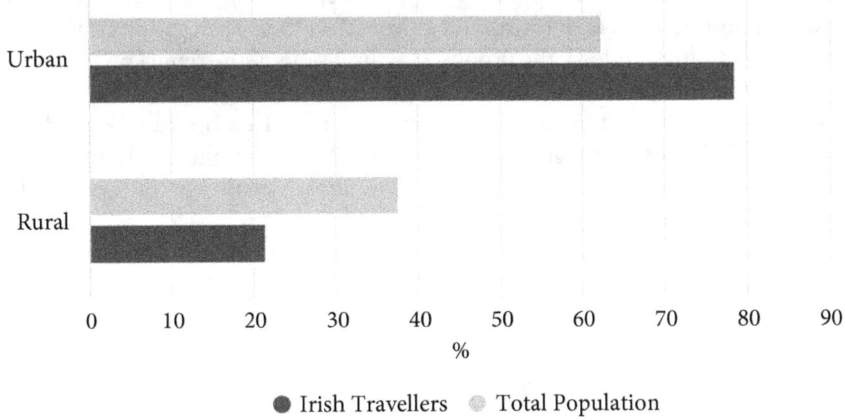


*Source*: CSO Ireland.

A complete breakdown of locations of halting sites and group housing schemes is not currently available. Yet many of the major sites of accommodation exist more in an industrialised landscape than an urban one.[17] However, this does not reflect the majority of Travellers who now live in settled housing, primarily local authority-provided or private rental accommodation. While homelessness has become an increasing problem in recent years, Travellers are

> strikingly over-represented in the general homelessness population … experienc[ing] multiple forms of homelessness, such as doubling up on sites or roadside, sleeping rough or in cars, in emergency accommodation (including refuges), as well living in the most egregious site conditions.[18]

[17] See, eg, Labre Park in Balllyfermot; Carrowbrowne in Galway; Spring Lane, Cork City; and St Oliver's Park in Cloverhill. All of which are peripheralised and either next to busy motorways or within industrial or brown site zones generally disconnected from amenities and the settled community. In the case of Spring Lane, the site is located within a disused quarry and beside a busy ring-road. St Oliver's is located next to the M50 and Cloverhill and Wheatfield Prisons. Carrowbrowne is next to a dump. The geographical significance of these locations is not lost on the Community members themselves. As the Travellers living at the Carrowbrowne site said, '[T]his is an example of what they really think of Travellers. That of all the land that they had to give, they gave us the place beside the dump.' See 'Travellers have a right to a home that is culturally appropriate' *The Journal* (23 November 2017). Note that despite recognition that older halting sites are largely unsuitable and should be taken out of commission, they are still used by councils to deal with overcrowding. An example of this is the wholly unusable Brennan's Glen in Kerry, which, despite recognition of its unsuitability as an unserviced and dangerous site (located next to the main Killarney to Tralee road), was still used in 2005 as an overflow. This was in spite of such comments from Councillors as 'If it was used as a dog pound, the ISPCA would be down. It is not a fit place for anybody to send anybody.' Cllr Brian O'Leary, cited in 'Glen to be made a temporary halting site' *Kerry Times* (6 October 2005) at www.independent.ie/regionals/kerryman/news/glen-to-be-made-a-temporary-halting-site-27364805.html.

[18] B Harvey, *The Traveller Community and Homelessness* (Pavee Point Traveller and Roma Centre, 2021) 7.

Despite this geographic urbanisation, the reality of life in Ireland for the Traveller Community is different from that of the settled community. Traveller experiences of living in or on the edge of towns and cities reflect their segregation from established communities. Indeed, the proposed assimilation of the report on itinerancy created enforced urban and societal marginalisation,[19] while the lack of access to services because of deep-rooted discrimination and racism has resulted in a community living on the edge of society, where facilities might be within walking distance but remain entirely inaccessible. The unmet legal need of the Traveller Community in Ireland, mirroring the exclusion from both advice and representation experienced by those residing in rural areas, arises from both a scarcity of demand and fundamental issues of accessibility.

## IV. Barriers to Justice for Travellers

Within the Irish legal system there are considerable barriers in place for those victims of discrimination who wish to legally challenge their treatment. An insufficient and overburdened legal aid system,[20] and overreliance on pro bono and public interest law projects,[21] is compounded by a limited number of specialist equality practitioners.[22] This is in turn is exacerbated by the general inability of the equality system to protect and vindicate victims of discrimination.[23]

Amidst this general lack of resources, Traveller litigants must attempt to secure representation within a system from which they are largely excluded, both socio-economically and also culturally. For Travellers seeking justice, 'a legacy of prejudice and discrimination means that legal empowerment for these groups poses particular challenges that a focus on "the poor" alone will obscure'.[24] This is compounded by the generalised nature of legal aid cuts, scarcity of public interest

[19] Donohue et al (n 12).

[20] Gaps in legal aid provision unfortunately fall to community law and advice centres such as Free Legal Advice Centres (FLACs), Mercy Law, and Community Law and Mediation (CLM). As a result, these organisations are vocal about the need for reform and enhancing funding to ensure an adequate legal aid framework. See E Barry, 'Access to justice requires much more than access to legal aid' *Irish Times* (16 May 2019) at www.irishtimes.com/opinion/access-to-justice-requires-much-more-than-access-to-legal-aid-1.3893413; Community Law & Mediation, Press Release: Civil Legal Aid Scheme must be reformed in next Programme for Government (May 2020) at https://communitylawandmediation.ie/civil-legal-aid-scheme-must-be-reformed-in-next-programme-for-government/.

[21] FLAC Annual Report 2020, *Remote Justice*, at www.flac.ie/publications/flac-annual-report-2020/; and see also 'Nearly 12,500 calls last year for free legal advice – with big increase in employment concerns' *The Journal* (29 June 2021) at www.thejournal.ie/flac-annual-report-2020-free-legal-advice-5479815-Jun2021/.

[22] TEJP (n 3).

[23] Morgan-Williams and Donson (n 3).

[24] DM Brinks, 'Access to What? Legal Agency and Access to Justice for Indigenous Peoples in Latin America' (2019) 55(3) *The Journal of Development Studies* 348, 349.

and equality practitioners, and overreliance by the state on non-governmental organisations (NGOs) and free legal advice services.

As Eilis Barry, CEO of FLAC has aptly noted:

> Ireland's court and legal system is designed by lawyers for lawyers. The procedures and processes of the courts restrict access because they are off-putting, complex and costly. Access to the courts is built around the assumption that litigants will have legal representation, and increasingly legal representation is beyond what most individuals can afford. The more marginalised and disadvantaged individuals are, the more inaccessible justice becomes.[25]

Notwithstanding the general nature of this issue, core factors that prevent Travellers from accessing justice mirror those facing other legally-excluded groups,[26] including the centring of human rights practice, administrative and jurisdictional barriers, and exclusion from specific legal services. Traveller experiences of justice 'are the paradigmatic example of the intersection between social and economic exclusion and group identity'.[27]

## A. Centring of Human Rights Practice

In Ireland, the centring of legal services around the capital, Dublin, has created substantial issues for people outside of this catchment area, including those residing in smaller towns and within rural areas. While access to justice is problematic generally, those seeking to vindicate their human rights are particularly poorly served. Although no clear data exist on the breakdown of human rights-focused law firms, most human rights practitioners and specialists are based in the capital.[28] Similarly, legal information and advice clinics run by NGOs such as FLAC, CLM[29] and Mercy Law are also predominantly based in Dublin, although FLAC does operate national advice clinics.[30] In many ways, this may be unsurprising, as the Dublin

[25] ibid.

[26] Legally-excluded groups can include those othered by the legal system (justice-involved persons, Travellers, socio-economically deprived individuals, minority groups and asylum seekers). It can also include those considered outside of the jurisdiction of legal services, eg those residing in 'unserviced areas' such as rural communities.

[27] Brinks (n 24) 349.

[28] Large to medium firms with established human rights profiles, such as Arthur Cox, A&L Goodbody, KOD Lyons, are all based within Dublin. While it is difficult to record exactly, a solid indicator as to the location of practitioners who are willing to engage, or have in the past engaged, in human rights, equality and public interest work can be found by looking at the Public Interest Law Alliance (PILA) Pro Bono Pledge. The PILA Pledge is signed by firms and individuals willing to accept an allocated number of pro bono hours via a referral scheme managed by PILA. The majority of large firms who have signed up to the PILA Pledge, such as Matheson, McCann Fitzgerald, are based in Dublin. Of the other initial 45 PILA Pledge signatories in 2020, only seven are based outside of Dublin.

[29] CLM also has an office in Limerick; see https://communitylawandmediation.ie/.

[30] While FLAC runs FLAC Clinics and is partnered with Citizens' Information, these have been suspended during the Covid-19 pandemic.

region accounts for more than 25 per cent of Ireland's population.[31] However, the practical result of this distribution is that those living outside of Dublin in rural environs are presented with significant issues in accessing much-needed legal information and support, creating a legal desert that results in a significant unmet legal need. Crucially, however, this unmet legal need appears to arise regardless of whether a Traveller resides in Dublin or in a more rural location. In practice, physical proximity to Dublin as a perceived human rights 'hub' does not equate to access to justice for Travellers, or indeed for other minority groups. Access to services is an issue regardless of geographical proximity to recognised legal service providers. Traveller-specific legal supports are not widely available to meet demand, with only one dedicated service available to Travellers within Ireland.[32] There is a need for increased Traveller-specific legal advice providers in light of the variances in legal needs between the Traveller Community and the settled community in terms of perceived justiciable problems.[33] While the settled community will predominantly seek advice on family law, conveyancing and probate issues, the Traveller Community will generally need advice regarding accommodation, equality and social welfare issues. Familiarity with the unique justiciable problems that arise for the Traveller Community is a prerequisite that is unfortunately widely unrealised.

## B. Administrative and Jurisdictional Barriers

In addition to this scarcity of specialised service provision, the Traveller Community also faces structural barriers to accessing justice, based on system design and operation. By way of example, the equality system,[34] the key framework for promoting inclusion and challenging discrimination, itself operates as a core barrier for Travellers.

Central to this is the divide between the Workplace Relations Commission (WRC) and the District Court. The WRC is a quasi-judicial tribunal, established in 2015 to replace the Equality Tribunal. The title is misleading and can result in an assumption that the Tribunal is primarily concerned with employment matters. Instead, it has a wider remit, including equality and equal status cases. Indeed, the WRC has a broad scope, focused not only on complaints and referrals but also on promoting good practice through a range of actions (research, advice, promoting information, etc).

The District Court, on the other hand, is the main court of summary jurisdiction in Ireland, responsible for hearing small civil claims (lower than €15,000),

[31] The 2016 Census (n 6) reported that Dublin region/county accounted for 28.3% of the total population of Ireland.

[32] Free Legal Advice Centre, Traveller Legal Unit at www.flac.ie/news/2020/07/27/flac-to-launch-only-dedicated-traveller-legal-serv/.

[33] H Genn, *Paths to Justice: What People Do and Think About Going to Law* (Hart Publishing, 1997) 12.

[34] Namely, concerned with the Equal Status Acts 2000–2018.

liquor licensing cases, and minor criminal cases and some family law. It has been described as the 'workhorse'[35] of the Irish legal system. It is organised on a regional basis, with 23 districts that are in turn subdivided. These courts hear a large volume of cases but are subject to little scrutiny in practice.[36]

The equality framework's current structure means that the WRC is responsible for deciding a wide range of first-instance discrimination claims, including employment and goods and services. It hears cases relating to discriminatory treatment that occurred somewhere other than 'on or at the point of entry to' a premises that sells alcohol. Unsurprisingly, given it replaced the Equality Tribunal, the WRC appears to be a preferable, non-adversarial, mediation-led body within which to hear cases. It holds hearings in hotels, and since the onset of Covid has been operating remote hearings, which has the potential to make it more accessible assuming access to appropriate IT resources. In addition, the WRC is faster and, unlike the District Court, there are no fees for commencement of a complaint. Hearings are informal in nature and allow complainants a suitable environment in which to represent themselves. Unfortunately, there is no provision for legal aid for hearings before the WRC, which often results in an inequality of arms where the other party is represented:

> [L]egal Aid is not provided in cases before the tribunals which deal with equality cases and social welfare appeals. Employers and businesses can often afford to pay for private legal representation in equality cases before the WRC; however persons making complaints often cannot. Where a person alleging discrimination does not have such financial means and is faced with an experienced legal team on the other side, this can give rise to an inequality of arms in practice.[37]

While it is not clear whether this is a contributing factor, the WRC has nevertheless seen a significant drop in cases in recent years. There was an 11 per cent reduction in complaints under the Equal Status Acts received by the WRC in 2018 (compared with 2017) and a further 26 per cent reduction in 2019 (compared with 2018).[38]

Notwithstanding this, a core space within which Travellers experience discrimination is in pubs and clubs. The introduction of section 19 of the Intoxicating Liquor Act 2003 means that discrimination alleged at or at entry to licensed premises must be heard in the District Court. Although District Courts are geographically well-distributed throughout Ireland, including in the majority

[35] DB Rottman, *The Criminal Justice System: Policy and Performance* (National Economic and Social Council, Dublin, 1984).

[36] C O'Nolan, *The Irish District Court: A Social Portrait* (Cork University Press, 2013). As District Court cases are largely unreported, there are also issues in understanding the type of cases and outcomes that come before the courts. This is problematic for an area such as equality law litigation.

[37] FLAC Factsheet – 3rd cycle Universal Periodic Review of Ireland 2021 on 'Legal Aid' at www.flac.ie/publications/flac-legal-aid-fact-sheet/.

[38] FLAC Factsheet – 3rd cycle Universal Periodic Review of Ireland 2021 on 'Equality' at www.flac.ie/publications/flac-equality-fact-sheet/.

of townlands, in practice they present significant accessibility issues.[39] While a complainant can self-represent, District Court proceedings are adversarial, and their operating environments are challenging and uncomfortable, particularly for those such as Travellers from marginalised communities. While little research has been carried out on the day-to-day functioning of these courts, they have been described as follows:

> District Court proceedings often take place with a background hum of noise which at times can reach such a volume that the intervention of the presiding judge is required to restore it to a tolerable level. The seating arrangements adopted could be described as tribal in nature and contribute to the ever-present buzz of noise.[40]

District Court judges, who sit alone on the bench, are unusual in comparison to other common law lower-tier adjudicators, in that they are full-time, permanent appointees recruited from the legal professions. They are described by O'Nolan as being 'a small elite and privileged group whose day-to-day decisions greatly impact [the Irish legal system] and the wider Irish society'.[41]

Given this court environment, any suggestion that Travellers would be able to self-represent is unrealistic. Yet the cost of legal representation is a significant barrier for the Traveller Community. The idea that self-representation is an option that offers people access to justice in the face of costs and poor legal aid cover has consistently been rejected. In *Airey v Ireland*,[42] the Irish Government had argued that the absence of legal aid did not prevent access to justice under Article 6 of the European Convention on Human Rights because self-representation was an option. In practice, however, it is essential that access is real and effective rather than 'illusory', as the European Court of Human Rights noted in its judgment.[43] While legal aid is available to bring equal status cases, until recently this was not widely acknowledged by the Legal Aid Board, leading to a general unawareness of this within the Community.[44] In addition, there is a very low uptake in practice due to considerable delays and a low threshold to qualify for means testing. This has a considerable effect on the ability of individuals to access representation and raises serious concerns about the limited number of individuals who have the resources to access the courts:

> Increasingly, access to the Irish courts is limited to wealthy individuals and corporates, as well as a small number of people who receive legal aid or where lawyers are prepared

[39] There are 23 District Courts in Ireland. The District Court consists of 64 judges, including a President.

[40] O'Nolan (n 36) 23.

[41] ibid 30.

[42] *Airey v Ireland* [1979] 2 EHRR 305.

[43] ibid para 24.

[44] Morgan-Williams and Donson (n 3). Respondents within research focus group on 'Barriers to Justice' noted that they were unaware of legal aid for such cases. 'Are Travellers aware that there is legal aid for cases before the District Court?' All: 'No.'

> to act on a 'no win no fee' basis. This compromises the kinds of cases that our courts hear and adjudicate on. Injustices are left ignored and our laws and human rights infrastructure are left unenforced.[45]

More broadly, self-representation, or lay representation from a support organisation, is generally not recommended due to the prohibitive nature of court costs, the length of time cases can take to progress, and difficulties with navigating the complex forms and court rules (something that at times can seem like proceeding in the dark because of a lack of understanding). Furthermore, Travellers with experience of the courts note the barriers these administrative barriers can place before an unsure lay litigant:

> You're torn left right and centre fighting to get your evidence, make your statements, write your letters, and still at the end of it you don't even get an apology … The paperwork is a barrier for Travellers, keeping records so it can stand up in court it wasn't easy for people to know how to do it. The other thing is that you could be discriminated against by 10 people daily and the system is so slow.[46]

The very structure of the equality framework itself also acts as a barrier, with a litigant having to understand which forum is appropriate to their case. The current divide between the WRC and District Court was the result of significant yet highly contentious[47] reform of the equality system. In 2011, the Equality Tribunal was wound down and its jurisdiction transferred to the WRC, while section 19 of the Intoxicating Liquor Act 2003 transferred jurisdiction for equality claims arising within a licensed premises to the Court. The implications of these reforms and transfer from a specialist equality body to an adversarial court system were noted by campaign groups:

> In 2003, cases under the Equal Status Acts 2000–2008 involving licensed premises were moved to the District Court under the Intoxicating Liquor Act 2003. Research on the impact of this transfer found that 'the change in Jurisdiction has resulted in an almost complete reduction in complaints taken under the law in relation to prohibited acts of discrimination'.[48]

The impact on Traveller access to justice was extensive. The Equality Tribunal had been considered an accessible and fair space within which to bring a claim:

> In the Tribunal, unlike the District Court, neither the complainant nor the respondent has to mobilize or present legal arguments. They merely have to present the facts of the

[45] E Barry, 'Realising equal access to justice for all' (17 May 2019) at www.flac.ie/news/2019/05/17/realising-equal-access-to-justice-for-all/.

[46] Morgan-Williams and Donson (n 3) 29.

[47] T Pegram, 'Bridging the Divide: The Merger of the Irish Equality Authority and Human Rights Commission' (2013) at www.tcd.ie/policy-institute/assets/pdf/Studies_Policy_29_web2September.pdf.

[48] S Gogan, 'From the Equality Tribunal to the District Court', Clondalkin Travellers Development Group (2005) 5, cited in Equality and Rights Alliance, Consultation Response to 'Blueprint to Deliver a World-Class Workplace Relations Service' (2012) at www.workplacerelations.ie/en/publications_forms/blueprint_consultation_responses_-_may_2012.pdf 62.

> case and the equality officer then investigates these facts, applies the relevant law and makes a finding. This is key to the accessibility of the Equality Tribunal.[49]

The District Court, however, with costs, the need for legal representation and the adversarial nature of proceedings, was a more intimidating venue at which to bring a claim. The impact of this is clear and was reflected in available (but limited) data on the number of cases brought both pre- and post-reform. Between September 2004 and February 2005, only nine claims of such discrimination were lodged compared to an average of 514 claims taken annually with the Equality Tribunal between 2000 to 2003.[50] More recently, data from the Courts Service highlighted that 'in 2017, 51 out of 52 applications [under the provisions of section 19 of the Intoxicating Liquor Act] were introduced by members of Traveller communities, and 50 out of 52 were struck off, withdrawn or adjourned'.[51]

These jurisdictional and administrative barriers are compounded by the experiences of Travellers within the District Court. Travellers generally do not trust the Court to provide justice, a view fostered by repeat occurrences of discrimination experienced by the Community. This reflects the Travellers' belief that the Courts cannot provide an effective remedy:

> Travellers are a small community. When we hear of other Travellers going through the stress of bringing a place to court for discrimination and it changes nothing, that means we feel it's not worth taking cases.[52]

In practice the marginalisation of Travellers becomes reinforced by the toothlessness of the current equality framework, leaving them with a clear sense that the system neither protects the right to equal treatment, nor offers an effective remedy for victims; it just entrenches exclusion.

## C. Exclusion from Legal Services

Travellers have rights to both equality and access to justice within Irish domestic and international legislative frameworks.[53] Similarly, access to justice and the associated access to an effective remedy are considered central and enabling rights afforded to all individuals. As Brinks has noted, access to justice and adequate legal representation are central to the advancement of ethnic minorities such as the Traveller Community, yet 'in spite of this rights-rich normative framework,

[49] ibid 64.

[50] M Clifford, 'Travellers pub claims fall to nine' *Sunday Tribune* (19 June 2005).

[51] *Advisory Committee on the Framework Convention for the Protection of National Minorities Report* ACFC/Op/IV(2018) 005.

[52] Morgan-Williams and Donson (n 3) 43.

[53] Art 40.1 Irish Constitution; Equal Status Act 2000–2018; Employment Equality Act 2000–2015; Art 14 ECHR; RED 2000/43/EC, etc.

indigenous groups still experience a high likelihood that their rights will be violated with impunity, and a concurrent inability to make effective use of this plethora of rights to pursue their most fundamental goals as peoples'.[54] However, as seen in preceding sections, many Travellers are unable to access traditional legal services, or to access legal representation directly. The result is an advice desert,[55] arising from significant unmet legal need.

Nationally there is only one 'Traveller-specific' legal service, based within FLAC.[56] Aside from the Traveller Legal Unit, a number of small legal information projects complement other general access to justice initiatives such as the TEJP, CLM Service, Mercy Law and FLAC. While these projects are general in scope, Mercy Law undertake a monthly legal advice clinic at Exchange House for Travellers. Notwithstanding the excellent work of these projects, there is a significant gap in Traveller-specific legal services.

Furthermore, as was noted in section IV.A, the majority of these advice services are based within urban environs, most notably in the capital, Dublin. Consolidation of specialist legal services in the capital creates significant access gaps for those residing in rural areas.[57] Thus, the advice desert that underlies Traveller access to justice is compounded by a further justice desert within which victims of discrimination are unable to find the representation needed to challenge discrimination through the relevant legal channels. These deserts increase mistrust and add to a perception that the system cannot or will not bring about much-needed resolution.

Newman recognised that rural communities experience advice and justice deserts as a result of their geographical removal from legal services.[58] However, the exclusion of the Traveller Community from access to justice evidences how these deserts, indicative of unmet legal need, are not only a result of the urban/rural divide but can also follow the entrenched marginalisation of formerly rural groups despite their geographical relocation to the peripheries of urban centres. As explored in section III, the majority of Travellers are resident in Dublin and theoretically should have access to legal advice via the available services, but this is not the case. Urban is not necessarily better in terms of access to justice for the

[54] Brinks (n 24) 350.

[55] Pruitt et al (n 2).

[56] The Traveller Legal Service (TLS) was established in 2019. The TLS is supported by The Community Foundation for Ireland and was established in cooperation with a Steering Group made up of representation from the national Traveller organisations. Although a welcome development, it remains the only Traveller-specific legal service nationally, and at present is run by a single solicitor for all national case referrals.

[57] Although not common, practitioners based in Dublin can and will travel to other Court districts, particularly those in major cities. However, it is difficult to find practitioners who are willing to travel to remote rural district courts or townlands. This is particularly the case where practitioners are for legal services that are already overwhelmed representing clients within their existing catchment and client bases.

[58] D Newman, 'Attitudes to justice in a rural community' (2016) 36(4) *Legal Studies* 591.

Traveller Community. Extreme marginalisation results in the same exclusion from access to justice regardless of location.

## V. 'Rediscrimination' within the Equality Framework

The lived experience of the Traveller Community reflects the inability of the equality system to ensure justice and to prevent recurrence of discrimination. The inability of Travellers to find representation and access the courts indicates that the equality system is itself a discriminatory forum, whereby the most vulnerable are excluded from seeking both assistance and redress:

> Justice systems more often than not incorporate the pathologies of their surrounding political and social systems, and it is difficult if not impossible to turn those who are second-class citizens outside the justice system, into first-class citizens inside.[59]

At its core, the legal system is excluding groups who cannot, whether for socio-economic, social-exclusion or other access reasons, such as residing in rural communities, make a claim. This exclusion from challenging discrimination via the courts can be considered 'rediscrimination'. This is exacerbated by the general failure of the system more broadly to respond robustly to discrimination against Travellers (and other minority rights-holders). Unfortunately, litigation is not a significant deterrent, with many pubs and service providers continuing to discriminate despite having cases successfully brought against them:

> Even if you win your case and get compensation money, it's no good because when you go back to that venue, they will still discriminate against you again. And just because you won for that one pub doesn't mean the pub next to them is going to let Travellers in.[60]

This is a common lived experience of other global indigenous or ethnic minorities who seek to vindicate legal rights.[61] Being excluded from service access, the result is that 'for individuals who bear the burden of social discrimination and prejudice the problem is not simply a lack of access but inequality within the system itself'.[62] The current framework is too weak to combat this sense of impunity and resulting repeated discriminatory conduct. With the system unable to produce a just outcome for victims of discrimination, 'rediscrimination' is inevitable.

[59] Brinks (n 24) 355.

[60] Morgan-Williams and Donson (n 3) 43.

[61] For example, the experiences of indigenous groups in many South American states show significant overlap with those of the Traveller Community detailed here. For an overview of these, see also the excellent work of Brinks (n 24). See also the experiences of First Nations as detailed by Allison and Cunneen in ch 6 of this volume.

[62] Brinks (n 24) 348.

## VI. Conclusion

As this volume makes clear, those residing in rural areas must navigate significant barriers to justice when seeking advice and just outcomes. Unfortunately, the majority of legal resources centre around urban hubs, and legal support systems are often dependent on 'technological, professional, and infrastructural capacities that simply do not exist in many rural regions'.[63] These legal deserts occur as a result of significant unmet legal need caused by uneven distribution of resources. As Statz et al note, 'rural access is not only impeded by well-documented phenomena such as rural distance and limited or nonexistent broadband, but also less examined challenges like rural legal deserts'.[64] These deserts lead to inability to source representation and a resulting failure to secure just outcomes when justiciable problems arise.

The experience of the Traveller Community in Ireland is beset with many such barriers, caused by the centrality of specialist legal services, structural obstacles and exclusion from legal services. Although traditionally a rural community, state policy intended to 'assimilate' Travellers has resulted in the majority of the Community now residing in urban areas.[65] The Travellers' right to access justice is denied through scarce resource allocation and inability to access legal representation and advice when needed. Despite recognition of this stark unmet legal need,[66] this inaccessibility is systemic.

In facing considerable barriers in accessing legal services, Travellers' exclusion from the legal system mirrors that experienced by rural communities, particularly in relation to physical access to a court and legal professionals.[67] Yet, as this chapter outlines, the barriers for Travellers move beyond geographical remoteness, as Travellers are unable to find both legal information and representation owing to the scarcity of suitable Traveller-specific resources. This lack of appropriate legal service provision creates an advice desert, which in turn gives rise to a justice desert, in which victims of discrimination experience rediscrimination by virtue of their exclusion from effective remedies by the equality system.

This is problematic on a number of fronts given the vulnerability and exclusion of Travellers within Irish society:

> Socially excluded groups within the general population are more likely to suffer justiciable problems (meaning problems for which there is a potential legal remedy within a civil and/or criminal justice framework) and the lack of effective and accessible mechanisms for resolving legal disputes prevents individuals from protecting and asserting their rights.[68]

[63] Statz, Friday and Bredeson (n 2).

[64] ibid 4.

[65] See section III.A.

[66] G Lee, 'State urged to bring back Traveller law centre' *Law Society Gazette* (December 2021) at www.lawsociety.ie/gazette/top-stories/2021/12-december/state-urged-to-bring-back-traveller-law-centre.

[67] Newman (n 58).

[68] FLAC Presentation to the Joint Oireachtas Committee on Justice and Equality on Reform of the Family Law System, 13 March 2019.

Where the legal system itself also acts as a fundamental barrier to accessing justice, resulting in systemic obstruction, the result is mistrust, harm and lack of belief in the system to ensure legal remedy and justice. Travellers therefore do not trust in the ability of the courts to provide them with justice:

> We never brought a case because you don't hear of Travellers getting any justice and its draining to have to fight every day of your life when the system that is supposed to be there to help you doesn't work. You could be years fighting and never get anywhere.[69]

These trust-based problems are exacerbated by the legal issues faced by Travellers. Their cases engage with more acute legal needs – regarding justiciable problems and the urgency of these – yet the system has not only failed to respond to these but further embedded the harms caused. The legacy of prejudice within and exclusion from society is perpetuated by the very system designed to overcome this, and domestic efforts made to overcome barriers to justice have failed to account for the needs of marginalised groups such as Travellers. In particular, modernisation attempts, such as shifts to remote hearings and greater digitisation of processes,[70] further alienate minorities who may not have access to the required technology. Clearly, future attempts to overcome the systemic barriers in place for marginalised groups seeking justice must centralise their voices and lived experiences in order to adequately respond to, and provide for, their unique needs. Inclusion of Traveller voices within this chapter is revealing as to their adverse lived experiences and the entrenchment of their exclusion from the current equality system.

[69] Morgan-Williams and Donson (n 3) 27.

[70] While such modernisation efforts, like the overhaul of the Court's IT system, pre-date the Covid-19 crisis, the shift to online hearings and submission of court documents electronically was made necessary by the pandemic. For more, see 'Life in Technicolour' at www.lawsociety.ie/gazette/in-depth/virtual-courts. Such shifts are welcome, not least where they improve access to WRC hearings, as allowing greater specialist representation for Travellers, yet special measures must be introduced for those unable to attend online hearings by virtue of socio-economic issues, including access to services such as broadband and computers.

# 8

# Older Victims, Legal Need and Access to Justice in Rural Communities in Northern Ireland

FAITH GORDON AND KEVIN J BROWN*

## I. Introduction

Older people's experiences of victimisation remain a relatively under-researched area. The voices and views of older people in criminal justice systems are often hidden, and their opinions are typically marginalised in policy, practice and in academic inquiry. While several existing contemporary studies have focused on specific crimes perpetrated against older people,[1] there has been very little emphasis on exploring whether location and place play a key role in older people's experiences of victimisation. Nor has there been an in-depth critical analysis of whether residing in rural locations impacts upon older people's legal needs, access to justice and tailored support services.

This chapter sets out to directly address this gap in the research-based literature, by considering specific issues for older people in rural communities when seeking access to justice following their victimisation. Northern Ireland is employed as a case study and the chapter draws on an extensive body of research conducted by the authors.[2] The discussion is derived from a larger study on access to justice and crime clearance rates for older victims in Northern Ireland, commissioned by the Commissioner for Older People and published as a report in 2019, along with a series of recommendations.[3] The study adopted a mixed-methods

* The authors are grateful to the Commissioner for Older People for Northern Ireland for funding the larger study from which this chapter is derived and to Dr Daniel Newman for his feedback.

[1] For example N Chivite-Matthew and P Maggs, 'Crime, Policing and Justice: the experience of older people' (Home Office, 2002) 1; H Bows, 'Age and Victimisation' in K Corteen et al (eds), *A Companion to Crime, Harm and Victimisation* (Policy Press, 2016) 1.

[2] KJ Brown and F Gordon, *Improving Access to Justice for Older Victims of Crime: Older People as Victims of Crime and the Response of the Criminal Justice System in Northern Ireland* (QUB and COPNI, 2019).

[3] ibid.

approach combining analysis of quantitative and qualitative data, which included analysis of statistics from the Police Service of Northern Ireland (PSNI) and the Public Prosecution Service (PPS) of Northern Ireland and semi-structured qualitative interviews and focus groups with older people including those who had been victims of crime, as well as family members. This chapter revisits that original qualitative interview data and data from focus groups, as well as Gordon's field diary notes from interviews with older people. The data have been revisited, specifically with a focus on exploring the areas of legal need and access to justice for older people living in rural locations in Northern Ireland. As such, they address this collection's framing question, looking at how people experience the institutions of justice in rural areas and how this rural experience differs from an urban experience.

The chapter commences with a review of the existing literature on older people and crime, with a particular focus upon rural communities. It then outlines the current service provision arrangements for older victims of crime in rural communities in Northern Ireland. The chapter then draws upon the voices of interviewees and focus group participants, to explore their legal needs and their experiences of victimisation, access to justice and services in their rural communities. Lastly, the chapter outlines several proposed future directions, and calls for the need for tailored reforms and sufficient expertise and resources to be allocated to older people in rural communities.

## II. Older People as Victims of Crime

Older people have been largely neglected in research-based studies on victims of crime. There is a wealth of existing academic literature that has focused on young people and their experiences as either perpetrators or victims within the criminal justice system (including the excellent chapter 12 by Mouhiddin in this volume).[4] However, older people appear to represent a particularly marginalised and hidden social group.[5] Over two decades ago, Brogden and Nijar published an important study that explored why the criminal justice system has effectively ignored older people.[6] Their research was critical of 'traditional criminology', stating that it 'has by-passed a population caricatured by ageist stereotyping and

[4] P Omaji, *Responding to Youth Crime* (Hawkins Press, 2003); S Brown, *Understanding Youth and Crime: Listening to Youth?*, 2nd edn (Oxford University Press, 2005); S Walklate, *Criminology: The Basics* (Routledge, 2006); D Finkelhor, *Childhood Victimization: Violence, Crime, and Abuse in the Lives of Young People* (Oxford University Press, 2008); RH Burke, *Young People, Crime and Justice* (Willan Publishing, 2013).

[5] See J Powell and A Wahidin, 'Old Age and Victims: A Critical Exegesis and an Agenda for Change' *Internet Journal of Criminology* (2007) at www.internetjournalofcriminology.com/_files/ugd/b93dd4_d06f3884b67a47d6ba1921c650dcf0b0.pdf.

[6] M Brogden and P Nijhar, *Crime, Abuse and the Elderly* (Taylor and Francis, 2000) 8.

by assumptions about inviolate private space'.[7] Their insights demonstrated how older people's victimisation has been overlooked and marginalised in academic, policy and practice spheres. While over two decades old, the key messages in this study still resonate today.

According to official statistics, the risk of an older person in Northern Ireland being a victim of crime is relatively low. That said, not all crimes are reported, and therefore not all incidents are officially recorded and included in the statistics. Data from Police records in Northern Ireland demonstrate that there was an average of 36 recorded crimes per 1,000 of the population in 2017/18, excluding the crime of fraud, as the recorded figures are not broken down by age for that category.[8] In that year the likelihood of recording a crime with the police was the highest for the 20–24 age group (68 per 1,000) and lowest for the 65+ age group (15 per 1,000).[9] The Northern Ireland Crime Survey, which records victims' experiences of crime, also finds that older people are the group least likely to be the subject of a crime. These findings from Northern Ireland are replicated in many other jurisdictions.[10] These overall figures do need to be unpacked and a thorough exploration of the offence categories needs to be considered. It is evident that older people are significantly less likely to be the victims of a violent crime compared with other adult age groups; however, in relation to crimes such as burglary, criminal damage and some forms of theft, the risks of an older person being a victim of crime are similar to those for other adult age groups.[11]

Research demonstrates that older people's perceptions of crime and the criminal justice system are typically based on their personal experience of being a victim of crime; contact either directly or indirectly with someone who has been a victim of crime; the presence of family members who are concerned on behalf of older relatives; outreach programmes and initiatives; and the media reporting of crimes.[12] Certain characteristics and circumstances make older people as a group more vulnerable to the harm that being a victim of crime can cause in comparison to other adult age groups. These factors include: a higher rate of fear of the impact of crime; a higher rate of physical and mental impairment and disability; a greater likelihood of living alone; a greater likelihood of the absence of support networks; higher rates of feelings of insecurity.[13]

The crimes of which older people are most likely to be victims are burglary, criminal damage and vehicle-related theft, excluding an insight into fraud statistics as these are not broken down by age in Northern Ireland. Burglary, criminal

[7] ibid.

[8] PSNI, *Trends in Police Recorded Crime in Northern Ireland 1998/99 to 2017/18* (PSNI, 2018).

[9] ibid.

[10] See A Rice and P Campbell, *Perceptions of Crime: Findings from the 2016/17 Northern Ireland Crime Survey* (Department of Justice, 2018); Scottish Government, *Pre-recording Evidence of Child and other Vulnerable Witnesses: Consultation Analysis* (Scottish Government, 2017).

[11] Brown and Gordon (n 2) 5.

[12] ibid.

[13] KJ Brown and F Gordon, 'Older victims of crime: Vulnerability, resilience and access to procedural justice' (2019) 25(2) *International Review of Victimology* 201.

damage and vehicle-related theft are categories of crime that involve intrusion into a person's 'safe space', and this can cause long-term serious harm.[14] As demonstrated by existing research, being a victim of crime can cause significant harm, emotionally, psychologically, physically and financially, which can negatively impact a victim's overall quality of life and can also exacerbate other issues.[15]

## III. Older People and Access to Justice

As a social group, older people have been described as more vulnerable to the effects of crime;[16] however, our study from Northern Ireland found a reluctance amongst older people to self-identify as vulnerable for the purposes of accessing additional support when journeying through the justice system.[17] The word 'vulnerable' was interpreted by many interviewees and focus group participants as a stigmatic label and was frequently rejected, even where objectively the justice system would categorise the persons as vulnerable. While participants would describe other older people as 'vulnerable', they typically rejected the use of the word to describe their own personal characteristics. However, the criminal justice system and the victim support service providers employ the word 'vulnerable' to assess support provision, and there exists a disconnect between older people's views and the system's descriptions.

In the European context, the preamble to the 2012 EU Directive establishes the minimum rights, support and protection of victims of crime,[18] to ensure that they receive equal access to justice, as it is deemed a fundamental right. Equal access requires that all victims should be treated with dignity and respect. In the context of Northern Ireland, the 2015 Victim Charter gave effect to the 2012 EU Directive, and it outlines that all victims will be 'recognised and treated in a courteous, dignified, respectful, sensitive, tailored, professional and non-discriminatory way'.[19] Yet an exploration of older people's experiences of access to justice in Northern Ireland demonstrates that there are issues that negatively impact upon that access. One such significant issue was the collection of evidence

[14] ibid; KJ Brown and F Gordon, 'Improving access to justice for older victims of crime by reimagining conceptions of vulnerability' (2022) 42(3) *Ageing & Society* 614.

[15] KJ Brown and F Gordon, 'Exploring and overcoming barriers to justice for older victims of crime' (2020) 12 *Criminal Law Review* 1127.

[16] S Fraga Dominguez et al, 'Elder Abuse Vulnerability and Risk Factors: Is Financial Abuse Different From Other Subtypes?' (2022) 41(4) *Journal of Applied Gerontology* 928.

[17] Brown and Gordon, 'Improving access to justice for older victims of crime' (n 14) 614.

[18] Directive 2012/29/EU of the European Parliament and of the Council of 25 October 2012 establishing minimum standards on the rights, support and protection of victims of crime, and replacing Council Framework Decision 2001/220/JHA [2012] OJ L315/57.

[19] The Victim Charter (Justice Act (Northern Ireland) 2015) Order (Northern Ireland) 2015 (SI 2015/370).

in cases that involved older people, which did impact upon their ability to access justice. As a Victim Support Officer interviewed for the study stated:

> It'll be the elderly person that suffers at the end of the day. They've gone through this trauma; they've had this burglary, they've had this criminal damage, they did the right thing, reported it to the police, given their statements and all of a sudden somebody's saying, 'We don't think you'll make a good witness so therefore we're not going to prosecute'.[20]

This was one of several significant issues negatively impacting older people's access to justice in Northern Ireland. Other issues identified in the research as causing problems for older victims of crime included the identification of vulnerability within the older population, communication between older victims and criminal justice agencies, and the length of time taken for cases to reach a resolution.[21]

## IV. 'Hidden' and 'Neglected': Older People in Rural Communities

Just as a focus on older people as a social group has been long neglected in criminology, so also have rural communities.[22] Moody employs the phrase 'rural neglect' to describe the discipline's lack of focus on crimes committed in rural locations.[23]

Our study specifically explored crimes against older people in Northern Ireland and responses to it by the criminal justice system. It explored how the PSNI and the PPS responded to crimes involving older people as victims. Several of the interviewees lived in rural areas in different parts of Northern Ireland. Semi-structured interviews and focus groups were also conducted with staff from the PSNI, PPS, Victim Support NI, and the Victim and Witness Crime Unit. The published research report made recommendations based on the research findings, with older people's experiences central to the suggestions for tailored reform.[24]

As noted previously, the crimes of which older people are most likely to be victims include burglary, criminal damage and vehicle-related theft, with the collected data excluding fraud statistics. These three categories of crime involve intrusions into supposedly safe spaces. Being a victim of a crime that undermines

[20] Brown and Gordon (n 2) 101.

[21] ibid.

[22] One of the few studies on rural access to justice in the UK includes the voices of older community members who believe their experiences are ignored in decision-making around legal service provision. See D Newman, 'Attitudes to Justice in a Rural Community' (2016) 36(4) *Legal Studies* 591.

[23] S Moody, 'Rural neglect: the case against criminology' in G Dingwall and S Moody (eds), *Crime and Conflict in the Countryside* (University of Wales Press, 1999) 23.

[24] Brown and Gordon (n 2) 216.

that sense of a safe space can cause serious and lasting harm, and there is an additional layer of isolation and distress if an older person lives in a rural location:

> '[W]e would see the age of the victim when they are in much later years as an aggravated feature in the case especially whenever they are an elderly person living in a rural setting and things like that where they feel isolated, where for instance they are ill or there's other vulnerabilities, that all compounds it. I'm just not so sure that that's always reflected in sentencing but probably no more so than other features aren't reflected properly reflected in sentencing.' Interviewee: PPS Prosecutor.[25]

Fear in relation to potential additional victimisation following the incident was mentioned by one interviewee, who described the possibility of retaliation for his interactions with the PSNI in reporting the incident of 'rural crime':

> 'I would love to catch the person that done it but in the long term I sort of think there has been somebody coming just some knock on your door some night saying we'll learn you, you boy you, sometimes you have to just bite your lip and say it's a loss but hopefully it will not happen again. I would say it is, I would still be saying to myself to the same wee house and say who's going to be here the night? Or who's going to land?' Interviewee: Older Victim of Crime.[26]

> 'I'd be looking at the bigger picture; I'd be saying yes, I would love to catch that person that done it but … I'm saying that then my life will be in danger [after that] so I nearly had to kiss the hare's foot and say it's water under the bridge but it's not good enough at the end of the day that these boys can just do that there and get away, it's not good enough.' Interviewee: Older Victim of Crime.[27]

One interviewee who had been the victim of what would be described as a 'rural crime', in that he had livestock stolen,[28] referred to his victimisation as a less serious crime and recounted that during his interactions with the PSNI he had stated:

> 'I said to the policeman, I said more or less this is only a minor thing to you, it's like penny halfpenny job, sure you's have more to do with your time.' Interviewee: Older Victim of Crime.[29]

In the context of Northern Ireland as a post-conflict society, there was evidence of a perception in some communities that criminals felt at greater liberty to carry out crimes against vulnerable individuals than they would have during the conflict in Northern Ireland, which lasted for over 30 years.[30] For some older people, the lack of paramilitary 'policing' in their communities heightened feelings of insecurity.

[25] ibid 210.

[26] ibid 58.

[27] ibid.

[28] This is one of the most popular topics of rural justice literature; eg, there are multiple chapters on it in one of the leading works, R Mawby and R Yarwood (eds), *Rural Policing and Policing the Rural* (Ashgate, 2011).

[29] Brown and Gordon (n 2) 65.

[30] ibid 59.

The formal criminal justice agencies were not viewed as offering the same level of protection in some of the communities. There was a view put forward during interviewees and focus groups that the post-conflict era made older people feel more vulnerable to the risks of 'everyday crime'.[31] This is an interesting and important observation of which the criminal justice agencies and support services need to be conscious, and it had an additional layer of meaning for participants living in smaller and more rural areas.

The authors interviewed coordinators from Victim Support Northern Ireland. The participants covered a range of geographical localities in Northern Ireland. Both participants had extensive experience of the difficulties that victims and witnesses can encounter in the criminal justice system and the support services that Victim Support provides, which were further exacerbated if older people resided in rural locations. These insights from service providers, advocates and practitioners provided details into the challenges for older people in rural communities, particularly in relation to transport and travel to large towns and cities. Further, the insights shone a light on to the need for tailored reform and resources to be directed to addressing the specific needs of older people living in rural locations.

## V. Need for Tailored Reform and Resources

The research study from which this chapter is derived has identified the significant short- and medium-term negative impacts that being a victim of crime can have on older people. Older people living in rural locations who participated in this research had specific needs, which typically had previously not been recorded or listened to. We assert that further research needs to be conducted to explore the long-term effects being a victim of crime can have on the health and well-being of older people, with the additional layer of feeling isolated and alone in the process of navigating the criminal justice system if they do not have a support network and access to service providers, which are typically located in towns and cities. If research were to be conducted that focused on health and well-being, the findings of such a study would help inform the approach taken to supporting such victims, with a clear focus on the challenges for those living in rural communities.

There is clearly a specific need for tailored services for older people to be available and accessible for those living in rural areas. As the qualitative research demonstrated, navigating the criminal justice system can be traumatic for victims of crime and can result in individuals experiencing secondary victimisation. Older people identified that they have specific needs that relate to their age and their

[31] ibid.

access – or in many instances lack of access – to available support networks. Also, for those living in rural and regional areas they have additional specific needs in relation to access to justice, which range from access to service provision, access to transport and access to support networks.[32] The introduction of an older person's victim advocacy scheme in Northern Ireland, as exists for other groups within society, would provide a forum for older people from rural areas to express their needs and concerns.

Of the quantitative data available, it was evident that certain measures have not been recorded. We recommend that the Victim and Witness Care Unit should introduce a recording practice that allows data on levels of engagement by different demographic groups of victims and witnesses to be gathered and published to inform research and practice. This should include location. The role of the Victim and Witness Care Unit is to provide a single point of contact within the criminal justice system. Its primary role is to keep victims and witnesses fully informed of the progress of the prosecution case throughout the criminal justice process, and it can make referrals to other service providers if required. Further, whilst PPS resources are limited, the implementation of an outreach programme or public engagement strategy may prove beneficial, especially for those living in rural locations, who often find it challenging travelling to towns and cities to access service support.

The Judicial Studies Board[33] and the Lord Chief Justice's Sentencing Group[34] should work with the Commissioner for Older People for Northern Ireland to identify how to raise awareness amongst the older population of the sentencing guidelines and the process of sentencing more generally, as this would assist with older people's perceptions of the criminal justice system and the outcomes. This dialogue should include work on the need for greater and specific tailored information, advice and service provision for older people living in rural areas, who are often situated a distance away from centres in which they could access information and services in person.

Community Impact Statements, similar to Victim Impact Statements, are available in Northern Ireland but rarely used: they are designed to capture the impact of a crime on the wider community and in rural communities that typically are small and close-knit; this would be a key avenue to record the impact on the individual and on the wider community. It is recommended that the Commissioner for Older

[32] Work on the civil justice system in England and Wales, for example, has highlighted that older service users have struggled with the increasing move towards remote access since the Covid-19 pandemic; these users can find the technology confusing, but also see the importance of face-to-face contact to develop trust. See J Mant, D Newman and D O'Shea, *Access to Justice and Blended Advice: A Report for the Access to Justice Foundation* (Access to Justice Foundation, 2022) 1.

[33] The role of the Judicial Studies Board in Northern Ireland is to ensure that judicial officers are equipped with the skills and knowledge to conduct their duties. The Board provides information and training in a way that preserves judicial independence and promotes confidence in the justice system.

[34] The Lord Chief Justice's Sentencing Group assesses what, if any, improvements could be made to the sentencing guideline arrangements in Northern Ireland.

People for Northern Ireland consult with stakeholders on the potential utility of Community Impact Statements as a mechanism for bringing to the attention of the justice system the wider impact some crimes can have on the older population of a locality.

## VI. Conclusion

Older people have long been a hidden and neglected social group in criminological and socio-legal studies. Older people's experiences of victimisation, the criminal justice system and access to justice have not been critically analysed in previous studies. The large qualitative and quantitative study from which this chapter's discussion and evidence base are derived, demonstrates that although older people are not homogeneous as a social group, there are common aspects to the experience of older victims of crime of which agencies of the criminal justice system should be aware and that policymakers should seek to address.[35]

As explored in this chapter, for older victims of crime in rural communities in Northern Ireland, location and place do impact upon access to justice, and typically these contextual factors shape aspects of older people's legal needs. Criminal justice agencies need to engage in regular dialogue with older people living in rural communities, and their advocates or representatives, to ensure that their voices and experiences inform future reforms. The introduction of an older person's victim advocacy scheme in Northern Ireland would provide a forum for older people from rural areas to express their needs and concerns. Adopting reforms that are based on the needs of older people living in rural locations would be a demonstration of the adherence of the criminal justice system in Northern Ireland to the principles that all victims should be treated with dignity and given equal access to justice, irrespective of age and in addition, we argue, irrespective of location.

[35] Brown and Gordon (n 2) 1.

# 9

# Litigants in Person and Rural Family Justice in England and Wales

JESS MANT

## I. Introduction

This chapter contributes an insight into how people in rural areas experience the family court process in England and Wales. Drawing upon original empirical data from interviews with 23 individuals who were representing themselves in family court hearings, the chapter emphasises the differential impact of legal aid policy on those living in rural communities, as compared with those living in large cities in England and Wales. In doing so, it indicates the extent to which the availability and accessibility of legal support is demarcated by geographical factors, and the differential experiences that litigants in family cases had as a result. It also provides an insight into the different strategies that people in rural areas may employ when they are faced with a dearth of service provision in their local area. Ultimately, the findings presented provide a basis for reflecting upon the differential impact of UK legal aid policy for those in rural areas of England and Wales.

## II. Litigants in Person and Family Justice

The notion of family justice is broadly defined. At some times, this term is used to describe the concept of access to justice as it relates to family law, and at other times, it is used to refer to the specific systems by which justice is achieved, such as the family court process. Both are relevant during the process of family breakdown.[1] This is because when a family breaks down, there are several issues that need to be decided – where children should live, how often they spend time with each parent, and how any property or assets should be divided. Although these decisions are often difficult and emotional, most parents work these issues out by negotiating

[1] A Barlow et al, *Mapping Paths to Family Justice* (Palgrave, 2017).

between themselves and do not seek legal advice.[2] Some families will use mediation, where a mediator will help them to work through the issues and come to agreements. However, informal negotiations are often not possible for those families where former partners are struggling to communicate effectively, contending with complex circumstances, high levels of conflict, power imbalances, or even safety concerns and domestic abuse.[3] Traditionally, these would be the families most likely to find themselves in the family court, which has traditionally operated as a safety net, providing a formal environment in which court orders can be made to secure safe and appropriate arrangements in otherwise chaotic and difficult family circumstances.[4] This safety net has, however, been placed under significant strain by swathes of legal aid reforms, including the almost complete removal of eligibility for funded advice and representation for private family law problems under the Legal Aid, Sentencing and Punishment of Offenders Act (LASPO) 2012. Now, approximately 80 per cent[5] of cases that reach the family court involve people who are representing themselves as 'Litigants in Person' (LIPs), and many of those arrive for their hearings without prior legal advice or an advocate to help them navigate the family court process.

The four aims of LASPO stipulated in the UK Government's initial policy consultation were to: discourage unnecessary litigation, target legal aid at those who need it most, make significant savings to the cost of the legal aid scheme, and deliver better overall value for money for the taxpayer.[6] The aims were to be achieved by withdrawing legal aid eligibility for several legal problems, including social welfare law, employment law, and several issues relating to immigration, clinical negligence, debt and housing law. Funding to support advice and representation in private family law[7] was to be entirely removed, on the basis that such disputes were best resolved privately and did not necessitate the involvement of the justice system.

[2] See generally M Maclean and J Eekelaar, *After the Act: Access to Family Justice after LASPO* (Hart Publishing, 2019).

[3] M Hester et al, Domestic Violence: A National Survey of Court Welfare and Voluntary Sector Mediation Practice (Policy Press, 1997).

[4] J Birchall and S Choudhry, 'What About my Right Not to be Abused?' Domestic Abuse, Human Rights and the Family Courts (Women's Aid, 2018).

[5] In the year following the implementation of LASPO, the number of cases involving LIPs increased from 43% to 74%, and since then, this number has remained steady at around 80%. See Ministry of Justice, *Family Court Statistics Quarterly: October–December 2021* (Ministry of Justice, 2021).

[6] Ministry of Justice, Proposals for the Reform of Legal Aid in England and Wales (Ministry of Justice, 2010).

[7] Private family law concerns disputes between family members, such as between parents over arrangements for children. It is distinct from public family law, which refers to situations where local authorities intervene due to concerns about the safety of children. Nevertheless, it should be noted that the distinction between public and private family law is far from clear-cut, with many 'private' family law cases involving cross-cutting allegations and safety concerns. Under LASPO, there is a narrow exception to the bar on eligibility for those who can corroborate that they have experienced such domestic abuse, but this must be done through prescribed forms of evidence. See further R Hunter, 'Doing Violence to Family Law' (2011) 33 *Journal of Social Welfare and Family Law* 343.

As the UK Ministry of Justice stated during the LASPO consultation, the Government's view was that the availability of legal aid for family disputes has been an incentive for people to litigate their family disputes unnecessarily:

> Legal aid has expanded far beyond its original intentions, available for a wide range of issues, many of which need not be resolved through the courts. This has encouraged people to bring their problems to court when the courts are not well placed to provide the best solutions.[8]

After LASPO, disputing families on low incomes are now only able to access public funding to support their participation in mediation. If families want to consult a solicitor for legal advice or they need to use the family court, they must do this at their own expense. The default position is therefore one of non-eligibility, where individuals may not expect state-funded legal support in relation to their family disputes and using law or courts as a route to obtaining resolutions is generally stigmatised.

The narrative that legal advice acts as a gateway to unnecessary litigation is, however, inaccurate. In reality, legal advice has traditionally played an important role in ensuring that family disputes do *not* escalate to the point of requiring extended engagement with the legal system.[9] Gaining a realistic overview of one's legal position means that people are better equipped to negotiate privately or to participate in mediation on an equal footing. In very difficult circumstances where court proceedings are necessary, legal advice can serve to narrow down the issues, give individuals an understanding of what to expect when they go to court, and streamline the process to avoid prolonged and protracted hearings.[10] Now, many more people are self-representing in the family court as LIPs, attempting to navigate a system that is still premised upon the expectation that litigants have lawyers to guide them.[11]

The implementation of LASPO can therefore be understood as a significant turning point for family justice because it has fundamentally altered the ways that people engage with family law. Underpinned by the objective of reducing expenditure on legal aid, LASPO has further entrenched the idea that family disputes are personal matters that should be resolved without recourse to state-funded assistance. It has also intensified existing cynicism about the legitimacy of lawyers' involvement with family law issues, constructing reliance on legal support as individualised failures on the part of citizens.[12] All of this means that legal advice

[8] Ministry of Justice, Reform of Legal Aid in England and Wales: The Government Response (Ministry of Justice, 2011).

[9] K Wright, 'The Divorce Process: A View from the Other Side of the Desk' (2006) 18 *Child and Family Law Quarterly* 93.

[10] See generally R Ingleby *Solicitors and Divorce* (Oxford University Press, 1992); J Eekelaar et al, *Family Lawyers: The Divorce Work of Solicitors* (Hart Publishing, 2000).

[11] J Mant 'Placing LIPs at the Centre of the Post-LASPO Family Justice System' (2020) 32 *Child and Family Law Quarterly* 421.

[12] H Sommerlad and P Sanderson, 'Social Justice on the Margins: The Future of the Not-for-Profit Sector as Providers of Legal Advice in England and Wales' (2013) 35 *Journal of Social Welfare and Family Law* 305.

(in its traditional format) has become practically inaccessible for those who cannot afford to instruct lawyers privately. Rather, individuals must prepare for family court proceedings by piecing together the free or affordable support that they can find – much of which, of course, depends upon the extent to which information or advice is available and accessible in their local area.

This chapter contributes an insight into what family justice looks like for those based in rural areas of England and Wales. It does this by drawing upon data from 23 interviews with LIPs during 2017, undertaken as part of a larger empirical research project that sought to investigate the accessibility of family court proceedings after LASPO.[13] Due to the timing of these interviews, it is possible to capture a unique insight into how LIPs experienced the family court process as the implications of LASPO were beginning to manifest, but before the impending impact of the Covid-19 which came in 2020. Of course, an inevitable limitation of this data is that it cannot indicate how these experiences may have been intersected by the Covid-19 pandemic, which rapidly accelerated existing trends towards increasingly digitalised court processes.[14] Nevertheless, the issues raised here are likely to endure, if not worsen, given that a significant minority of the UK population are categorised as digitally excluded.[15]

Within these interviews, LIPs in both rural and urban areas talked extensively about their experiences of navigating what is now a deeply fragmented landscape of legal and non-legal support in preparation for their court hearings. A prominent theme of these discussions, identified during thematic analysis, was the way in which their experiences differed according to where LIPs lived in England and Wales. The purpose of this chapter is to provide an insight into these differences with a view to reflecting on what these experiences can reveal about the differential impact of this legal aid policy for those living in rural communities.

In terms of recruiting LIPs for interviews, it is difficult to identify and locate LIPs as a population group outside of the court environment. There are also specific ethical implications associated with cold-approaching people at court buildings, given that this is likely to be a very stressful and emotional time. Therefore, two main methods were used to recruit LIPs to the project. First, LIPs were recruited through leaflets and information sheets about the project, which were displayed at prominent face-to-face advice services across England and Wales, including the Citizens Advice Bureaux and Support Through Court, which each have offices in most major cities. Second, LIPs were recruited through posts about the project in relevant social media groups and online forums about family law and the court process. The sample that emerged through these methods consisted of 16 mothers

[13] For further detail of this wider project, see J Mant, *Litigants in Person and the Family Justice System* (Hart Publishing, 2022).

[14] See generally N Creudzfeldt, 'Towards a Digital Legal Consciousness?' (2021) 12 *European Journal of Law and Technology* 1.

[15] Local Government Association, *Tackling the Digital Divide* (House of Commons, 4 November 2021).

and seven fathers, with ages ranging between 18 and 45 years old.[16] The sample was disproportionately represented by those who identified as white British, with just one man who identified as black African, one woman who identified as white European, and two women who identified as South Asian. English was a second language for the last three LIPs. Crucially, for the purposes of this chapter, 14 LIPs were based near or within large cities across England and Wales – hereinafter referred to as 'urban LIPs' – and nine were from small towns and rural areas – hereinafter referred to as 'rural LIPs'.

The experiences of these nine rural LIPs will be central to the discussions in this chapter, but comparisons will also be drawn with the experiences of the other LIPs in order to demonstrate the significance of geographic location for the accessibility of legal support. In doing so, the chapter will argue that experiences of preparing for the family court may be significantly demarcated by barriers relating to limited service provision in rural areas, and that people in rural areas may take a range of different strategies when facing these barriers. It will argue that by examining these responses and perceptions, it is possible to expose a deeper understanding of what access to justice looks like for those living in rural communities.

In terms of structure, the chapter will proceed as follows. First, it will outline the different experiences that rural LIPs and urban LIPs had in terms of accessing advice and support when trying to prepare for their court hearings, and the specific challenges that were faced by those in rural areas with limited face-to-face service provision. Second, it will explore how rural LIPs responded to these challenges by seeking ad hoc and sporadic support, and the potential implications of partial and incomplete advice. Finally, it will conclude by reflecting on what the experiences, perceptions and responses of rural LIPs can reveal about the current state of family justice, and the future trajectory of access to justice concerns for rural communities.

## III. Sourcing Support: Advice Deserts

During interviews, LIPs identified several different kinds of legal support that they sought out in preparation for their impending court hearings. First, LIPs need a *legal* understanding of their position, which includes an awareness of how the relevant law might apply to their circumstances, their legal entitlements and how the legal framework works in relation to decisions about children. This is particularly important for those who are being summoned to a court hearing by the

[16] All names used in this chapter are pseudonyms chosen by LIPs during interviews. Given the challenges associated with recruiting LIPs discussed here, this is a relatively small sample. However, it is broadly aligned with similar small-scale qualitative studies on LIPs that have been undertaken after LASPO. See, eg, K Leader, 'Fifteen Stories: Litigants in Person and the Civil Justice System' (PhD thesis, London School of Economics, 2017); KA Barry, 'The Barriers to Effective Access to Justice Encountered by Litigants in Person in Private Family Matters Post-LASPO' (2020) 42 *Journal of Social Welfare and Family Law* 416.

other parent, who may be in a stronger economic position and may have already accessed advice that led them to commence proceedings. Second, LIPs require an insight into the *procedural* functions of the family court. For instance, this might include guidance on how to prepare or respond to an application for a court order, how the different types of family court hearings fit together as part of a broader process and what will be expected from them at a court hearing. Third, LIPs require *practical* and *emotional* support during these preparatory stages. This is especially important in family law given the high proportion of court cases that involve allegations of domestic abuse, safety concerns and high levels of conflict.[17] Evidence also suggests that LIPs disproportionately include those with learning difficulties and mental-health issues, which may mean that some individuals require bespoke or additional support.[18]

While the extent and nature of the assistance required necessarily varies depending on the individual and their circumstances, across interviews LIPs indicated the challenges they faced accessing these different types of support. Crucially, the availability of support across all categories was strongly demarcated by geographic location, with all nine of those in rural areas facing distinctive challenges in accessing all four types of support due to a lack of available face-to-face services in their local areas. Of these rural LIPs, five were unable to access any face-to-face advice services at all. These LIPs explained that their town or village had no services that could help them, or that the advice services in their area had closed. To understand the scale of this problem, it is possible to draw together an understanding of how legal aid policies have affected the sustainability of advice services in rural areas.

Even before LASPO, concerns about the cost of providing state-funded legal advice meant that the legal aid scheme was a common target for cost-saving policy measures.[19] During the lifetime of the scheme, these measures have come in two forms: those geared towards reducing cost by limiting the availability of legal aid for individuals, and those seeking to reduce cost by incentivising legal aid providers to work more cost-effectively. In terms of the former category of policies, the legal aid scheme has been reformed multiple times by successive governments to limit eligibility through increasingly strict means testing. In practice, this has always meant that even those who were historically eligible for legal aid have often been excluded from its benefits because they were expected to pay expensive and sometimes unaffordable contributions towards the cost of legal services.[20] In terms

[17] CAFCASS and Women's Aid, *Allegations of Domestic Abuse in Child Contact Cases* (CAFCASS, 2017); M Harding and A Newnham, *How do County Courts Share the Care of children Between Parents?* (University of Warwick and University of Reading, 2015).

[18] R Moorhead and M Sefton, *Litigants in Person: Unrepresented Litigants in First Instance Proceedings* (Department for Constitutional Affairs, 2005) 70; L Trinder et al, *Litigants in Person in Private Family Law Cases* (Ministry of Justice, 2014) 27.

[19] S Hynes, *Austerity Justice* (Legal Action Group, 2012); S Hynes and J Robins, *The Justice Gap* (Legal Action Group, 2009).

[20] S Cretney, *Family Law in the 20th Century* (Oxford University Press, 2005).

of the latter, measures have also frequently been targeted at legal aid providers themselves. This is because from the point that the legal aid scheme was originally introduced, demand for legal advice and representation grew rapidly as people began to access legal services for a broad range of problems. The increasing demand for advice and representation that was funded through legal aid meant that the cost of reimbursing service providers escalated beyond the expected confines of the legal aid scheme.

Taken within the developing context of family law, it is unsurprising that demand for advice and representation increased. With greater complexity of the law and growing numbers of separated parents managing childcare across different households came more need for family dispute resolution and orders under the Children Act 1989.[21] However, this increased demand for legal aid also raised suspicions of 'supplier-induced inflation', whereby lawyers claiming legal aid reimbursement were suspected of drawing cases out or encouraging litigation to maximise their income from the scheme.[22] These concerns indicated a shift in the relationship between lawyers and the state, in which government policy became geared towards promoting efficiency and greater scrutinisation of firms working in legal aid, as well as limiting renumeration for legal aid work. While some of these policies did improve the efficiency and standards of legal aid provision, these managerialist and bureaucratic procedures were widely cited as reasons for lawyers moving away from legal aid work, and many small providers found it unviable to rely on legal aid work as a source of income.[23] Cumulatively, this meant that there were fewer solicitors able to provide services through legal aid, and those that remained were overburdened and poorly remunerated.

The LASPO scope changes, which came into force in April 2013, dealt another blow to already-struggling legal aid providers, with entire areas of law being removed from the scheme. Statistics indicate that the number of not-for-profit legal advice centres in England and Wales has almost halved since 2005, and since LASPO came into force, data suggest that services offering civil legal aid have decreased by a third.[24] The UK Ministry of Justice does not collect data on what proportion of these civil providers are family law firms, but there is evidence to suggest that family law services have been disproportionately affected. For example, post-LASPO observations of family law firms suggest that smaller firms and those that have traditionally relied on legal aid clients are facing significant challenges sustaining their businesses now that they cannot derive an income from legal aid.[25] Due to the shortfall caused by LASPO, large numbers of firms have had to

[21] Maclean and Eekelaar (n 2) 10–11.

[22] R Moorhead, 'Legal Aid and the Decline of Private Practice: Blue Murder or Toxic Job?' (2004) 11(3) *International Journal of the Legal Profession* 159, 177.

[23] ibid 168–75.

[24] A Ames et al. Survey of Not-for-Profit Legal Advice Providers in England and Wales (Ministry of Justice, 2015); Ministry of Justice, Legal Aid Statistics Quarterly: October–December 2021 (Ministry of Justice, 2021).

[25] M Maclean and J Eekelaar, Lawyers and Mediators: The Brave New World of Services for Separating Families (Hart Publishing, 2016).

diversify their income streams either by moving away from legal aid work entirely, or by moving into offering other services like mediation.[26] As a result, 'advice deserts' are now common, with some geographical areas having no organisations at all willing to take on a legal aid contract.[27] These areas are disproportionately likely to be rural, post-industrialist or economically-deprived areas, where people are heavily reliant on welfare payments and public service employment and have been hit hardest by concurrent austerity measures.

For those living in rural areas, locating any sources of face-to-face advice at all was a significant challenge. Importantly, these experiences of rural LIPs starkly contrasted with those of the 14 urban LIPs who were interviewed for this project. For LIPs living in and around large cities, experiences of accessing support were quite different. Rather than being faced with a dearth of services, urban LIPs were faced with the challenge of navigating complex and fragmented networks of services and organisations around their city, including drop-in pro bono clinics and a myriad of non-legal face-to-face services. For example, LIPs in cities frequently relied upon student-led advice clinics, which were based at major universities. Several of them also made use of city-based services like Citizen's Advice Bureaux and Support Through Court, which can each provide practical and procedural help with paperwork and court forms. Support with private family law paperwork now forms almost half of the work undertaken by Support Through Court volunteers, and these services frequently employ local level networks with local law firms to which they can refer clients for legal advice.[28] Despite a greater availability of services in cities, accessing advice and support in this context was by no means straightforward. In practice, the task of piecing together a variety of different sources requires significant investment of time, energy and resources that several urban LIPs did not have, due to many of them having full-time caring responsibilities for children and precarious working arrangements and financial situations, which all existed as barriers to effectively accessing available support. Nevertheless, the disparity between urban and rural LIPs was significant, with decades of austerity-informed measures having hollowed out the ecosystem of advice services available to those outside major cities.

## IV. Sporadic Support: Is it Enough?

Among the LIPs who participated in this project, the differential impact of LASPO on LIPs in rural areas of England and Wales was stark. As noted earlier, all rural LIPs were unable to locate any advice services in their area, and this significantly

[26] S Wong and R Cain, 'The Impact of Cuts in Legal Aid Funding of Private Family Law Cases' (2019) 41 *Journal of Social Welfare and Family Law* 3.

[27] E Marshall et al, *Family Law and Access to Legal Aid* (Public Law Project, 2018).

[28] Personal Support Unit, Report and Financial Statements for the Year ended 31 March 2018 (Personal Support Unit, 2018).

framed their experiences of the family court process. As Trinder et al note, the preparatory stages of family court hearings can often be considered the most crucial for ensuring success within the court process. This is because accessing sufficient support in advance of entering the court process can often be vital in terms of narrowing down the issues that need to be decided, managing expectations for what can be achieved through the court process and emotionally preparing oneself for compromise within this process.[29]

Despite the challenges among rural LIPs in terms of accessing ongoing support from advice services, three rural LIPs did manage to locate some face-to-face assistance by searching beyond the traditional remit of free advice services that typically serve urban locations. For these LIPs, support came not from an advice service but from family law firms. One LIP (Joan) paid privately to instruct a lawyer on an 'unbundled' basis, and two LIPs (Ikraa and Grace) were able to access a pro bono appointment at local law firms.

Unbundled services involve individuals in instructing a lawyer on an ad hoc or selective basis to assist them with specific tasks, such as preparing an application to start proceedings, drafting paperwork, giving them a specific amount of legal advice, or even coming with them to represent them at a specific hearing. Importantly, these services are not comprehensive, and clients will agree the pricing and scope of these defined tasks in advance. During interviews, Joan revealed that she had relied upon a local lawyer via an unbundled arrangement as a safety net throughout her family court proceedings, and gave the following advice:

> [I]f you're paying for any advice, make sure you put everything in one email to your solicitor, don't send loads of small ones because they measure their costs in time, so if you save it for one, they might just charge you for an hour rather than the time it takes for them to open five small ones.
>
> **Joan**

Although Joan would have preferred to have her lawyer manage her case comprehensively, she was aware of her limited funds and was also conscious that her abusive ex-husband was in a much stronger economic position. This created a significant power imbalance in which he would drag proceedings out as much as possible, meaning that she had limited resources to use for legal support during her case. Joan's coping strategy was therefore to undertake as much independent research and preparation as she could using books, leaflets and the Internet, and to then rely upon her lawyer if she faced particularly difficult tasks or questions that she could not manage by herself.

This sporadic method of using of legal services is not a new phenomenon. Rather, even before LASPO this was a common solution for litigants faced with delays obtaining legal aid, or finances running out before a case was completed.[30]

[29] Trinder et al (n 18).

[30] Maclean and Eekelaar (n 25); L Webley 'When is a Family Lawyer a Lawyer?' in M Maclean et al (eds) *Delivering Family Justice in the 21st Century* (Hart Publishing, 2015) 305.

Now that the majority of people are categorically excluded from legal aid, there is some emerging evidence to suggest that there is an increasing demand for these unbundled services in family law.[31] However, Joan's experience of maximising the amount of advice she could receive, combined with similar evidence of LIPs using unbundled services alongside their hearings in Trinder et al's study, deepens current understandings of how unbundled services may be used in the future.[32] It suggests that accessing services on an unbundled or fixed-fee basis can also be a strategic approach used by LIPs who are completely excluded from legal aid and know they can only afford a certain amount of assistance.

This is, however, only possible for LIPs who have some financial resources that they can afford to spend on legal services. In practice, due to the LASPO reforms, there are also now likely to be a range of LIPs from extremely deprived backgrounds who cannot afford to pay for any help at all and will be entirely reliant on free assistance. This is because even those who would previously have met stringent means tests are now excluded on the basis of the type of case they are pursuing, rather than their income. While unbundled legal services may meet some support needs of LIPs after LASPO, there is therefore a concern about what free advice and support is available for those who cannot afford to pay anything towards the cost of support when they find themselves involved in family court proceedings.

During interviews with Ikraa and Grace, it became quickly apparent that locating a source of free legal advice was only one component of the challenges they each faced when attempting to access support:

> There is some help, but you really have to push to find it, it isn't readily available – like it doesn't come with the court papers. You have to go find it yourself, and the face-to-face advice you get is limited to the odd half hour or just 20 minutes.
>
> **Ikraa**

A common practice among family law firms, especially those that offer legal aid services, is to provide some free advice for clients seeking assistance. This might be to assess whether a potential client is eligible for legal aid and can then be taken on as an ongoing client, or simply to provide a baseline level of advice to an ineligible individual who otherwise has nowhere to turn. Since the implementation of LASPO, the number of people seeking free advice from law firms has significantly increased, as they now frequently arrive at firms to find that there is no legal aid available for family law problems.[33] Therefore, although some firms are continuing to offer pro bono advice to clients who find themselves ineligible for legal aid, the majority have been overwhelmed since LASPO, and simply cannot meet the current level of demand. As Ikraa's experience demonstrates, locating a family law firm that offers free advice is extremely difficult in the absence of any joined-up system of referrals. Additionally, due to the increased burden on

[31] Wong and Cain (n 26) 7–11.
[32] Trinder et al (n 18) 13–15.
[33] Maclean and Eekelaar (n 2).

these already-struggling services after LASPO, it is likely to be even more difficult to access appointments that are heavily oversubscribed and frequently held at set times, such as 'drop-in' advice evenings.

When describing the strategies that they had employed to seek advice from law firms, both interviewees also raised that they had experienced difficulties relating to the appointment format. For Ikraa, the limited time she was permitted with the advisor meant that she left her appointment feeling like she had spent most of her allotted time explaining her circumstances rather than receiving advice, and that she had insufficient opportunity to ask questions about the advice she had received. As existing literature demonstrates, advice giving is often a holistic exchange, through which advisors deploy a range of techniques, including the collection of relevant information, identification of clients' knowledge gaps, correcting clients' misconceptions about the law and offering clients a realistic view of what might be achieved in their case.[34] While experienced advisors are undoubtedly skilled in undertaking these tasks efficiently, the task of advice giving nevertheless requires degrees of flexibility, sensitivity and spontaneity in order to ensure that the client is equipped to deal with the next stage of their problem. Achieving this within the confines of a strict time limit is therefore likely to be extremely challenging for advisors attempting to support LIPs who are arriving with no prior understanding and are unlikely to be able to subsequently follow up on any point of advice or information given during the session.

The implications of this are particularly stark for the high proportion of LIPs who have learning difficulties or mental-health problems.[35] Grace, for example, had learning difficulties, which meant that she required more time when processing both written and oral information. As a result of this, she explained that she had made initial attempts to gain advice in her town, but after experiencing an appointment at her local law firm, had quickly decided not to engage with any further face-to-face services because she would have struggled to make use of the limited time that was available. For LIPs with mental-health problems or learning difficulties, therefore, this time-constrained method of accessing free advice may be entirely inappropriate.

Although there were key differences between the levels of resources available to these three LIPs, their experiences reveal some common concerns about the withdrawal of holistic, state-funded legal advice for family law, especially for those who cannot access the myriad of services available in cities. First, it risks potentially leaving vulnerable LIPs with only partial or incomplete understanding of their legal position and uncorrected misconceptions about the law or what to expect from the court process. The consequences of these gaps may be that LIPs

[34] E Kirk, 'Justice and Legal Remedies in Employment Disputes: Adviser and Advisee Perspectives' in S Kirwan (ed), *Advising in Austerity: Reflections on Challenging Times for Advice Agencies* (Bristol Policy Press, 2017) 91.

[35] Trinder et al (n 18) 27; L Cusworth, *Uncovering Private Family Law: Who's Coming to Court in England?* (Nuffield Family Justice Observatory, 2021).

employ inappropriate or disadvantageous strategies to self-representation once they arrive at court. Second, it cannot encapsulate the emotional and practical forms of support that are vital for LIPs' perceptions of fairness, their ability to meaningfully participate with the legal system, and the tools with which they can feel able to assess and accept the legitimacy of family court outcomes.[36]

## V. Conclusion

The accessibility of the family court is an issue that transcends the physical locations of the courtroom. This chapter has provided an indicative insight into the differential impact of legal aid policy on LIPs living in rural areas of England and Wales. For those who are able to pay privately for comprehensive legal services, the accessibility of family law advice has been largely unchanged by reforms such as LASPO. For the majority, however, the traditional format of instructing a lawyer to oversee the dispute from start to finish is unaffordable without the subsidisation of legal aid, and legal aid reforms have had a significant impact on both the availability and the accessibility of legal services, especially for those in remote or rural areas. In addition to the way in which LASPO has caused an increase in the number of people who are self-representing in the family court process, it has therefore also significantly impaired the availability and accessibility of the services that support people to use this process.[37] Now, those who find themselves acting as LIPs must find a way of preparing for their court hearings within a deeply fragmented context of advice services and law firms that are struggling to stay afloat and decreasing in number.

Crucially, this chapter has demonstrated that experiences of this context are also strongly demarcated between those living inside and those living outside of the major cities in England and Wales. While urban LIPs may be overwhelmed by the task of having to navigate several different services and piece together the different sources of information and advice they receive, others who live in small towns or rural areas have completely opposing experiences. These LIPs are faced with a distinct lack of available services in the areas to which they can travel. The consequences of these 'advice deserts' are significant, with many LIPs arriving at their court hearings with limited or no prior advice or understanding of their proceedings. Further, even when rural LIPs can access some sporadic support in rural areas, this carries the crucial risk of their engaging with the legal system on the basis of partial or incomplete advice, which may leave the LIPs ill-equipped to manage their proceedings.

Ultimately, this chapter has provided only a snapshot of the deleterious impact that legal aid reforms have had on those living in rural communities. Nevertheless,

[36] TR Tyler, *Why People Obey the Law* (Princeton University Press, 1990).

[37] See ch 13 of this volume, which more broadly explores some of the changes in how justice services have been delivered over recent years.

this indicative insight into the challenges faced by rural LIPs provides a basis for reflecting upon the current state and future trajectory of family justice in England and Wales. In particular, the findings presented here raise concerns about how support barriers may be further perpetuated in the coming years, as services continue to diminish and law firms struggle to meet the gaps in rural advice provision through pro bono services. Starting from this baseline, it is also essential that future research into the impact of Covid-19 on the accessibility of advice or the court process does not omit the significant consideration of rural versus urban location from its analysis. The findings presented here also emphasise the importance of learning from the perceptions and experiences of those who are forced to navigate the rural advice context. As indicated by the experiences discussed above, it is not always possible to predict how individuals may respond to the challenges they face, with some likely to look to alternative sources of advice, or to take purposeful strategies to maximise the small amount of support they can find. As such, it is vital that future research not only considers the scale of the advice deserts that characterise rural areas, but also gains a qualitative understanding of how individuals encounter rural family justice, and how this may affect their perceptions of the broader legal system that is designed to act as a safety net during the tumultuous process of family breakdown.

# 10

# Overcoming Geographic Barriers: Towards a Framework for Facilitating Legal Service Delivery in Rural Communities in Canada

LISA MOORE*

## I. Introduction

Location matters in Canada. Where Canadians live, the relative convenience and opportunities that a location provides, and the cost of living of an area carry immense significance.[1] We form strong attachments to the places that we recognise as 'home', often interweaving features of our community or a location with our identity. We might use our place of birth or residence to exemplify certain individual traits or more broadly equate generalisations about a place with its residents. It is common, for example, to reference 'city life' or to speak generally about being from the country. As with other demographic markers – ethnicity, age, race, etc – location is assumed to reveal something about an individual's character, their lifestyle or even culture. Nowhere are these characterisations of place more pronounced than in discussions centred on urban and rural areas.

Perceptions of this urban-rural dichotomy colour interactions and choices related to different types of locations. A lawyer's apprehension about relocating to a practice in a rural area, or a rural litigant's misgivings over engaging an

* The author is grateful to Ab Currie, PhD and Nicole Aylwin for their helpful comments on an early draft of this chapter.

[1] The importance of location is further reflected in the cost to own or rent a home in different parts of Canada. These costs vary greatly and include prices at both extremes. Canada is currently home to two of the most expensive housing markets in the world. The cities of Vancouver and Toronto are currently ranked the 6th and 12th most expensive housing markets in the world respectively. See Commercial Real Estate Services, *Global Living 2019* (Commercial Real Estate Services, April 2019) 6, at www.cbreresidential.com/uk/sites/uk-residential/files/property-info/FINAL%20REPORT.pdf. Similarly, it is not uncommon for people in some rural areas to own their home and have an annual income that is below the poverty level. See K Cohl and G Thomson, *Connecting Across Language and Distance: Linguistic and Rural Access to Legal Information and Services* (Law Foundation of Ontario, December 2008) 33.

urban-based lawyer or interacting with a judge in an urban setting, might be grounded in this divide. The broader landscape of legal experiences also reflects place-based distinctions. In Canada's justice sector, where there is a dearth of empirical evidence on impacts, outcomes and experiences, it can be difficult to determine the extent of these justice challenges and how much further we might have to go to address existing gaps. To that end, and in the absence of actionable data, perceptions about small-town living and rural dwellers can drive assumptions about legal need and how best to facilitate access to justice services and information.

In actuality, there is little difference between the kinds of legal problems that people experience in urban and rural areas.[2] Unmet legal need is prevalent in both types of location.[3] With regard to civil justice matters, which is the primary area of focus in this chapter, people in both rural and urban areas in Canada routinely experience civil justice problems in any of 16 legal categories, including family, housing, employment, debt, social assistance, disability assistance, consumer and medical treatment problems.[4]

[2] As an example, the 2019 study in rural Ontario that is referenced throughout this chapter identified 25 legal problem categories among rural residents seeking legal help, including problems related to family, employment, wills and power of attorney, housing/landlord-tenant and disability assistance. The problem categories and specific problem types in the study parallel those identified across decades of national legal needs research in Canada, with variations in the frequency of problem types and more specificity in how problems were categorised. Education problems, for instance, were identified as a distinct legal problem category in the 2019 rural legal outreach study, where education problems are more commonly categorised as (other) family problems in national legal needs studies. See A Currie, *Someone Out There Helping – Final Report of the WellCoMs Mobile Van Project* (Canadian Forum on Civil Justice, December 2019) 10–11 at www.cfcj-fcjc.org/wp-content/uploads/Someone-Out-There-Helping-Final-Report-Of-The-WellCoMs-Mobile-Van-Project-by-Ab-Currie.pdf. Discussing broadband access in rural Canada, the Federation of Canadian Municipalities in their 2014 report makes a similar point on the broader issue of the needs of rural populations relative to their urban counterparts. The report states that, '[t]he actual needs of these communities are the same as other, larger population centres, but the economics and geography often pose substantial challenges'. See Federation of Canadian Municipalities, *Broadband Access in Rural Canada: The role of connectivity in building vibrant communities* (Federation of Canadian Municipalities, 2014) 21 at www.fcm.ca/sites/default/files/documents/resources/report/broadband-access-rural-canada.pdf (hereinafter 'Connectivity Report').

[3] A 2022 Statistics Canada report *Experiences of Serious Problems or Disputes in the Canadian Provinces* reveals that 17% of people in rural locations across Canada, compared with 18% of people in urban locations indicated that they had experienced at least one *serious* dispute in the previous three years. See L Savage and S McDonald, *Experiences of Serious Problems or Disputes in the Canadian Provinces, 2021* (Statistics Canada, 18 January 2022) 18, at www150.statcan.gc.ca/n1/pub/85-002-x/2022001/article/00001-eng.pdf. A similar pattern was identified by the Canadian Forum on Civil Justice in their *Everyday Legal Problems: Canadian Regions* report, which found that provinces with almost 50% of rural residents and provinces with a much greater urban-rural population divide had a statistically similar scope of legal problem experiences. L Moore, *Everyday Legal Problems and the Cost of Justice in Canada: Region* (Canadian Forum on Civil Justice, August 2017) 7 at www.cfcj-fcjc.org/sites/default/files//docs/REGION%20-%20Everyday%20Legal%20Problems%20and%20the%20Cost%20of%20Justice%20in%20Canada.pdf.

[4] In this chapter, civil justice problems broadly refer to non-criminal problems, including family justice problems. The 16 problem types referenced are based on the civil justice problem types included as part of Canada's 2016 national problems survey, which asked Canadians about their experiences with 16 types of civil justice problems and criminal charges. See TCW Farrow et al, *Everyday Legal Problems and the Cost of Justice in Canada: Overview Report* (Canadian Forum on Civil Justice, 2016) 7–8 at www.cfcj-fcjc.org/sites/default/files/Everyday%20Legal%20Problems%20and%20the%20Cost%20of%20Justice%20in%20Canada%20-%20Overview%20Report.pdf (hereinafter 'CFCJ Overview Report').

While there are few differences to be found among the broader categories of legal problems experienced by urban and rural populations across Canada, other place-based distinctions do exist within the civil justice landscape. Much of the discourse around access to institutions of justice in the urban context is grounded in the gap between what people have and what they reasonably need to equitably and effectively meet their justice needs. Financial, temporal, personal and other resources commonly determine level of access to institutions of justice. In the rural context, 'access' is shaped in key ways by an *absence* of institutions of justice. Courts, tribunals, and the diversity of legal information services, law offices, legal clinics, alternative dispute resolution services and other legal service models available in urban centres are generally absent from the rural landscape, complicating the experience of barriers identical to those of urban populations and the ability of rural populations to meet their justice needs. To the extent that these distinctions between the rural experience and the urban experience can be encapsulated through a single notion, it is perhaps that geography and distance – two features that define life in rural and remote areas – amplify adversity and existing access to justice obstacles. As rurality increases, access to justice obstacles also increase. This is one of two underlying themes in this chapter.

The second theme is that rural Canada is not homogeneous. Across Canada's provinces and territories, rurality *looks* different.[5] The history, economy, regional and geographic aspects, culture and demographic characteristics of a given rural population combine in distinct ways to influence perceptions and experiences of institutions of justice and determine a population's specific justice needs. A rural community with a large non-English-speaking immigrant population, for example, will have different legal needs than a community with a high rate of youth out-migration and an aging population. For some rural communities, restorative justice will be an important way to engage with the law; other communities will have adapted their local infrastructure to facilitate remote service delivery or access to formal justice mechanisms in other locations. There are various factors that set Canada's rural communities apart; and in some cases, these distinguishing features among rural areas will more closely resemble features that are commonly associated with urban areas. In highlighting this diversity, the second theme in

[5] For example, in eastern Canada, over 50% of the population of Prince Edward Island reside in rural areas and almost 40% of rural dwellers in Prince Edward Island are under 35 years of age; rural economies in the province subsist primarily on small-scale agriculture. Ontario, in central Canada, is home to approximately 1.8 million rural residents who account for roughly 13.8% of the province's total population. This population is demographically diverse, including communities where people predominantly speak languages other than English or French. Canada's largest province – Quebec – has more than 1.5 million rural residents with an almost equal number of people who are under 35 years of age and 55 years and older. Just over 15% of Albertans live in areas that are considered rural. That is an estimated 639,000 people in the Western province. In Canada's north, many rural areas are home to Indigenous peoples. For more about Canada's diverse rural areas, see generally B Moazzami, *Strengthening Rural Canada: Fewer & Older: Population and Demographic Challenges Across Rural Canada, a Pan-Canadian Report* (Strengthening Rural Canada, 2015) at www.strengtheningruralcanada.ca/file/Fewer-Older-Population-and-Demographic-Challenges-Across-Rural-Canada.pdf.

this chapter seeks to communicate what Canada's rural communities might want people to better understand about their experiences of the justice system – that although there is a shared landscape of legal problems, the legal needs of a given rural community and how they are best addressed will vary. To meet the legal needs of Canada's rural populations requires approaches to legal service delivery, multidisciplinary dispute resolution and methods of disseminating legal information that consider the nuances of the place and population being served. Because of the diversity within Canada's rural landscape, place-based generalisations such as those referenced at the outset of this chapter will often miss the mark or exacerbate existing issues when broadly applied to policy decisions on rural and remote areas.

Through an examination of geographic barriers and place-based strategies for facilitating access to justice in rural areas, this chapter will first seek to explore present-day meanings of 'rural' and 'access to justice'. I then discuss a promising pilot project in rural Ontario through the lens of our current understanding of barriers to access justice in rural areas, with a view towards identifying learnings to measure and potentially address access to justice challenges in other rural areas in Canada.

## II. Rurality and Access to Justice in Canada

In order to explore what it means to overcome legal services and legal information barriers and address the legal needs of people outside of Canada's urban areas, it is important to have a clear understanding of what constitutes rurality and remoteness in Canada, who resides in these areas and the extent of the obstacles that they face. The various elements that contribute to applications of 'rural' and 'access to justice' merit consideration here.

### A. Rural and Remote

'Rurality' has long resisted a single, universal definition. Communities, small towns and reserves[6] throughout Canada display geographic, social, economic and demographic dissimilarities that make them distinct within the collective of rural areas. Language, culture and customs that are unique to a given rural population further delineate rural areas. There is, of course, a standard definition of the term 'rural' that exists as part of the accepted terminology to differentiate between urban and non-urban areas in Canada; interestingly, this definition was further refined quite

[6] A reserve is land set aside by the Canadian Federal Government for the use and occupancy of a First Nation group. See Indigenous Awareness Canada, 'What is a Reserve?' at www.indigenousawareness canada.com/indigenous-awareness/what-is-a-reserve/.

recently, in 2017.[7] Notwithstanding parameters related to population size, population density and distance from population centres that qualify locations in Canada as rural, it is the specific dynamics of each rural area that more precisely influence quality of life, way of life and access to amenities for these populations. It is for this reason that these locations are best served by programmes and services that, while attentive to the general aspects of rural areas, are attuned to the specific needs of the place and population being served.

It bears noting that rurality in Canada is also often discussed in terms of degree of rurality. That is to say, in many contexts, a distinction is made between rural and remote areas, where the latter possess similar, qualifying traits to rural areas but are located further from population centres. The distinction is an important one, particularly around questions of access and availability. In general, it is typical for people in rural locations to live further from local amenities and services than people in urban areas. It is also common for there to be limited access to public transportation in rural areas and for travel by road to be subject to weather conditions. Where these issues exist to varying extents within different rural areas, they are often universal and carry greater impacts within remote and isolated areas. Scholarship on this divide in the Canadian context suggests that greater distances from remote and isolated locations to services in other areas creates a shared landscape of challenges that can be more readily identified as a defining aspect of these locations.[8]

From one rural area to another, however, differences more closely relate to the availability of local services and supports within each community, and the proximity to services located in other communities or urban areas. In the justice context, these distinctions for rural communities often manifest in varied cost, transportation and service provider barriers for litigants, with obstacles more broadly present in access to alternative dispute resolution services, court services and non-legal services that support holistic problem resolution. Obstacles are especially acute in areas such as family law, where there might be supervised access and exchange requirements, meetings with assessors, mandated mental-health assessments or other in-person requirements. Distance can also present challenges for legal professionals in rural areas, with the nearest courthouse often located several hours away by car, or a ferry ride away in some rural areas of Atlantic Canada.

[7] This standard definition refers to that used by Canada's national statistical agency – Statistics Canada. As of 16 January 2017, the definition adopted by Statistics Canada for 'urban' areas applies to small population centres with a population of between 1,000 and 29,999; medium population centres with a population of between 30,000 and 99,999; and large urban population centres consisting of a population of 100,000 and over. Population density is also a factor in the characterisation of an area as urban or rural. The two new criteria adopted to further delineate population centres are the use of a secondary population density threshold as well as employment density. Along with these criteria, urban population centres are further designated as having at least 400 residents per square kilometre. All areas outside of population centres continue to be defined as rural areas. See Statistics Canada, 'Population Centre and Rural Area Classification 2016' at www.statcan.gc.ca/eng/subjects/standard/pcrac/2016/introduction.

[8] J Nuffield, *The Challenges of Youth Justice in Rural and Isolated Areas in Canada* (Department of Justice Canada, April 2003) i at Justice Canada www.justice.gc.ca/eng/rp-pr/cj-jp/yj-jj/rr03_yj5-rr03_jj5/rr03_yj5.pdf>.

There are several, additional explanatory notes about rurality that are worth highlighting in order to offer further insight into the obstacles that Canadians face related to geography and distance factors and their impact on access to justice services. Almost one in six Canadians – approximately 6.1 million people – reside in a rural area; in Atlantic Canada, the estimate is closer to one in two.[9] The remainder of Canada's population is urban-dwelling. Within rural areas, there are few avenues to pursue an education beyond the primary or secondary level.[10] This same obstacle does not exist for a majority of Canada's population who reside in urban areas. Within urban areas, there are various pathways for academic and professional development – including in the area of law – and many of these pursuits are within reasonable, commutable proximity to areas where people live. Rapid globalisation and the proliferation of digital technologies in recent decades have further erased distance boundaries and expanded options and opportunities for Canadian residents, and in particular for urban dwellers, who are more likely than their rural counterparts to have dependable access to Internet and cell-phone services. Recently, there have been significant funding investments by governments aimed at facilitating the expansion of broadband and other digital technologies in rural and remote areas; the Covid-19 pandemic has brought this issue into greater relief, spurring further momentum.[11] In some areas, however, Internet and cell-phone connectivity continues to be limited or otherwise unreliable, with little expectation of forthcoming improvements.[12] As discussed in chapter 15 of this book regarding England and Wales, uneven access to technology has various implications within the justice landscape in Canada.

On the side of institutional justice mechanisms, limited access to dependable online and cell-phone services translates into a need for legal obligations, filings and interactions with courts, tribunals and their officers to almost exclusively be attended to in person. While accommodations have been made for remote

[9] The number and percentage of Canadians living in rural areas are based on data released by Canada's national statistical office in January 2021. See Statistics Canada, 'Population estimates, July 1, by census metropolitan area and census agglomeration, 2016 boundaries' (release date 14 January 2021), at www150.statcan.gc.ca/t1/tbl1/en/tv.action?pid=1710013501.

[10] A high rate of out-migration among youths aged 20–24 in Canada's rural communities has been explained as the result of a need to leave rural areas in order to pursue (post-secondary) educational opportunities. N Rothwell et al, 'Migration to and from Rural and Small Town Canada' (2002) 3(6) *Rural and Small Town Canada Analysis Bulletin* 12 at www150.statcan.gc.ca/n1/en/pub/21-006-x/21-006-x2001006-eng.pdf?st=byfUp_21. Students in rural communities also commonly face school closures. See, eg, S Burgess, 'School closures will turn villages into ghost towns, rural residents warn' *CBC News* (28 March 2017) at www.cbc.ca/news/canada/ottawa/stone-mills-township-fears-prospect-of-school-closures-1.4038494; and K Yarr, 'Urban-rural divide highlighted over school closure proposals' *CBC News* (11 January 2017) at www.cbc.ca/news/canada/prince-edward-island/pei-school-closure-reaction-1.3930391.

[11] Government of Canada, 'High-speed Internet for all of Canada' (date modified: 28 April 2020) at www.ic.gc.ca/eic/site/139.nsf/eng/home. See also, eg, K Lightning-Earle, 'We need access to justice and the internet' *CBA National Magazine* (29 April 2021) at www.nationalmagazine.ca/en-ca/articles/law/access-to-justice/2021/access-to-the-internet-for-access-to-justice.

[12] See, eg, A Desmarais, 'Northern MPs say virtual parliament is opportunity to tackle broadband challenges' *CBC News* (28 April 2020) at www.cbc.ca/news/canada/north/northern-mps-virtual-parliament-opportunity-tackle-broadband-challenges-1.5547279.

administration during the Covid-19 pandemic, it remains to be seen whether many of the changes will remain in place. As of late 2021, some court services already signalled a return to pre-pandemic modes of operation. Outside of the justice system's formal dispute resolution framework, a lack of available or reliable Internet service also inhibits distance learning and professional development in rural areas, including paralegal, mediation or arbitration certification, and continuing professional development for lawyers. This in turn complicates another existing problem in the justice sector – the decline in the number of lawyers and legal service professionals who practise or offer legal assistance in rural areas.[13] Legal practice in rural areas comes with benefits and challenges. New lawyers in particular might be attracted to the breadth of experience that is possible in a rural practice, with greater first-hand insights into the impacts of legal assistance in people's lives. The pace of life may be slower in rural areas, offering a better work-life balance than may be possible in many metropolitan centres. Conversely, there are fewer networking opportunities for new lawyers in rural areas. With shoddy access to online tools to engage in programmes for professional development in some rural and remote areas, as well as other obstacles, aspiring or trained legal professionals may opt for urban areas for the opportunities that they provide and the absence of digital and other barriers that are prevalent in many rural and remote locations.[14]

Barriers to cellular service and Internet connectivity also present challenges for justice seekers in rural and remote areas. An inability to readily or reliably connect to online and cell-phone services for extended periods limits people's options to access legal information or legal help remotely. This too is noteworthy. In a national legal problems survey by the Canadian Forum on Civil Justice (CFCJ), one in three people reported searching online for help with their civil justice problem(s).[15] Further, data from the same study revealed that approximately 20 per cent of people in Canada search the Internet as the first step to resolving their civil justice problem(s).[16] Insomuch as the civil justice problem types experienced by rural and remote residents are the same as those experienced by people in urban areas, the importance of access to all available avenues for information and assistance to address a serious civil justice problem is also the same. Owing to Internet and cell-phone service barriers, however, rural and remote residents are at a significant disadvantage in this regard compared to their urban counterparts.

There is a final, instructive note about access to online and remote legal services for non-urban residents that is worth considering now, in the era of Covid-19. Internet and cellular services are invariably more widely available and of a higher

[13] J Baxter and A Yoon, 'No Lawyer for a Hundred Miles? Mapping the New Geography of Access of Justice in Canada' (2014) 52(1) *Osgoode Hall Law Journal* 9.

[14] See, eg, H Douglas, 'Incentivizing New Lawyers to Work in Rural Communities' *Slaw* (10 April 2019) at www.slaw.ca/2019/04/10/incentivizing-new-lawyers-to-work-in-rural-communities/.

[15] See CFCJ Overview Report (n 4) 9.

[16] L Moore, *Everyday Legal Problems and the Cost of Justice in Canada: Cost of Justice Survey Data* (Canadian Forum on Civil Justice, 2018) 112–16, at www.cfcj-fcjc.org/wp-content/uploads/Everyday-Legal-Problems-and-the-Cost-of-Justice-in-Canada-Cost-of-Justice-Survey-Data.pdf.

standard in urban areas. Notwithstanding, in our increasingly connected world, there are many online tools and remote technologies that our justice systems have failed to embrace. Many are devices that are proved to effectuate more efficient and cost-effective outcomes, for both governments and users of the justice system. Online dispute resolution services and other remote services that also offer timelier and cheaper options for the public to resolve their civil justice problems have been slower to materialise in much of Canada. One development stemming from the Covid-19 era may be that some of the antiquated systems that the legal sector has steadfastly embraced might now be acknowledged as grossly inadequate, particularly in light of how quickly other sectors were able to pivot to virtual and remote services at the start of the pandemic, while courts and justice services struggled.[17] If more court and legal services become available online, it will be even more important for rural and remote areas to be developed to meet an increased reliance on remote services. If not, they stand to face similar or even greater access to justice obstacles in the immediate future. Further, there is increased pressure for models for Internet service delivery in rural areas to more closely resemble options that are broadly available in urban areas, including unlimited data packages and higher connectivity speeds. If these options do not materialise, there is a risk that limited availability of Internet services in rural and remote areas will be more consistently replaced by a prohibitive cost barrier of accessing the Internet. We will have effectively exchanged one obstacle for another.[18]

## B. What Does Access to Civil Justice in Rural Canada Entail?

A significant challenge to facilitating better access to justice lies in the fact that there is no single route to doing so. Early scholarship on this subject discusses access to civil justice predominantly in terms of access to courts.[19] Access to justice is now more broadly equated with: fairness; equality; legal empowerment; understanding the language of the legal system; access to lawyer assistance and alternative dispute resolution mechanisms; and avenues to understand and address the diverse legal, social, economic, health and personal impacts that derive from or are exacerbated by experiences of justiciable problems.[20] Within rural areas, these notions of access to justice can be especially difficult to achieve.

[17] See B McLachlin, 'Access to Justice: Justice in the time of social distancing' *The Lawyer's Daily* (31 March 2020) at www.thelawyersdaily.ca/articles/18386/access-to-justice-justice-in-the-time-of-social-distancing-beverley-mclachlin.

[18] See, eg, H Douglas, 'Rural internet users frustrated with high overage charges during COVID-19 restrictions' *Huntsville Doppler* (1 April 2020) at www.doppleronline.ca/huntsville/rural-internet-users-frustrated-with-high-overage-charges-during-covid-19-restrictions/.

[19] Access to law here denotes having a general awareness of one's legal rights as well as the financial means to exercise those rights to resolve legal disputes, with the assistance of lawyers or through the courts.

[20] See TCW Farrow, 'What is Access to Justice?' (2014) 51(3) *Osgoode Hall Law Journal* 957.

Like the definitions of 'rural' and 'remote' that have been refined in recent years, this understanding of 'access to justice' has evolved to better reflect people-centred perspectives.[21] The complexities of facilitating pathways for meaningful access to justice for rural residents also become clearer with this present-day understanding. The resulting challenge lies in adopting ways to deliver legal services and information that effectively address legal needs; reflect present-day understandings of access to justice; and accommodate geography and distance considerations of rural locations.

This tension – between what people expect, want or require of the justice system and the difficulties or failure of the systems to deliver – lies at the heart of an ongoing crisis in access to justice. Generally, barriers to access to civil justice in Canada result from a combination of factors, including complex legal procedures, prohibitive costs, a lack of public consciousness about everyday legal problems, delays and limited use of modern technologies for legal processes. Within rural areas, these obstacles are prominent realities of the justice landscape. Complicating this problem is the fact that historically, justice sector investments have focused on formal legal service delivery methods in lieu of investments in front-end, early dispute resolution processes where costs are lower and problems may be less complex. These issues each play a role in fuelling an increasingly inefficient, unaffordable and inaccessible civil justice system. Like many large-scale social problems, the physiognomy of this crisis looks disproportionately low-income, racialised, disabled, Indigenous and otherwise representative of a vulnerable or marginalised group.[22]

This crisis in access to civil justice is largely a crisis of everyday legal problem experiences. The ordinary transactions and occurrences in daily life are the birthplace of most justiciable problems. Accordingly, people often do not recognise the legal underpinnings of their everyday problems and do not treat them as potentially serious legal problems at the outset. This sets the stage for many problems to escalate in cost and gravity. Vulnerable and marginalised groups are especially susceptible to civil justice problems and their adverse consequences. Within any given three-year period in Canada, people experience approximately 36,000,000 separate, everyday civil legal problems.[23] Many of these problems represent clusters of legal problems experienced by vulnerable populations whose initial problems triggered other serious civil justice problems. With almost 20 per cent of Canada's population living in non-urban areas, it is easy to surmise the extent of civil justice problem experiences within these communities.

[21] For a brief discussion on people-centred access to justice, see Action Committee on Access to Justice in Civil and Family Matters, *Access to Civil and Family Justice: A Roadmap for Change, Final Report* (Action Committee on Access to Justice in Civil and Family Matters, 2013) 2–3 at www.cfcj-fcjc.org/sites/default/files/docs/2013/AC_Report_English_Final.pdf.

[22] See generally A Currie and L Moore, 'Social and Economic Adversity Experienced by Canadians and Everyday Legal Problems' (Canadian Forum on Civil Justice, December 2018) at www.cfcj-fcjc.org/wp-content/uploads/Social-and-Economic-Adversity-Experienced-by-Canadians-and-Everyday-Legal-Problems-Ab-Currie-Lisa-Moore.pdf.

[23] See CFCJ Overview Report (n 4) 7.

What we understand about experiences with civil justice problems, access to justice and the dimensions of place in Canada can be instructive in informing pathways for better access to justice in rural areas. One model to do so involves mobile legal services. This approach integrates outreach with aspects of holistic service delivery to address civil legal needs within rural areas. The goal is to meet people where they are. To highlight the potential for this model to address some of the access to justice challenges facing rural residents, section III of this chapter examines a mobile legal service pilot project in rural Ontario. This project is a recent and fitting example that shows promise as a way to address geography and distance barriers and facilitate greater access to civil justice for rural residents.

## III. Facilitating Access to Justice Through Mobile Service Delivery in Rural Areas

If people have trouble accessing legal help or information in person, one option is to bring the legal help and information to them. This is the simple concept behind the WellCoMs Mobile Van (the 'mobile van') project, which launched as a pilot project in May 2019.[24] Legal services across Canada are largely offered through traditional brick-and-mortar access points; a law van would be considered a rarity in most settings. The Mobile Van project was conceived by the Legal Clinic of Guelph and Wellington County located in Southwestern Ontario to address a longstanding gap in the availability of legal services within the County's rural areas.[25] With virtually no public transportation between communities, and the distance between some communities exceeding an hour by car, rural residents also face obstacles to accessing legal services outside of these communities. The goal of the Mobile Van project was to provide access to legal information, legal advice and related non-legal supports across 12 rural communities in Ontario, with populations ranging from approximately 800 people to almost 20,800 people in the largest rural community in the County.[26] As it relates to the themes of this

[24] The project has since received funding to support at least three years of year-round service.

[25] Guelph and Wellington County are located in Southwestern Ontario. Combined, the areas have a population of approximately 230,000 people. The Legal Clinic of Guelph and Wellington County opened in 2002 and, according to a report on the WellCoMs Mobile Van project, 'the legal needs of the population of rural Wellington … have been perceived to be unmet since the establishment of the Clinic'. A Currie, *The WellCoMs Mobile Van Project: Building Paths to Justice in Rural Wellington County Interim Report* (Ontario, August 2019) 1 at https://cfcj-fcjc.org/wp-content/uploads/The-WellCoMs-Mobile-Van-Project-Building-Paths-to-Justice-in-Rural-Wellington-County-Interim-Report-August-2019-by-Ab-Currie.pdf.

[26] The average age of the population of Guelph is 39.3 and the average age of the population of Wellington County is 40.2. See Statistics Canada, 'Census Profile, 2016 Guelph, City [Census subdivision], Ontario and Wellington, County [Census division], Ontario' (Statistics Canada, 29 November 2017) at www12.statcan.gc.ca/census-recensement/2016/dp-pd/prof/details/page.cfm?Lang=E&Geo1=CSD&Code1=3523008&Geo2=CD&Code2=3523&Data=Count&SearchText=guelph&SearchType=

chapter, it is an especially relevant case study in that it applies a model for outreach in rural communities that mirrors present-day understandings of the importance of early intervention, addressing the legal and non-legal dimensions of problems, and legal empowerment for better access to justice.

During the initial six-month period of the pilot project, up to three service providers, which at times included a paralegal, lawyer or other legal professional, travelled by van to a different community each weekday. The van was then parked at a public, local site where visitors could receive information, assistance or referrals for civil justice matters. People passing by en route to complete an errand might stop by, or, as was the case when the van's schedule was shared more widely among residents and the van's services became known within each community, residents would be referred by friends or family or visit of their own volition for help with one or more specific legal problems. Importantly, by incorporating frequently visited local sites such as convenience stores and libraries as part of an overall strategic outreach plan to connect with rural residents, the Mobile Van project navigated geography and distance barriers that often contribute to unmet legal need or stand in the way of access to legal assistance in rural areas.

The project was directed at assisting as many low-income rural residents as possible, aligning with legal needs studies that have shown that low-income populations often have diverse unmet legal needs.[27] Further, the project adopted a 'no wrong door' policy – an assurance that, regardless of the type of legal problem or legal information request from individuals who approached the mobile van, there would be at least some attempt to provide meaningful assistance. In addition to facilitating legal problem resolution for a range of problem types, a 'no wrong door' policy encourages legal empowerment. People seeking legal help learn more about their legal problem, how the problem can be resolved, and better understand the role of law in their lives. A 'no wrong door' policy generally fosters a more positive interaction with and perception of the law, and it also spurs the resolution of hidden problems – legal problems that may have been misidentified as non-legal and could potentially become more serious or lead to other problems. As a result, the project saw impressive levels of success at assisting people with a range of civil justice problems, including family law, landlord-tenant, wills and power of attorney, employment, disability assistance and other types of problems.[28]

Begins&SearchPR=01&B1=All&TABID=1. Between 5% and 15% of adults in the communities served by the mobile van were low-income earners. The mean age of the population may explain the higher rates of family and landlord-tenant problems across communities and comparatively lower levels of disability support problems. Currie (n 2) 12.

[27] Communities served by the Mobile Law Van had between 1.3% and 15.3% of their population living below the poverty level. Currie (n 2) 8. For a discussion of experiences of low-income earners and legal problems, see Currie and Moore (n 22).

[28] Currie (n 2) 11.

## A. How Mobile Legal Services Facilitate Access to Justice in Rural Communities

Complex problems often demand multifaceted solutions. Facilitating better access to justice is one such problem, which requires efforts on multiple fronts. Insomuch as we now understand access to justice to be more than a problem of access to court services, it is important to consider developments that show promise in addressing the diverse legal and non-legal aspects of everyday legal problems.[29] For rural areas – as in urban areas – these considerations should extend beyond ensuring that legal services can be reasonably accessed to also facilitating access to alternative methods of dispute resolution and auxiliary services that are equipped to deal with the non-legal dimensions of civil justice problems. The most common obstacles that rural residents face to accessing these services stem from transportation, cost and temporal barriers, made worse by geography and distance.[30] In six months, the WellCoMs Mobile Van saw almost 600 visitors, many of whom received information and assistance related to a range of legal and non-legal problems. When necessary, outreach workers on the van connected justice seekers, through Skype, to a lawyer at the regional legal clinic for legal advice related to their specific problem(s).[31] If legal services are made available locally, at places that people regularly visit, little additional effort will be required to connect with these services. People need groceries; they often visit their local library, parks and other community spaces, as well as the other locations where the mobile van sought to operate. These locations were chosen strategically, and in consultation with and with approval from local authorities. For many rural residents, the mobile van offered convenience in a way that may not often be seen in their community.

To amplify the efforts of the mobile legal service, a mix of modern and traditional communication tools were used to advertise the mobile van's presence within the communities and the exact location where the van would be stationed. Videos, announcements and other related content about the mobile van's services were regularly shared through the Facebook pages of local community organisations. An infographic was created; and posters that included the van's schedule were shared in many of the same locations where the van operated, as well as in the local offices of elected representatives, local food banks, coffee shops, garages and stores. News about the van also appeared in local and regional publications;

[29] According to Cohl and Thomson, 'people rarely experience legal problems without facing non-legal problems at the same time'. See Cohl and Thomson (n 1) 5.

[30] Additional resources may also be required to facilitate the dissemination and delivery of information and services in languages other than French or English that may be widely spoken within a rural or remote area. Language barriers extend beyond the availability of legal help in Canada's two official languages – French and English – including among many Aboriginal populations. While interpreters can be helpful, information should be made available in the language of the person receiving help. See further ibid 5.

[31] This model, whereby an intermediary is the primary point of contact, can also be helpful for self-help and to promote legal empowerment, in particular for self-help resources that are provided at a distance. See ibid 50.

and community leaders were invited to visit the van. Further, a large pop-up tent was set up beside the van at each location with signage promoting free legal services and information. Word-of-mouth was also an important tool in advertising the van's services within each community. The collective merits of this level of outreach are two-fold. A significant number of people with legal problems, or who knew people experiencing legal problems,[32] were made aware of this newly available, local and accessible resource. Second, and especially pertinent to our discussion of what it means to access justice, this type of outreach often results in increased legal awareness and legal empowerment among residents of the communities served. It stands to reason that even among the 122 passers-by (or 21 per cent of the mobile van's visitors) who did not have a legal problem, there was still some benefit – they were now aware of a place to seek help for a legal problem should one arise or where to refer others for help; many also walked away with plain-language materials.

Notably, some visitors and justice seekers who visited the van were able to get assistance with legal matters in the early stages of their problem, before they became more costly, complex and difficult to resolve.[33] The van was also successful at helping people with the non-legal aspects of their legal problems. During the mobile van's six-month pilot project, outreach workers referred visitors to 28 different community programmes and services for assistance with the non-legal dimensions of their problems. This included food banks, family health services, local offices of members of parliament, literacy centres, support services for women in conflict with the law, an organisation to help reintegrate and improve conditions for previously incarcerated persons, mental-health associations and various local community resources centres.[34]

## IV. Conclusion

The mobile van operated five days per week, made a total of 128 visits to designated sites within 12 rural communities, and helped hundreds of people with legal and related non-legal problems. The total cost to operate the van, including salaries, rental of the van and operating costs, was approximately CAD $50,000.[35]

[32] According to the CFCJ's Everyday Legal Problems and Cost of Justice survey, approximately 61% of people went to friends and family for advice on legal problems. See CFCJ Overview Report (n 4) 9. See further Currie (n 2) 15.

[33] Complex legal problems that merit resolution through formal legal channels will generally be more expensive and time-consuming to resolve. Further, unresolved legal problems tend to form clusters of multiple, serious legal problems. Resolving a legal problem early and outside of the formal justice system will generally mean lower costs. For an overview of the process and potential benefits of early problem resolution, see Action Committee (n 21) 11–12.

[34] Community resources centres provide assistance on a range of matters to people of all ages. This may include access to health and social services programmes, employment services, educational support, tax and financial services, information on housing support, transportation information and assistance, and recreational programmes.

[35] Approximately US $40,400 or £30,000 (rates as at 30 October 2021). The WellCoMs Mobile Van project was able to operate through a combination of funding from a Law Foundation of Ontario grant,

The noteworthy outcomes achieved by the Mobile Van project are the result of an extensive and well-executed outreach strategy, spurred by questions about the extent of unmet legal need in the communities being served, and further shaped by a present-day understanding of access to justice and an appreciation of the specific dynamics of the 12 rural communities where the van operated. These elements together served as complements for a robust strategy to improve access to legal help among low-income residents in the communities served by the mobile van.[36] Notwithstanding, it is the project's use of the particulars of the locations served that fundamentally shapes the story of the mobile van's success. The local connections that were made, the community spaces where the van's services were promoted, and the well-known and oft-visited local sites where the van parked to offer help to passers-by are a testament to the importance of local, place-based solutions that speak to the needs of a community rather than simply cater to general conceptions of 'rural' and 'remote'.

Running through a checklist of the access to justice barriers that exist or are amplified within rural areas, this mobile legal services approach offers a promising way to address a range of these issues, including the presence of fewer lawyers in rural areas, temporal and cost barriers related to travel to connect with service providers in other communities or regions, some digital barriers given that the van offered a way to remotely connect with a lawyer through Skype, access to relevant public legal education and information resources, and generally a way to identify and receive assistance, without delay and related to various types of civil justice matters. As an additional consideration, this model of mobile legal services delivery model could potentially be adapted to other rural areas across Canada, including areas with different language or cultural norms.[37]

As a pilot project, the Mobile Van project was also an exercise in learning about what works, what is possible and what is needed to improve access to justice in the rural areas served. This is significant, in particular because of the lack of empirical evidence on access to civil justice generally. Along with recent developments related to large-scale investments in providing access to broadband services in more rural and remote communities, it is hoped that these efforts represent a shift in greater focus to meeting the needs of rural and remote residents, and a desire to steer Canadian communities in the right direction to offer better support for remote service delivery.

There is still a long way to go before achieving more broad-based access to justice services and information in rural and remote communities. The ongoing

assistance from volunteer staff, and support from the regional Legal Clinic of Guelph and Wellington County.

[36] Specifically the report notes 'The van is intended to draw people out, helping them overcome the barriers that prevent them from obtaining timely assistance with their everyday legal problems.' See Currie (n 2) 4.

[37] The final report of the WellCoMs Mobile Van project is available online: Currie (n 2). Due to the success of the Mobile Van pilot project, the Legal Clinic of Guelph and Wellington County has extended it for a three-year term.

crisis in access to justice continues to have impacts for a growing number of low-income and middle-income earners in Canada. With a lack of affordable pathways for low- and middle-income earners to resolve their civil justice disputes through formal channels, or independent of them, many people are priced out of our justice system. The result is a stark rise in pro se litigants across Canada's urban and rural areas. Cost is one of the central obstacles to access to justice for these populations and one that, so far, continues to prove difficult to overcome.

As a final note, while the achievements of the mobile van are to be commended and examined further for the insights that they may offer, there remain place-based limitations to this service delivery model that might inhibit broader application within remote areas. Harsh winter conditions make it unfeasible to operate the van in the same way throughout the year as well as beyond some readily accessible routes and rural sites. This, in conjunction with limited cellular and Internet availability in remote areas, means that there continue to be few options for adults, at any income level, to reasonably address their legal problems within remote areas. This exemplifies an earlier point that as rurality increases, so do access to justice barriers. While mobile legal services can offer some support in rural areas, it is more challenging and likely more costly for them to operate in remote areas, if at all.

Adapting to the dynamics of a location is important to improve the delivery of justice services and the dissemination of information in rural areas. From this vantage point, it is possible to also envision a future with improvements to access to justice in remote areas.

# 11

# Conceptualising Rural Access to Justice as Supply Chains Primed for Transformation

AMANDA L KOOL AND HANNAH HAKSGAARD

## I. Introduction

The justice gap persists in many rural parts of the world due to a confluence of economic, cultural and professional factors at play throughout the justice system and society at large. This justice gap means that people in rural areas experience institutions of justice – including access to lawyers and other legal advice – differently than people in urban areas. Travel, distance, the rural lawyer shortage and other factors create this difference. No single factor or institution can be blamed for the rural lawyer shortage or the inability of many rural people to otherwise adequately resolve the legal issues in their lives,[1] nor can any single person or programme fix the rural lawyer shortage or meet presently unmet rural legal needs.[2] In prior literature on rural legal access, authors have collected data, detailed existing services (or the lack thereof) and articulated potential solutions – both narrow and far-reaching – regarding specific aspects of the rural justice crisis.[3] In this chapter, however, we propose an alternative understanding of the rural lawyer shortage and the rural access to justice crisis, one that frames the myriad rural access to justice challenges as a host of opportunities yet to be leveraged in concert rather than as a series of discrete legal resources intended to address discrete legal

[1] LR Pruitt et al, 'Legal Deserts: A Multi-State Perspective on Rural Access to Justice' (2018) 13 *Harvard Law & Policy Review* 15, 18–22.

[2] M Statz and J Bredeson, 'Concerned about Rural Access to Justice? Start Here First' (2020) *Northland Access to Justice* at www.northlandproject.org/the-rural-a2j-guide.

[3] We have each taken part in writing this literature. See Pruitt et al (n 1) 121; H Haksgaard, 'Rural Practice As Public Interest Work' (2019) 71 *Maine Law Review* 209; H Haksgaard, 'Court-Appointment Compensation and Rural Access to Justice' (2020) 14 *University of St Thomas Journal of Law & Public Policy* 88; and LR Pruitt and AL Kool, 'It's Time to Heed the Call of Rural America' (5 May 2017) *National Law Journal* at www.law.com/nationallawjournal/almID/1202785103651/Opinion-Its-Time-to-Heed-the-Call-of-Rural-America/?slreturn=20210610210351.

problems. Through this broader lens, the entirety of the rural justice gap can be conceptualised as a poorly calibrated supply chain, ready for transformation.

## II. Supply Chain Framework

Supply chain management focuses on the active administration of supply chains in order to most efficiently and effectively deliver products to where they are needed. Here, the product is lawyers and related legal services, and the destinations needing that product are rural communities. We recognise that ensuring the presence of lawyers and other legal resources in rural areas does not cleanly fit into the prevailing conceptualisation of supply chain management in the business world, which focuses on the development and movement of goods towards the consumer rather than the development and movement of people providing (or receiving) needed services.[4] We nevertheless find the concept of supply chain management to be a useful approach for holistically examining the system of legal resources intended to address the many legal needs of rural communities.

The concept of supply chain management rests upon two core tenets.[5] The first tenet recognises that the delivery of a particular product to an end user relies upon the cumulative effort of all links in the supply chain that lead to the delivery of that product to the end user.[6] The second tenet posits that the various organisations that represent individual links in a particular supply chain too regularly fixate on their own internal operations and too rarely consider the function and efficiencies of the supply chain as a whole and their place within it.[7] These connections between stations in the supply chain function in two critical ways: one, as a means to drive the development and location of product through the supply chain; and, two, as a means to drive information through the various links in order to control flow and calibrate long-term plans along the chain. Increased efficiency and functionality along the supply chain result in better outcomes for all parties involved along the chain, including the recipient(s) of the product or service, whose demand has been met.[8]

Through this lens, the rural justice gap lies at the nexus of two supply chains: the supply chain that produces and supplies new lawyers and related legal services

[4] See KC Tan, 'A Framework of Supply Chain Management Literature' (2001) 7 *European Journal of Purchasing & Supply Management* 39, 39–40 (providing various definitions of supply chain management).

[5] See R Handfield, 'What is Supply Chain Management (SCM)?' (19 February 2020) at https://scm.ncsu.edu/scm-articles/article/what-is-supply-chain-management-scm,.

[6] ibid.

[7] ibid.

[8] ibid.

in rural areas (Figure 11.1), and the supply chain that links rural people facing legal needs to potential solutions for those legal needs (Figure 11.2).

**Figure 11.1** Supply Chain 1: Delivering future lawyers to rural legal practice (macro)

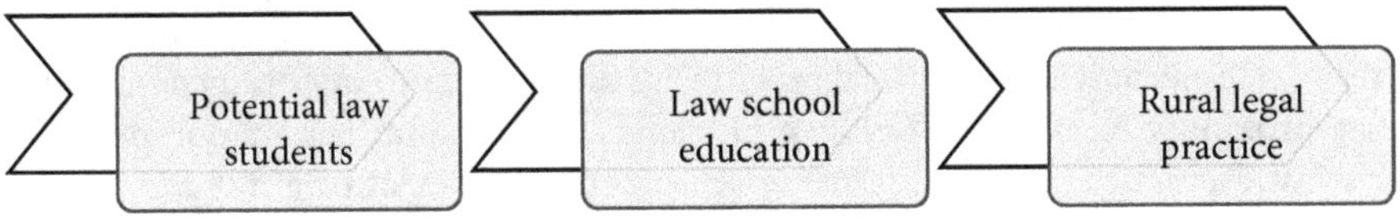


**Figure 11.2** Supply Chain 2: Delivering legal needs to legal resolution (macro)

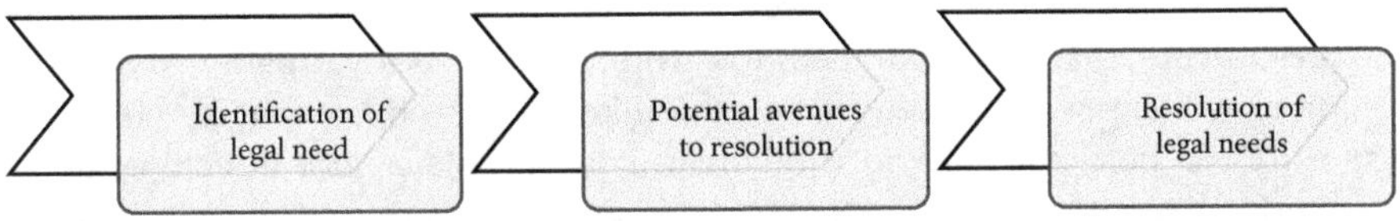


The two core tenets of supply chain management create a helpful framework for these two supply chains involved in the rural justice gap. Regarding Supply Chain 1, every lawyer available in a rural area lives and practises in that area due to the cumulative effort of a host of organisations, including undergraduate schools, law schools, licensing authorities, mentors, other social service institutions and beyond. Regarding Supply Chain 2, every legal need arises due to a host of legal and non-legal causes and must be addressed by one or more legal resources. The links in each of these rural access to justice supply chains are often disjointed, however well intentioned. By examining these supply chains as a whole and seeking ways to align efforts and improve connections between the links, the ultimate goal of achieving rural access to justice for all can be better realised.

This chapter continues by examining each of the two rural justice supply chains separately, and then considers the nexus between the two supply chains as a means to drive meaningful and sustainable rural justice for all.

## III. Delivering Future Lawyers to Rural Legal Practice

**Figure 11.3** Supply Chain 1 (micro)

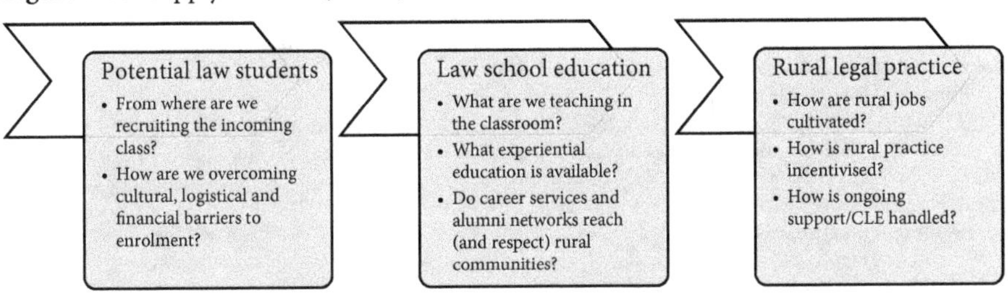

## A. Recruiting Future Rural Lawyers to Law School

The supply chain intended to place more lawyers into rural legal practice is long in terms of years. The creation of a meaningful and sustainable supply of rural lawyers begins with children in rural communities, as law students from rural areas are 'especially open to rural practice',[9] with students in one study explaining that 'proximity to extended family and friends' in jobs after law school incentivised rural practice, as did a desire to serve communities of origin.[10] Most rural lawyers are themselves products of rural communities,[11] perhaps because it is easier for those with rural roots to build connections and community (and therefore a book of business) in rural places.[12] Yet rural public school systems too often lack resources[13] that drive graduates toward professional career paths. Moreover, children with exposure to lawyers are more likely to attend law school,[14] but that exposure can be challenging in rural areas. Law schools cannot directly address the myriad issues that youth face in rural communities, but law schools do possess a unique ability to prime and expand the supply chain of future rural students entering their institutions and returning to legal practice. By working with State judiciaries, current students, alumni, bar associations, undergraduate institutions and rural school systems, law schools can drive outreach efforts designed to increase schoolchildren's exposure to rural legal practice.

As rural students prepare to leave high school, exposure to legal practice and legal education can become more targeted. Undergraduate schools – especially those schools located in or near rural communities – should advertise their pre-law programmes and hold advising visits in rural high schools, perhaps in tandem with a local law school. Law schools, perhaps in tandem with local undergraduate institutions, can pre-admit high school students to law school and can partner to provide scholarship programmes tailored to incentivise future rural lawyers through college.[15] Strengthening the connections from high school student

[9] LR Pruitt et al, 'Justice in the Hinterlands: Arkansas as a Case Study of the Rural Lawyer Shortage and Evidence-Based Solutions to Alleviate It' (2015) 37 *University of Arkansas Little Rock Law Review* 573, 633; see also T Mundy, 'A HECS Rebate? Ways to Attract and Retain Graduate Lawyers in Rural, Regional and Remote Communities' (2010) 35 *Alternate Law Journal* 99.

[10] Pruitt et al (n 9) 634.

[11] See, eg, D Gilbertson, 'Reflections on the Rural Practice of Law in South Dakota: Past, Present, and Future' (2014) 59 *South Dakota Law Review* 433, 434 (discussing attorneys going back to hometowns for practice); and JT Johnsen, 'Rural Justice: Country Lawyers and Legal Services in the United States and Britain' (1992) 17(3) *Law & Social Inquiry* 415, 418 (reviewing two books and noting rural practitioners as disproportionately coming from rural roots).

[12] Johnsen (n 11) 418.

[13] J Dayton, 'Rural Children, Rural Schools, and Public School Funding Litigation: A Real Problem in Search of a Real Solution' (2003) 82 *Nebraska Law Review* 99, 100; C Sielke, 'Rural Factors in State Funding Systems' (2004) 29 *Journal of Education Finance* 223, 232–34; A Kenworthy, 'A Common Thread: Rural America and Education Policy' *Rural Review* (19 July 2021) at www.ruralreconcile.org/ruralreview/educationpolicy.

[14] Pruitt et al (n 1) 147–78.

[15] University of Nebraska College of Law does both of these. Rural Law Opportunities Program, Nebraska College of Law at https://law.unl.edu/RLOP/.

through a career-focused graduate school programme carries significant potential in rural areas, where the calibration between these links is particularly poor: rural students remain both less likely to attend college and more likely to drop out of college than their urban and suburban counterparts.[16]

As the supply chain brings potential future lawyers into college, future employers should interact with students to expose them to career paths they might not have otherwise considered. Because more undergraduate colleges than law schools exist in rural areas,[17] any rural-based organisation that regularly hires lawyers – government agencies, court systems, non-profit organisations, law firms and bar associations – should hire local undergraduates. Recruiting a local college student into a rural summer internship is likely easier than drawing in a law student attending school in a more-distant city, as the law student's present circumstances and future plans are likely more established than those of the undergraduate student. Exposing local undergraduate interns to careers in law can increase the odds those students will consider attending law school, return to intern during law school and even return to the community to practise law after graduation. By scaling the model of rural lawyer recruitment to begin prior to law school, aligning incentives around the related causes of rural revitalisation and rural access to justice and reaping the gifts of time, the supply chain links between rural schoolchildren and law schools can work in concert to demonstrably expand the number of young people who see rural legal practice as a known and viable career path, thereby increasing the numbers of new attorneys who may choose rural practice – and rural living – after law school graduation.

Once rural-focused students have developed an interest in law school, law schools can increase their chances of law school attendance by reducing barriers to admission. Many rural students considering law school will be the first in their families to attend law school, and likely even college.[18] Those first-generation students may need additional advice and financial support prior to applying to law school, as such advice and support may not exist in their familial and community networks. Organisations interested in rural lawyers can provide support to would-be law students via free Law School Admission Test (LSAT) prep courses for aspiring rural lawyers, for example. Law schools can develop programmes and market rural practice as a programmatic speciality to attract rural students, while also waiving application fees for rural students or those interested in rural practice. Better yet, law schools should develop scholarship programmes targeting students with a demonstrated interest in rural practice. Applicants considering rural

[16] E Nadworny and J Marcus, '"Going to Office Hours is Terrifying" and Other Tales of Rural Students in College' *NPR* (12 December 2018) at www.npr.org/2018/12/12/668530699/-going-to-office-hours-is-terrifying-and-other-hurdles-for-rural-students-in-col.

[17] CD Chavis, 'Location, Location, Location: Rural Law Schools and Their Role in the Rural Lawyer Shortage' *Legal Ruralism Blog* (14 July 2017) at http://legalruralism.blogspot.com/2017/07/location-location-location-rural-law.html.

[18] R Buddin, 'First-Generation College and Low-Income Families by School Location' (April 2014) *ACT Research & Policy Information Brief 2014–2016* at www.act.org/content/dam/act/unsecured/documents/Info-Brief-2014-16.pdf.

practice may be more cost-conscious than most law school applicants, as salaries and family median incomes tend to be lower in rural areas and rural lawyers tend to be in private practice, which means they do not qualify for many loan forgiveness programmes.[19] Law schools' provision of critical support to rural students considering law school and post-graduation rural practice increases the likelihood that rural students will apply to – and then attend – law school,[20] fortifying critical links in the rural justice supply chain.

## B. Educating Future Rural Lawyers

In order to ensure an output of rural lawyers after graduation, law schools must develop 'sustained and immersive rural educational experiences'.[21] This involves many arms of a law school in working together to foster rural careers among its student body: marketing and communications teams that highlight and promote rural practice; a career services office that helps students identify internships, fellowships and post-graduation employment in rural areas;[22] hands-on clinical legal education programmes that reach and serve rural communities; and an administration that facilitates positive conversations about rural practice, offers relevant coursework (such as law office management courses and seminars on rural legal issues) and includes rural perspectives within otherwise urban-centric doctrinal courses. Sufficient faculty must be primed and well-suited to mentor and support students interested in rural practice, which ideally includes faculty members who themselves possess rural practice or other rural life experience. Because of distance, rural lawyers are likely less able to serve as adjunct faculty, but schools can invite rural lawyers to speak on employment panels, guest lecture in classes, teach classes remotely or otherwise engage with students in ways that obviate the need for frequent travel to campus.

Law schools – especially elite law schools – too often uphold an academic culture that nudges students toward large firms in urban areas. The spatial intimacy between urban-based law schools and their adjacent employers and the attraction of law schools toward large-scale employers (such as large law firms, which tend to concentrate in urban areas) often leaves small firms and other small-scale employers without engagement with law students; this is especially

[19] Haksgaard, 'Rural Practice' (n 3) 219–20.

[20] Although our ideas are not based on his list, we note similarities to Professor Mitch Crusto's list of ways law schools can support Black students. M Crusto, 'Supporting the Next Generation of Black Lawyers: Steps Law Schools Can Take' *Scholastica Blog* (24 November 2020) at https://blog.scholasticahq.com/post/supporting-next-generation-black-lawyers/?utm_source=The+Abstract&utm_campaign=573d1f08ee-EMAIL_CAMPAIGN_LR_Abstract_Nov20_COPY_01&utm_medium=email&utm_term=0_9e1c242ede-573d1f08ee-343442893.

[21] M Statz and P Termuhlen, 'Rural Legal Deserts are a Critical Health Determinant' (2020) 110 *American Journal of Public Health* 1519, 1521 at https://ajph.aphapublications.org/doi/10.2105/AJPH.2020.305807.

[22] Pruitt et al (n 1) 147–78.

true for firms and other employers in rural areas that are geographically distant from campus. Moreover, too many law students internalise implicit and explicit messaging within law school communities that equates 'success' with the highest-paid law firm jobs located in the largest cities.[23] The draw of on-campus interview programmes for large urban firms[24] paying high salaries,[25] often in tandem with student concerns about student debt and relatively low rural salaries,[26] serves to discourage rural legal practice. Law schools must directly combat this pervasive and limiting mentality by actively and intentionally framing rural practice as a known, viable and worthwhile career path.

Though smaller and more rural-based law schools are often further ahead on promoting rural legal practice,[27] those schools also tend to lack the expansive networks and related resources that elite schools could wield to foster larger-scale change. For example, elite schools are better positioned to pay law students for rural internships and extend loan forgiveness to students entering rural practice, both making the option of rural legal practice more financially feasible and signalling its validity.[28] Funders interested in addressing the rural justice gap should consider investing in smaller law schools with more direct relationships with rural practitioners and rural areas.

Absent additional resources, law schools can leverage other pathways to exposing students to rural practice, including structuring networking and recruitment events by region (of the State in which the law school is located, for example) rather than by practice area, which reflects the outsized role that geography – rather than a specific practice area – often plays for students who are looking to live and practise in a particular rural community. Schools should integrate rural practice into discussions about career options and can invite rural practitioners to on-campus interviews. Many State bar associations and individual law schools facilitate programmes to connect law students with rural firms, generally through summer internships[29] or networking opportunities.[30] These programmatic offerings further signal the importance and viability of rural practice to law students actively weighing post-graduation decisions.

[23] L Laird, 'In Rural America, There are Job Opportunities and a Need for Lawyers' *ABA Journal* (1 October 2014) 42 at www.abajournal.com/magazine/article/too_many_lawyers_not_here._in_rural_america_lawyers_are_few_and_far_between (quoting Bruce Cameron, a Hamline Law graduate, as saying '[t]here seemed to be a concentration on one standard career path – practice for a law firm in a metropolitan area').

[24] H Barnes, 'Top 10 Reasons Most Law Students and Lawyers Prefer Large, Famous Firms' *BCG Attorney Search*, at www.bcgsearch.com/article/900043069/Top-10-Reasons-Most-Law-Students-and-Lawyers-Prefer-Large-Famous-Firms/.

[25] *Salary Distribution Curves*, NALP, at www.nalp.org/salarydistrib.

[26] Pruitt et al (n 9) 634–42.

[27] Pruitt et al (n 1) 146.

[28] Haksgaard, 'Rural Practice' (n 3).

[29] *Rural Practice*, Drake University Law School at www.drake.edu/law/careers/resourcesforstudents/ruralpractice/.

[30] *Rural Practice Committee Program*, The Iowa State Bar Association at www.iowabar.org/page/RuralPracticeProgram.

## C. Delivering Law School Graduates to Rural Legal Practice

Over the last decade, many American jurisdictions have experimented with how to attract new lawyers to rural communities.[31] In chapter 2 of this book, Beskin and Pruitt provide a comprehensive survey of programmes and policy responses instituted by various States, and we will not revisit that work here. Instead, we highlight how these programmes, intended to address rural lawyer shortages, fit into the larger supply chain framework. We also note the important roles that individual lawyers and firms have in recruiting new lawyers to rural communities independent of policy intervention.

To ensure the supply chain brings lawyers to rural areas and keeps them there, funded programmes are important. Yet after a decade of attempts, only South Dakota and North Dakota have funded an extensive stipend for rural practitioners.[32] Notably, South Dakota's programme requires buy-in from various points on the supply chain: the State bar, the State judiciary, the local government and the individual attorney must collaborate to align community needs with the attorney's practice before incentives are authorised.[33] Other types of legislative intervention can incentivise rural practice, such as targeted loan forgiveness,[34] State-sponsored health care, higher hourly rates for appointed court work[35] and expanded broadband access to facilitate rural and remote legal practice.[36] Where legislation falls short, law schools, judiciaries or State bars can provide direct support, such as research assistance from libraries,[37] or free or reduced-cost access to research databases.[38] It is critical that lawyer associations support rural lawyers as they grow and develop their practices, long past when they first arrive in the community. Because short-term support risks attrition of practitioners once support ends,[39] recruiting and retaining rural attorneys requires a long-term, collaborative approach to continued mentorship, camaraderie and education for rural practitioners.

Individual lawyers also can directly and fundamentally impact the rural lawyer supply chain by hiring new associates or otherwise helping new lawyers find

[31] Laird (n 23).

[32] Beskin and Pruitt, ch 2 of this volume.

[33] PG Goetzinger and RL Morris, 'Project Rural Practice: Its People & Its Purpose' (2014) 59 *South Dakota Law Review* 444, 456.

[34] Haksgaard, 'Rural Practice' (n 3).

[35] Haksgaard, 'Court-Appointment Compensation' (n 3).

[36] Statz and Termuhlen (n 21).

[37] T Sneed, 'The Academic Law Library's Role in Cultivating the Rural Lawyer' (2019) 64 *South Dakota Law Review* 213, 230–31.

[38] Handbook for New Members, State Bar Association of North Dakota at https://cdn.ymaws.com/www.sband.org/resource/resmgr/docs/resources/new_members_handbook_dec.202.pdf, 3 (noting bar membership comes with free access to Casemaker, an online legal research service).

[39] W Davis, 'No Country for Rural Lawyers: Small-town Attorneys Still Find it Hard to Thrive' (Feb. 1, 2020) *ABA Journal* (1 February 2020) at www.abajournal.com/magazine/article/no-country-for-rural-lawyers (noting the failure of Drake Law School's 'Rural Access to Justice Initiative' programme).

jobs in their communities. Existing rural lawyers can engage with a mentality of expansion rather than one of scarcity and competition by hiring new associates and seeking to grow the firm's overall book of business, providing mentorship, resources and financial stability to new attorneys. Rural lawyers planning for retirement can recruit new attorneys and plan for the transition of the business in the years to come. Rural lawyers who hire new associates may need to sacrifice time and money to make the firm's growth or transition successful, at least in the short term, such as by delaying the sale of their firm or forgoing a purchase price altogether,[40] recognising that new attorneys burdened with significant student loans often cannot afford to purchase a practice outright.[41]

If lawyers and law firms cannot hire new rural attorneys, they can still provide critical support to rural communities and rural lawyers in other ways. Law firms in nearby population centres can open satellite offices with dedicated staff in smaller markets. Attorneys in both urban and rural markets can mentor attorneys engaged in solo practice.[42] And bar associations and other organisations interested in supporting rural attorneys can establish networks of rural attorneys in particular regions, facilitating the share of information, forms and clients among a group of attorneys with various subject matter expertise. Creating resource and referral hubs can help rural legal specialists find sufficient clientele and elevate legal accessibility and standards of practice in a rural community to match the resources that exist within the context of larger law firms in an urban market.[43]

## IV. Delivering Legal Needs to Legal Resolution

**Figure 11.4** Supply Chain 2: Delivering legal needs to legal resolution (micro)

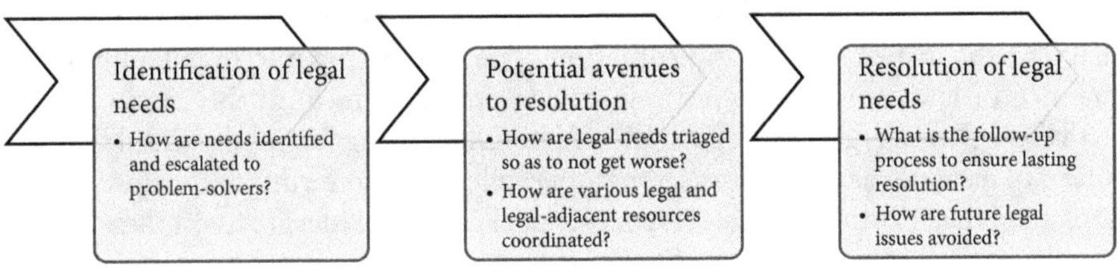


[40] J Karp, 'No Country for Old Lawyers: Rural US Faces a Legal Desert' *Law 360* (27 January 2019) at www.law360.com/articles/1121543/no-country-for-old-lawyers-rural-u-s-faces-a-legal-desert.

[41] Laird (n 23) 42 ('Debt also prevents brand new lawyers from buying an entire practice outright, one traditional way to get started.').

[42] Pruitt et al (n 1) 111 (discussing various existing mentorship programmes for rural attorneys).

[43] AL Kool, 'Legal Needs Assessment for Kentucky Entrepreneurs'(2018) *Kentucky Bar Association* 23 at https://cdn.ymaws.com/www.kybar.org/resource/resmgr/legalneedsassessment/LegalNeedsAssessmentforKentu.pdf (providing an approach for how lawyers can support rural entrepreneurs, an approach that should be used in other subject matter areas).

## A. Identifying and Escalating Rural Legal Needs

The first obstacle in addressing a legal need is to identify a need as both legal in nature and capable of recourse or resolution. In communities where low-cost legal resources are not available or otherwise well-known to the community, residents may fail to recognise that their problems (and in turn, potential solutions to those problems) are legal in nature.[44] A pervasive fear and distrust of the justice system further separates people facing civil legal needs from people who can help with those needs. Trusted and knowledgeable intermediaries must be present and equipped to bridge the gaps during the earliest, crucial stages of the supply chain.

As many problems are first exposed outside the family unit when they are presented to non-legal service providers – clergy, school administrators, librarians and the like – and framed as life issues rather than as legal issues, such trusted, 'front-door' service providers must be trained to identify legal needs within a person's broader set of challenges and refer those needs through appropriate channels.[45] In Kentucky, the State access to justice commission has developed two proposals designed to work in tandem as a means to link people with legal needs to potential resolution through front-door service providers. The first proposal would train public librarians and circuit clerks to identify and refer patrons with legal needs to appropriate services, and the second proposal details a unified branding strategy intended to raise awareness of those referral resources throughout the broader community.[46] Of course, a successful branding strategy would inherently increase the number of people bringing their legal needs to a front-door resource designed to recognise the need and refer toward resolution, which would necessitate increased capacity and efficiency along the subsequent links in the chain in order for such increased demand to be satisfied.

Front-door service providers are not immune to being fearful of and intimidated by the justice system, and sometimes fear of crossing into the unauthorised practice of law causes non-attorney service providers to limit their interactions with their clients regarding legal topics, further impeding the supply chain to resolution of legal needs. Unauthorised practice rules need to be drafted, enforced and explained in a way that empowers front-door service providers to assist their clients regarding legal issue-spotting and appropriate referral, especially for populations who have no other access to legal resources.[47] Moreover, as State bar associations and State legislators update unauthorised practice of law rules, they should work with front-door service providers to better understand the types of legal issues that these providers see in their organisations and identify which investments in legal

[44] Pruitt et al (n 1) 23.

[45] *Justice in Action: Kentucky's Justice for All Strategic Plan*, at 15–16 (pdf on file with authors).

[46] ibid.

[47] SR Benson, 'Assisting Rural Domestic Violence Victims: The Local Librarian's Role' (2016) 108 *Law Library Journal* 237 at www.aallnet.org/wp-content/uploads/2018/01/vol-108-no-2-2016-11.pdf.

education training would be best suited to assist those providers in their efforts to meet the needs of their patrons.

State bar associations and others who are well positioned to train front-door service providers and develop referral channels should be careful to avoid prescriptive training by those unfamiliar with the communities in which front-door service workers live and work. Because front-door service providers often better understand their communities' needs and wishes than those tasked with setting up training programmes and other supply chain interventions, local service providers should be intentionally included in the development of programmes. When outside organisations – like State bar groups – do show up in rural areas to establish programmes or services, local service providers must be kept front and centre at each step to ensure that constituents will feel comfortable and that any programmes offered carefully align with community needs.

## B. Potential Avenues to Resolution

The efficacy of developing open and accessible entry points via front-door service providers into a network of legal services requires that an adequate and varied set of legal services exists to meet the demand. Legal aid offices are often overwhelmed with more potential clients than can be represented by staff attorneys. That being so, legal aid resources must be reserved for the subset of cases that requires direct client representation to reach resolution. Other needs that fall short of necessitating full representation can be met through workshops, self-help centres, limited scope representation and other means.

Moreover, a data-driven,[48] coordinated body of legal and legal-adjacent resources provides opportunities for legal needs to be addressed during their earliest stages, but the data must be particular to the community to every extent possible – just as all cities are not the same, all rural areas are not the same.[49] It is better to address issues early rather than once the problems have been exacerbated, when potential avenues to resolution remain more plentiful and straightforward: 'As one faith leader stated in response to a spate of evictions among his parishioners, "I wish people would contact me before, not after, their belongings are on the street."'[50] Establishing and maintaining a nimble, connected network of service providers that feels comfortable referring clients to one another and understands one another's intake criteria, workflow and timelines fosters opportunities for needs to be met earlier, more quickly and more collaboratively, thereby further priming the efficacy and efficiency of the pipeline to justice.

Front-door service providers play an outsized role in introducing people with legal needs into various channels toward resolution, as well as ensuring that

[48] Pruitt et al (n 1) 129–35.
[49] ibid 138.
[50] *Justice in Action* (n 45) 9.

individuals continue to receive the assistance they need until ultimate resolution has been achieved. These service providers often understand the big picture of a person's myriad needs far better than an attorney involved in one aspect of that person's needs, and can serve a vital role by relaying such information to attorneys and other subject matter experts. For example, a monetary award in an eviction defence case may seem like a desired outcome for a law school clinic's client who is facing homelessness, but a sudden influx of cash into the client's bank account may unintentionally affect the person's public benefits, as the continued award of such benefits typically relies upon strict financial tests for indigency. A front-door service provider can relay key information to avoid such unintended consequences – in this case, by relaying to the law school clinic that the client receives certain public benefits that are subject to certain eligibility criteria – thereby positioning the front-door service provider as an important safeguard against unintended harm to the client.

Because the first referral made on behalf of a person seeking legal assistance rarely leads to full resolution, a trusted front-door service provider plays an integral role in keeping legal issues rolling toward resolution. In addition to relaying crucial information about public benefits or other client-specific circumstances to various stakeholders, front-door service providers can ensure that all referrals are 'warm' – meaning that more than a name, number or email address is given to the client, who is then left to proceed on their own – and can follow along with next steps between the person and the legal service providers to help connect dots between the person and subsequent service providers. While technology can certainly be helpful to scaling legal resources to reach as many people as possible,[51] available and trusted human interaction remains vital to guiding a person in crisis through to resolution of their legal and non-legal needs.

## C. Resolution of Legal Needs

The ideal resolution for any legal need is one that occurs before the court system is involved. Therefore, a ready and known front door to legal services, replete with alternatives to the courts, is the first step to resolving legal needs. For those needs that do reach the court system, many civil parties will be proceeding without counsel,[52] and so organisations would be wise to offer assistance to pro se parties to help parties comply with deadlines, complete forms and otherwise navigate the system without full (or any) representation by counsel. Access-to-justice advocates

[51] See, eg, LR Pruitt and BE Showman, 'Law Stretched Thin: Access to Justice in Rural America' (2014) 59 *South Dakota Law Review* 466, 523 (providing an example of using a telephone number to connect a front-door service provider and legal aid).

[52] M Statz, 'On Shared Suffering: Judicial Intimacy in the Rural Northland' (2021) 55 *Law & Society Review* 5, 7 (noting that unrepresented litigants are 'skyrocketing' in rural State and tribal courts).

should work through continuing education training on implicit bias and other relevant topics to ensure that judges and the broader court system do not unintentionally exacerbate the challenges faced by self-represented litigants.[53] Once a legal need has been addressed, a follow-up process should be activated as a means to ensure lasting resolution and avoid unnecessary repetition of similar legal issues in the future.

## V. Nexus between the Rural Justice Supply Chains

The two supply chains – one bringing lawyers to rural communities and one ensuring legal needs end in legal resolution – are connected in many ways, and sometimes the chains directly overlap. For instance, a law school clinic that provides legal services in rural areas exposes law students to rural practice, which increases the chances that law students will choose to practise in a rural community post-graduation and also helps to address existing legal needs in the community and bring them to resolution. Similarly, the more that organisations hire law school interns or sponsor recent graduates through fellowship programmes, the more those organisations can expand their own services and resolve legal issues while expanding the pipeline of practising rural attorneys.

Addressing obstacles and inefficiencies within one supply chain can also improve the functionality of the other supply chain. For example, when a network of legal resources measurably decreases the number of unresolved legal needs in a rural community, the economic health and vitality of a community increases, thereby increasing the attractiveness of the rural community to newcomers, including attorneys. Attorneys can prevent financial abuse[54] and other economically-detrimental behaviours between community members, increase legal compliance[55] and subsequently improve the economic opportunities of a community, thereby easing the supply chain of legal needs sent toward legal resolution. Because each supply chain drives the other, ongoing communication and collaboration between the stakeholders that comprise the two supply chains is critical to achieving holistic success in closing the rural justice gap.

We have framed the rural justice supply chains as a pipeline of attorneys into rural communities and a pipeline of legal needs into resolution, yet the nexus of these two pipelines reveals countless additional connections that span across the justice system and far beyond.[56] As just one example, healthcare providers often refer patients to legal services providers, meaning that the rural justice supply

[53] *Justice in Action* (n 45) 25 (proposing implicit bias training for judges).

[54] B Oltman, 'A Perfect Storm: Agriculture and the Crime of the 21st Century: Legal Implications of Elder Financial Abuse in the Agricultural Industry' (2016) 12 *NAELA Journal* 13.

[55] Statz and Termuhlen (n 21).

[56] ibid.

chains inherently intersect with the rural healthcare supply chains. While collaboration among stakeholders in a justice system is crucial for the system's success, developing broader awareness among community stakeholders is key to broader buy-in for legal aid funding and other efforts to improve the justice system and outcomes for community members. In South Dakota, for example, the State bar association developed relationships with non-lawyer stakeholders in rural communities as one of the first steps toward creating its incentive programme for rural lawyers.[57]

Many government officials and area leaders may not understand the ways in which unresolved civil legal needs prevent residents from reaching their fullest potential and contributing to the community in meaningful ways. Involving politicians, business leaders and non-legal service providers in championing the work of addressing civil legal needs further demonstrates the interconnectivity of the justice system with a healthy economy and community, and cements the working relationship between parties who too often fail to understand how their respective organisational efforts and challenges are aligned. Beginning with a discrete project in which interests intersect – projects focused on reinstating drivers' licences for formerly-incarcerated individuals who need to drive for meaningful employment, for example – can allow a diverse body of stakeholders to align their interests and efforts for actionable and tangible community good.

## VI. Conclusion

The ideal calibration for any community's civil justice system is one in which the optimal number of attorneys and related legal services are available, accessible and otherwise able to meet all the legal needs of the community's population. This ideal calibration also strives for local attorneys to find plentiful work and earn a worthwhile wage, pay off their student debt in short order and maintain work-life balance throughout their career, thus incentivising an eager pipeline of future attorneys to come. It is at this juncture of our idealistic pursuit of justice for all that we must acknowledge our supply chain's perpetual friction: even a perfect solution to the justice crisis hinges upon the existence of pervasive problems in an imperfect world. After all, a world without problems needs no system of justice, and a world without a system of justice (arguably) needs no attorneys. This is not the 'real' world, of course: just as the root causes of poverty and other problems that drive involvement with the justice system extend far beyond the purview of lawyers or even the law itself, market forces and other systemic, societal challenges that drive poverty and other problems in rural communities and elsewhere will continue to drive civil legal needs in those communities.

[57] Goetzinger and Morris (n 33) 452.

As a result, today's solutions may not meet tomorrow's challenges, and rural justice supply chains must accept outside forces and their evolving impacts on the justice gap as a constant.

Rural legal needs often arise from compounded circumstances, just as resolving those needs often requires multi-faceted solutions. Because our civil justice gap reflects broader dynamics within a capitalistic society, closing the gap requires a recognition of the innate complexities and interrelatedness of both the problems and their solutions, as well as a tolerance of enduring tensions within the civil justice system that ebb and flow with market forces outside the control of any link in the supply chain. Minimising the justice gap in a sustained way therefore demands that the links along these chains work together to remain agile against disruptive forces, recognise each legal problem and its potential solutions as pieces of a broader justice system, identify and leverage common ground among links and seek co-efficiencies along the chains. By working in concert rather than in silos, individual efforts made along these rural justice supply chains can drive holistic and sustainable metrics of success far greater than the sum of each link's individual efforts, thereby calibrating and priming the rural justice supply chains to deliver lasting, transformational change.

# 12

# 'Restorative What?' Young People's Experiences of Accessing Justice in Rural Syria

ADNAN MOUHIDDIN

## I. Introduction

Much of the research and literature on crime in Syria is concentrated on crimes whose conceptualisations and responses are rooted in international law (for example, war crimes, crimes against humanity and genocide).[1] Little, if any, of the existing research has explored street crime and homicide[2] in a country that has experienced one of the worst human tragedies of the twenty-first century. In March 2017, the war in Syria was described by Zeid bin Ra'ad, the High Commissioner of the Office of the United Nations High Commissioner for Human Rights (OHCHR), as 'the worst man-made disaster since World War II'.[3] Beside the basic infrastructure, which has been severely damaged, the impact of the war will affect the Syrian community for generations to come. Millions of children and young Syrians[4]

[1] See JJ Sarkin, *The Conflict in Syria and the Failure of International Law to Protect People Globally: Mass Atrocities, Enforced Disappearances and Arbitrary Detentions* (Routledge, 2021). Also see OE Ogunnowo, and F Chidozie. 'International Law and Humanitarian Intervention in the Syrian Civil War: The Role of the United States' *SAGE Open* (April 2020), doi:10.1177/2158244020919533.

[2] In this chapter, 'crime' refers to all kind of crimes, apart from the crimes of terrorism and the corruption of public officials. Both crimes are heavily politicised in Syria and therefore discussing them will require clarifications that are not within the scope of this chapter.

[3] D Collins, 'A torture chamber' *Aljazeera.com* (15 March 2017) at www.aljazeera.com/features/2017/3/15/syria-war-worst-man-made-disaster-since-world-war-ii (accessed 22 March 2022).

[4] In this chapter, 'youth' refers to those between the ages of 15 and 24. Following the guidance of the United Nations Educational, Scientific and Cultural Organisation (UNESCO), 'Definition of youth perhaps changes with circumstances, especially with the changes in demographic, financial, economic and socio-cultural settings; however, the definition that uses 15–24 age cohort as youth fairly serves its statistical purposes for assessing the needs of the young people and providing guidelines for youth development' (UNESCO, 2018). See UNESCO, 'What do we mean by "youth?' (UNESCO, 2018) at www.unesco.org/new/en/social-and-human-sciences/themes/youth/youth-definition/ (accessed 1 March 2022).

have been deprived of an education,[5] displaced from their domiciles and neighbourhoods and/or recruited as soldiers[6] in the course of the conflict. Children's and young people's extensive involvement in the war, whether as participants, witnesses or victims, has resulted in war-associated mental illnesses such as Post-Traumatic Stress Disorder (PTSD), and exposed them to the risk of involvement in dysfunctional behaviours and serious criminal conduct.

It is well established that civil-war societies experience a dramatic increase in crime rates during and after the war.[7] Syria is no exception. With a rise in crime since the eruption of the civil war in 2012, the Court of Appeal in Syria reported that youth crime has quadrupled.[8] Coinciding with international and humanitarian reports, these statements attribute such a rise to socio-economic factors.[9] This not only threatens the well-being of the youth and impacts upon their future opportunities, but it also places the development and the future stability of the country at stake, since the impact is likely to be evident during the coming decades. In 2010, the United Nations Development Programme (UNDP)[10] noted the lack of familiarity with juvenile issues within the court system in Syria. It also found that there is a lack of judges specialising in juvenile crime in Syria. Moreover, the destruction of the Syrian infrastructure has affected all sectors at unprecedented levels, including the judicial system and the ability of Syrians to access and rely on an effective legal system that provided them with fair and just remedies. The ongoing war has not only led to legal experts' being exiled and/or displaced, it has also divided the country into cantons, each being led by local forces that install their own court systems and apply justice as they see fit.

Generally speaking, crime impacts not only individuals but also the wider community. Besides the role of the wider society, local communities' adherence to their own valued norms and laws is a vital stage in building a post-conflict society. In this vein, tribal customary law has always been a significant means of resolving disputes and preserving order in Syria. In Iraq, for instance, the ongoing wars and turmoil in the country have strengthened the position of tribal law, which

[5] F Gordon and A Mouhiddin, 'Citizenship education in the conflict-affected societies of Northern Ireland and Syria: Learning lessons from the past to inform the future' in A Peterson et al (eds), *The Palgrave Handbook of Citizenship and Education* (Palgrave Macmillan, 2020) 449.

[6] Human Rights Watch, 'Syria: Opposition Using Children in Conflict' *Human Rights Watch* (29 November 2022) at www.hrw.org/news/2012/11/29/syria-opposition-using-children-conflict (accessed 01 March 2022).

[7] V O'Connor and C Rausch, *Model Codes for Post-Conflict Criminal Justice* (United States Institute of Peace Press, 2007)

[8] M Hmejo, 'Poverty and displacement are the most significant factors. Al Bakri: youth crime quadrupled' *Al-Watan* (14 November 2016) at http://alwatan.sy/archives/78259 (accessed 1 March 2022).

[9] Save the Children, Digital S, 'Invisible Wounds: The Impact of Six Years of War on the Mental Health of Syria's Children' (Save the Children's Resource Centre, 2017) at https://resourcecentre.savethechildren.net/library/invisible-wounds-impact-six-years-war-mental-health-syrias-children (accessed 1 March 2022).

[10] UNDP, 'Support to Juvenile Justice in Syria' (UNDP, 2010) at https://info.undp.org/docs/pdc/Documents/SYR/00060249_Juvenile%20Justice.pdf (accessed 1 March 2022).

has filled the gap left by the Iraqi Justice System and whose rules are rooted in the concrete, practical experience of the community, including restorative justice. Although not a country currently experiencing conflict, Jordan, which has a well-functioning justice system, also sees many crimes solved according to tribal law executed by the tribes themselves.

Discussing the role of tribal traditions is a very wide and rich topic, the size of which may be bigger than the capacity of this chapter. Therefore, this chapter will address how tribal mechanisms in rural Syria may provide alternative dispute resolution to the formal justice system. It will also explore the perception of young Syrians of tribal mechanisms and whether they respond well to the needs of young Syrians in conflict with the law in rural areas. This topic emerged during my doctoral research[11] on community crime prevention[12] among young Syrians. With a developed and keen interest in the use and implementation of restorative justice approaches in the United Kingdom, I explored whether this principle could be implemented in Syria. Unbeknown to me, similar traditions existed in rural areas in Syria. The chapter will also provide some context about rural areas in Syria and will explore why access to justice in these communities is vital. A key contribution of this chapter will be exploring how restorative justice may correlate with the values and norms of the Syrian rural and tribal communities, and where they fundamentally differ.

## II. Access to Justice in Syria

In Syria, the urban-rural division is as ancient as its communities. Historically, the urban-rural division occurred on social and cultural levels, whereby the rural areas lived 'at the mercy of the cities'.[13] Since the uprising in 2011, this division has deepened and has resulted in further challenges for Syrians in rural areas to access

[11] Data from practitioners who participated in my research will be provided in this chapter. The reference will provide the profession and the gender of the participant.

[12] With the lack of comparative studies in the field of the delinquent youth and crime in Syria, I opted to examine the correlation between the Syrian youth and their reliance on their society and communities in other societal activities that support not only their developments but also their vital needs. In 2007, research by N Kabbani and N Kamel, 'Youth Exclusion in Syria' (Middle East Youth Initiative, September 2007) reported a significant reliance among the Syrian youth (between the ages of 15–24) on family and community connections to secure employment, marriage and housing, where 90% identified 'family, relatives and friends' as the source for job searches: Furthermore, research conducted by International Alert, 'Why Young Syrians Choose to Fight: Vulnerability and resilience to recruitment by violent extremist groups in Syria' (International Alert, 2016), revealed the significant role of the family not only in the decision process leading to youths joining armed groups, but also in pulling them back into the community. The significance of role models and religion was also noted in the research. Another study conducted by Dawlaty, 'Transitional Justice from the Perspective of Syrian Youth' (Dawlaty, 2016) noted that young people's perception of what constitutes crime is affected by the existing stigma fused in their society and community views.

[13] H Batatu, *Syria's Peasantry, the Descendants of its Lesser Rural Notables, and Their Politics* (Princeton University Press, 1999).

justice mechanisms. This lack of access to justice has been exacerbated by the direct and indirect effects of the humanitarian crisis and the Covid-19 pandemic.[14] Before this chapter explores this area in further detail, it will first conceptualise the role of tradition in the Syrian justice system.

In essence, Syrian society remains tribal. Tribes in Syria have their own codes of ethics, morals and customs, and the 'tribal regions in Syria constitute 70% of the country's landmass'.[15] While Syria seemingly is a secular country, the role of religion and tradition in rural areas[16] and in the promulgation of Syrian laws is clearly evident. Islam has been the dominant religion in Syria since it was conquered by the Arab armies in AD 640, and this has had a direct impact on Syrian demography. In 1947, during the period in which the aforementioned laws were enacted, Sunni Muslims comprised 66 per cent of the Syrian population, which equated to nearly 3 million people.[17] As a majority, the laws reflected Sunni beliefs and understanding as to what law is, which echoes what Quinney observed as 'law-making represent[ing] the translation of specific group interests into public policy'.[18] Such interest was vested in the clerics, who during the 1950s assumed the position of the guardians of the country's morals and portrayed entertainments such as radio and the cinema as a form of moral corruption. In fact, 'traditionalists have always constituted the vast majority of the clergy'.[19] The traditionalists ensured their close observation of any attempts to alter the religiously conservative life in Syria. Therefore, their influence was not limited to education and endowment but extended to the political and social fields.[20] The committee of scholars had more influence on the laws passed by parliament than the international conventions had. In 1993, Syria ratified the United Nations Convention of the Rights of the Child 1989, with the following reservation:

> The Syrian Arab Republic has reservations on the Convention's provisions which are not in conformity with the Syrian Arab legislations and with the Islamic Shariah's principles, in particular the content of article 14 related to the Right of the Child to the freedom of religion.[21]

Despite this indication of the strong influence traditionalists have on law and its formulation in Syria, the juvenile justice system enjoyed some progressive measures that meet international standards. For instance, the Juvenile Delinquency Act

[14] The United Nations Office for the Coordination of Humanitarian Affairs, 'Humanitarian Needs Overview: Syrian Arab Republic' (March 2021) at https://reliefweb.int/sites/reliefweb.int/files/resources/syria_2021_humanitarian_needs_overview.pdf (accessed 17 March 2022).

[15] H Dukhan, *State and Tribes in Syria: Informal Alliances and Conflict Patterns* (Routledge, 2018) 2.

[16] Batatu (n 13).

[17] A Hourani, *Minorities in the Arab World* (Oxford University Press, 1947).

[18] R Quinney, *The Social Reality of Crime* (Little, Brown and Company, 1970) 43.

[19] T Pierret, *Religion and State in Syria: The Sunni Ulama from Coup to Revolution* (Cambridge University Press, 2013) 102.

[20] N Atassi, *The Evolution of The Syrian Society Between 1831–2011* (Atlas Books, 2019).

[21] United Nations Treaty Collection, 'Convention on the Rights of the Child' (UNRT, 2018) at https://treaties.un.org/pages/ViewDetails.aspx?src=IND&mtdsg_no=IV-11&chapter=4&clang=_en (accessed 18 January 2022).

of 1974 (and its amendment of 2003) is based on provisions that set the interests of the child and young people as a priority. Also, Article 5 invites the court to apply rehabilitative measures in the light of the social and psychological conditions of the juvenile, and Article 26 sets out the rehabilitative measures that should be available to the juvenile delinquent. These measures include care measures, education, vocational training, an appropriate job, and providing the appropriate guidance and advice for the juvenile to start their life and earn their living. Furthermore, the 1974 Act ensured that the privacy and the confidentiality of the juvenile are protected during their detention and trial (Articles 49 and 54) and that their offences are not recorded in the justice records (Article 58).

The practice and realities on the ground for children and young people, however, appear quite different from the ethos of the legislative framework. In 2010, the UNDP, in cooperation with the Syrian Government, assessed the juvenile justice system in Syria with a view to enhancing its performance and efficiency and reforming its institutions. The assessment noted the lack of familiarity with juvenile issues within the court system in Syria.[22] It also found that there is 'a lack of judges specialised in dealing with juvenile crime in Syria', although Article 34 of the Juvenile Delinquents Act 1974 clearly states that juvenile judges must be selected based on their experience in juvenile affairs.[23] The assessment then provided some examples that indicated shortcomings in the juvenile justice system. For example, the assessment revealed:

> [J]uvenile offenders between the ages of 15–18 are transported to the courts and back to the holding prisons with adult prisoners, exposing them to mental and physical abuse from older and more seasoned criminals. Furthermore, juvenile offenders are dragged through a sometimes-lengthy legal process leaving them in detention or holding cells often for longer than their offense and sentencing would dictate.[24]

In addition, the assessment highlighted what it called 'the weak follow up'[25] with juvenile cases, which relies on communication between the courts, the reform institutions, the probation officers and the families of offenders. It also observed:

> [R]eform institutions are often lacking strong in-house psycho-social and health expertise for offenders and often, staff at the centers are not trained to give specialized care or support to juveniles. Reform institutions do not have the capacity to particularly follow up with all the offenders or extend any specialized service.[26]

While this was the situation during a time of peace, one might question what the situation was after the eruption of the war. At the time of writing this chapter, Syria is divided into various factions and status quo authorities, and each applies

[22] UNDP, 'Support to Juvenile Justice in Syria' (UNDP, 2010) at https://info.undp.org/docs/pdc/Documents/SYR/00060249_Juvenile%20Justice.pdf (accessed 1 March 2022).

[23] ibid.

[24] ibid 4.

[25] ibid.

[26] ibid.

justice as it sees fit, therefore distinct approaches are applied depending on the area. Should the Syrian Government gain control over the entire Syrian territory, justice in Syria will encounter an extreme level of corruption, which has crippled the Syria justice system for decades.[27] In Afghanistan, corruption was the predominant reason why people lost their trust in the state to ensure security. Innocent people had to bribe their way out of prison, while drug mules dominated the market.[28] As in many war-affected societies, citizens lost trust in the criminal justice system, which in many instances had abused them. In its peacekeeping missions, the United Nations reported that judges, prosecutors and court officials in conflict and transitional societies abuse their powers in an environment of corruption, misconduct and lack of professional behaviour.[29] Moreover, state crime intervention, and justice policies and practices in general, in post-conflict societies is hampered by the 'the lack of statistical data by the state' and lacks understanding of the needs of victims and societies.[30] Such a lack of data might also mirror the fact that the criminal justice systems are outdated. As is often the case after a war, authorities concern themselves with establishing order and stability, while the state institutions, including the justice sector, are politically typically neglected.[31] These obstacles were common features observed in Cambodia, East Timor, Kosovo,[32] Afghanistan[33] and Burundi,[34] where the crippled justice systems could not reach the communities in rural areas, and therefore these communities resorted to alternative dispute resolution mechanisms that stemmed from the norms and customs of rural areas.

## III. Community Alternatives

In November 2016, a criminal law judge in the Syrian Appeal Court reported that homicide and theft committed by young Syrians had quadrupled in comparison to

[27] J Davis, *The Arab Spring and Arab Thaw: Unfinished Revolutions and the Quest for Democracy* (Routledge, 2016). Also see A Al-Sheikh and A Hamada, 'Corruption in Syria: Causes, Effects, and Anti-Corruption Strategies' (2014) Publication no 26m Syrian Economic Forum, at http://syrianef.org/assets/estimate_position/english/Corruption-in-Syria.pdf (accessed 1 March 2022)

[28] J Braithwaite and A Wardak, 'Crime and War in Afghanistan: Part I: The Hobbesian Solution' (2013) 53(2) *The British Journal of Criminology* 179.

[29] The Office of the United Nations High Commissioner for Human Rights, 'Rule-Of-Law Tools for Post-Conflict States: Mapping the justice sector' (OHCHR, 2006) at www.ohchr.org/sites/default/files/Documents/Publications/RuleoflawMappingen.pdf (accessed 1 March 2022).

[30] O'Connor and Rausch (n 7) 100.

[31] ibid.

[32] C Rausch, *Fighting Serious Crimes: Strategies and Tactics for Conflict-Affected Societies* (United States Institute of Peace Press, 2017).

[33] UN Office for the Coordination of Humanitarian Affairs, 'Afghanistan: Efforts to improve access to justice in rural areas' (Reliefweb, 2005) at https://reliefweb.int/report/afghanistan/afghanistan-efforts-improve-access-justice-rural-areas (accessed 1 March 2022).

[34] I Chaara, J-B Falisse and J Moriceau, 'Does Legal Aid Improve Access to Justice in 'Fragile' Settings? Evidence from Burundi' *Journal of Peace Research* (April 2022) at doi.org/10.1177/00223433211055633.

the rates found before the war.[35] The reasons for such rise, according to the judge, stemmed from the dire economic factors suffered by the country's youth.[36] He named unemployment and living hardships among those factors that led young Syrian to satisfy their daily needs via illegal means.[37] He added that 'psychological factors have played a significant role in the criminal behaviour among the juveniles'.[38] The Judge associated these factors with the 'horrendous depictions of homicide' young Syrians watch on various media platforms on a daily basis.[39] He also added other factors, such as the impulse for revenge and displacement from the neighbourhoods in which the young people were raised. In his elucidation of crime levels, the judge distinguished between 'deprived, rural and crowded areas' and urban areas.[40] For instance, he found that fewer crimes happen in Sha'alan and Abu-Rumanah (urban and rich quarters in Damascus) in comparison to the rural areas of the district of Damascus. This distinction is applicable to the rest of Syria, where rural areas are particularly vulnerable to victimisation. The proliferation of small arms is widespread in rural areas that are outside the control of the regime or the status quo powers, and law and order in these areas is enforced to serve the interests of certain powerful groups.[41]

In exploring responses to young people's involvement in crime in rural communities, it is important to draw on the experience of other countries that have survived an internal conflict and have successfully installed alternative programmes. The United Nations Office on Drugs and Crime found that the focus of legal empowerment 'should be on the community and building links to the formal system, rather than on the formal system itself'.[42] In this sense, justice that was delivered by tribal councils (*Jirga*) in Afghanistan competed with that delivered by both the Taliban and the corrupt state, and was appreciated by the population. The *Jirga* resolved disputes by observing local traditions,[43] even if these traditions were in opposition to the Afghani laws inspired by Islamic law, which holds a supreme status.[44]

As has been frequently found, and as noted in section I of this chapter, crime does not impact individuals alone but also the community.[45] Considering the level of crime in rural Syria according to the official estimates, rural communities'

[35] Hmejo (n 8).
[36] ibid.
[37] ibid.
[38] ibid.
[39] ibid.
[40] ibid.
[41] Judge, female.
[42] United Nations Office on Drugs and Crime, *Criminal justice reform in post-conflict States: A guide for practitioners*, (United Nations Press, 2011).
[43] Braithwaite and Wardak (n 28).
[44] H Khan, 'Islamic Law, Customary Law and Afghan Informal Justice' (United Stated Institute of Peace, 2015) at www.usip.org/publications/2015/03/islamic-law-customary-law-and-afghan-informal-justice (accessed 1 March 2022).
[45] J Wilson, *Thinking About Crime* (Basis Books, 2013).

adherence to their own valued norms and laws is a vital stage in building a post-conflict society in the country and providing effective and fair access to justice for these communities.[46] A similar approach was implemented in Iraq, where tribal customary law has always been a significant means for resolving disputes and preserving order in that country. The ongoing wars and turmoil in Iraq have strengthened the position of tribal law, which filled the gap left by the Iraqi Justice System and whose rules are 'rooted in the concrete practical experience of the community', including restorative justice.[47] Although not a country currently experiencing conflict, Jordan, which has a well-functioning justice system, also sees many crimes solved according to tribal law executed by the tribes themselves.[48]

Disorder, as is often the case, is one of the main outcomes of the war. The loss of social control,[49] which results from this situation, should be appreciated when establishing alternative access to justice in war-torn societies. In this sense, young Syrians are less likely to engage in crime if they have strong social bonds with their communities.[50] What is meant here by 'social bonds' is attachment (ties), involvement, belief (respecting the laws of the society) and commitment. Now, when the means of control are shifted from custody to community, they penetrate the social fabric; the community gets to act as the agent of its own rights,[51] and therein lies the importance of alternative access to justice that has its seeds in local communities, including in rural areas.

Community and social control are strong forces within Syrian society, especially in rural areas. In these areas, tribes have long had mechanisms in place to resolve disputes between their members, even before the war. The influence of religion and customs in the promulgation of Syrian laws is evident, as we have seen earlier in this chapter. For decades, subsequent Syrian governments and regimes looked upon tribal customs of conflict resolution favourably. By doing so, these governments came to 'structurally reinforce state control over society'.[52] Anleu[53] has referred to this as 'coexisting', while Mestura described this dynamic as making 'legal exceptions by acknowledging and accepting the existence of customary laws that may have a controlling force in certain circumstances'.[54]

Limited research exists that explores the role of restorative justice in community crime prevention in post-conflict societies. In examining the potential role of

[46] O'Connor and Rausch (n 7).

[47] P Asfura-Heim, 'Tribal Customary Law and Legal Pluralism in al Anbar, Iraq' in D Isser, (ed), *Customary Justice and the Rule of Law in War-Torn Societies* (United States Institute of Peace, 2011) 239.

[48] A Furr and M Al-Serhan, 'Tribal Customary Law in Jordan' (2005) 4(2) *South Carolina Journal of International Law and Business* 17.

[49] J Wilson and R Herrnstein, *Crime and Human Nature* (Simon & Schuster, 1985).

[50] T Hirschi, *Causes of Delinquency* (University of California Press, 1969).

[51] A Cohen, *The Symbolic Construction of Community* (Routledge, 1985).

[52] Pierret (n 19) 101.

[53] SL Roach Anleu, *Law and Social Change* (Sage Publications, 2000).

[54] M Mastura, 'Legal pluralism in the Philippines' [1994] *Law and Society Review* 28.

restorative justice in community crime prevention plans among young people, the author asked one of the interviewees[55] about restorative justice:

| | |
|---|---|
| Researcher: | 'What do you know about restorative justice?' |
| Participant: | 'Restorative what?' |
| Researcher: | 'Restorative justice.' |
| Participant: | 'Is this where you bring the victim and the offender together to discuss what happened?' |
| Researcher: | 'Yes, partly so.' |
| Participant: | 'We have local traditions and customs similar to restorative justice. Did you explore them?' |

Although some participants confused restorative with transitional justice,[56] the interviewee's definition was close to that of restorative justice. Restorative justice has been defined as a communication between victims and offenders within a controlled environment to talk about the harm that has been caused and finding a way to repair that harm.[57] In other words, it is an alternative that involves all the parties to the incident rather than excluding them.[58] Restorative justice does not view crime as a mere challenge to the order and the sovereignty of the state but sees it as a community issue where the latter is involved; an alternative that restores rather than punishes and whose core focus is on the well-being of the parties.[59]

Following the insight provided by the interviewees, the author explored tribal alternative dispute resolution in rural areas that may provide alternative access to justice for young Syrians who are in conflict with the law. One participant[60] introduced the concept of the 'Arfeh':

> Tribes are based on a particular moral system. When they encounter issues, and before they resort to the justice system, they refer these issues to what they call mediator. Tribes call this person the 'Arfeh'. The Arfeh is a tribal judicial system. They are still present in rural areas. Of course, you cannot refer to him in any case, like in the case of murder. In this case, the state has public right of action, and the state will handle it. But other disputes, such as disputes over land or livestock, are referred to the Arfeh. They exist east to Aleppo, east to Hama, east to Homs towards the Iraqi borders. All these areas have the system of Arfeh. The Arfeh should be well known in the area. He should also be known for his intelligence, wisdom, skills and experience. Both parties resort to him. They share their case and accept his judgment. You cannot appeal his judgment, and this is a tribal law.

[55] Youth practitioner and screenwriter, female.

[56] An emerging and growing concept in the Syrian context as an approach to atrocities that have taken place during the war.

[57] H Zehr, *Restorative Justice, Intercourse* (Good Books, 2002).

[58] ibid.

[59] J Braithwaite, 'Restorative Justice' in M Tonry (ed), *Handbook of Crime and Punishment* (Oxford University Press, 1998) 323.

[60] Lawyer, male.

Different rural areas in Syria have their different approaches to these mechanisms. For instance, a Syrian judge[61] from south of Syria introduced another tribal alternative dispute resolution mechanism that is used in all kinds of disputes, including to respond to youth involvement in crime. She referred to it as the '*Hamayel*' and explained that:

> It is a system whereby tribes solve their disputes without the interference of the justice system. This system ensures that parties to the dispute are happy with the outcome. Disputing parties, each called Hamayel, would meet and provide due apology or compensation or both and move on without any reference to the justice system. Lots of disputes are solved that way. Heads of Hamayel call disputing parties to sit and talk. This is a tribal practice. I have seen it myself. The family of the young offender and that of the victim meet and discuss what happened. They also discuss the appropriate compensation. The young offender is told off and is given the opportunity to apologize. This shows that local communities are capable of solving their own issues and disputes … Bear in mind that the Syrian society is tribal by and large.

Similar to these mechanisms is the role of the '*Mukhtar*', which literally means 'the chosen'. His role is like that of the 'Arfeh'. In many Middle Eastern countries, every single village, town and neighbourhood in big cities has its own *Mukhtar*:

> The Mukhtar is a tangible figure known by generations of local citizens within their neighbourhood. They operate a small office and are open 24/7 for the resolution of various problems. Due to his many roles and responsibilities, the Mukhtar can act as a legitimate intermediary for governments. Ultimately, he can link citizens to government.[62]

Each of these alternatives could act as arbitrators and as the last resort in the absence of authorities and formal control, particularly because Syrians in general distrust the justice system. They are independent and neutral, and they are a classic example of community solutions to a community problem (youth involvement in crime). The role of these alternatives and the tribal dignitaries that lead them has exceeded that of the state in resolving disputes,[63] but mainly in rural areas.[64]

## IV. Wisdom Has No White Hair

Despite their benefits, it is important to distinguish between restorative justice and these domestic tribal mechanisms in rural areas. While they do provide an alternative to formal justice for rural communities, their restorative nature remains

[61] Judge, female.

[62] R Fakhouri and B Chebaro 'Mukhtar: A solution for i-government in a developing country' *International Business Policy* (2017), Conference paper: Academy of International Business Annual Meeting, Dubai.

[63] Youth lawyer and community development, male.

[64] Youth practitioner, male.

unclear. Restorative justice is progressive and aims to understand why the crime happened and how to move forward, whereas these alternatives seek compensation, with fewer strategies concerning the future. When both the victim and the offender share a minimal interest in settling the aftermath of the crime, a significant level of engagement occurs with the parties to the crime. Such engagement, as the evidence demonstrates, impacts the emotional well-being of the parties involved:

> The emotions and the wellbeing of the parties are central in the restorative approach. Explicitly addressing issues of human emotion, connection and relationships, restorative practice is an amalgam of specifically targeted activities, theoretical and practical constructs to support individual wellbeing and repair harm, through the development of nurturing, robust families and communities.[65]

This emotional dimension in the rural mechanisms explained above remains unclear, and therefore they should be distinguished from restorative justice. The expression of emotions among Syrian males is hindered by stigma (expressing emotions is synonymous with being weak) and masculinity (man up!), even more so in rural areas.[66] Furthermore, offending in Syria involves shame that does not lead to reintegration. In his book *Crime, Shame and Reintegration*, John Braithwaite considered the conditions under which certain forms of social reaction can produce responses that enable offenders to become law-abiding and respectable citizens.[67] Shaming is a principal element in such process. However, he identified two aspects to shaming: disintegrative shaming and reintegrative shaming. The former labels and excludes the person being shamed, while the latter involves social disapproval followed by a process that subsequently aims to reintegrate the offender back into society, decertifying him as deviant. It is noteworthy, though, that shame is also experienced by the victim of crime. Tomkins argues that that shame is felt by a person whenever his or her experience of the positive effects of justice is interrupted.[68] So an individual does not have to do something wrong to feel shame. Rather, the individual may simply experience something that interrupts interest-excitement or enjoyment-joy. Shame in Syrian society is a liability, often washed away and/or dealt with by naming and shaming the culprit or shedding their blood in extreme cases (honour killing). In the case of sexual offences, victims cease to be an injured party and become a liability. They too are punished along with the perpetrator, to restore the family's or the tribe's honour. Therefore, the ability of these mechanisms to provide meaningful access to justice in rural Syria is questionable at best, but also impeded by social concepts such as masculinity, stigma, honour and shaming.

[65] K Vernon and M Thorsborne, *The Psychology of Emotion in Restorative Practice* (Jessica Kingsley Publishers, 2014) 155.

[66] H Daoud, 'Those Two Heavy Wings of Manhood: On Moustaches' in D Cohen-Mor (ed), *Cultural Journeys into the Arab World: A Literary Anthology* (State University of New York Press, 2018) 58.

[67] J Braithwaite, *Crime, Shame and Reintegration* (Cambridge University Press, 1989).

[68] S Tomkins, 'Shame' in D Nathanson (ed), *The Many Faces of Shame* (The Guilford Press, 1988) 133.

Beyond the conceptual question, these mechanisms unfortunately lost their legitimacy among the rural communities through action by the Syrian Government that aimed to weaken the tribal system after the outbreak of war. This action (weakening the tribal system) was taken systematically:

> Claims that tribal practices have their legitimacy in tribal norms and values are hard to comprehend. After decades of dictatorship, the regime floated every single thug in these tribes to the surface at the expense of wise and moral members. Tribes as community institutions lost their identity and legitimacy too. Those tribal positive moral values have been lost and they are insignificant where they are present. Tribes maintained order in the rural area despite their flaws here and there. I mean in some cases these flaws hindered the development of our society. But they had a positive role to play despite these flaws. Things have changed today. They joined forces with the regime, and they were transferred into fighting forces. They lost their social impact. They lost their legitimacy. I don't think tribes have a preventive role. Tribes' young members do not take their tribes and their values seriously anymore. Receiving aid and food basket has become the one and only benefit of being a member of some tribe. Young people have lost their sense of belonging and identity. I don't want to generalise, but I think the majority have lost that kind of sense.[69]

To establish an alternative to youth justice in rural Syria, we should seek the values the Syrian communities in these areas treasure and appreciate. In other words, something to start from; something people value and from which we can progress. This, unfortunately, does not appear to be a straightforward case when it comes to Syrian rural communities. As is often the case, communities that emerge from prolonged periods of conflict and war lack effective traditions of peaceful conflict resolution. The old non-violent ways of conflict resolution are often destroyed during prolonged conflicts and become irrelevant and ineffective. When under pressure, 'communities use the (often violent) methods the war has bequeathed them'.[70] Similarly, the Syrian conflict 'caused huge differences between individuals and communities regarding shared values and visions of the future, at both local and national levels'[71] but mainly in rural areas.[72] The meanings and contents of the dominant societal ways of behaving may vary among the members of the same community. In this case, Cohen argues, community boundaries become anomalous, and their integrity is severely impugned.[73] The ethnical and religious diversity of the Syrian communities will most likely trigger different perceptions as to what crime and justice may comprise, such as honour killings and revenge, which are widely practised in rural areas in Syria.[74] In the course of the war that erupted

[69] Judge, male.

[70] C Steenkamp, 'In the shadows of war and peace: making sense of violence after peace accords' (2011) 11(3) *Conflict, Security & Development* 357.

[71] Syrian Centre for Policy Research, *The Conflict Impact on Social Capital: Social Degradation in Syria* (Friedrich-Ebert-Stiftung, 2017) 10.

[72] ibid 29.

[73] A Cohen, *The Symbolic Construction of Community* (Routledge, 1985).

[74] H Dukhan, 'The end of the dialectical symbiosis of national and tribal identities in Syria' (2022) 28(1) *Nations and Nationalism* 141.

in 2011, these practices forged a tribal identity that clashed with the national identity and faith in the state institutions that are associated with the repressive Syrian regime.[75] Inevitably, this will impact not only the faith of rural communities in the justice system, but also their access to it.

Although now repealed, previous attempts to revoke Article 548 of the Syrian Penal Code of 1949 were vehemently opposed by Syrian communities. Article 548 had frequently been used as leverage to acquit men committing 'honour killings'. The intensity with which the concept of 'honour killing' is viewed may be traced to an earlier attempt in 2006 to survey public opinion on whether honour crime should be classified as a criminal and punishable offence.[76] The survey created an 'outrage in Syria'[77] and the researchers were 'banned from analysing [its] findings'.[78] This suggests that a broad cross-section of Syrian society does not view 'honour killing' as a crime, just as with domestic violence:

> The woman was covered in bruises and the judge lectured her on obeying her husband. I know why he did so. He comes originally from a rural area where it is OK to beat your wife black and blue and she is blamed if she dares to protest.[79]

Similar issues could be found within the Bedouin tribal system and the Druze community culture.[80] For example, when it comes to the crime of revenge, the duty of the avenger of blood is a sacred obligation among the Druze.[81] Moreover, homosexuality is not only illegal but is still a rejected concept in Syria, and responses to it often take a violent form.[82] This could potentially lead to tragic outcomes, where a gay person is condemned under these alternative mechanisms while someone who has committed an honour or revenge killing is protected. To this may be added the proliferation of weapons among young people (which is more common in rural areas)[83] and young people's displacement, which has undermined the role of these tribal mechanisms. As of today, Syrian society is

> divided into civil and military sections, and the outcome of any dispute is regulated under this division. In other words, if you have gun, you are stronger and you can win any argument. It is unclear how they [the *Arfeh* and *Hamayel*] could function in this environment.[84]

[75] ibid.

[76] K Abu Halawa, *Survey concerning the need to change the unfair laws toward women* (Karama Publications, 2006).

[77] ibid 45.

[78] R Maktabi, 'Gender, family law and citizenship in Syria' (2010) 15(5) *Citizenship Studies* 557, 563.

[79] Lawyer, male, sharing his observation from a trial he attended.

[80] B Johnson et al, 'Does adolescent religious commitment matter? A reexamination of the effects of religiosity on delinquency' (2001) 38(1) *Journal of Research in Crime and Delinquency* 22.

[81] ibid.

[82] United Nations High Commissioner for Refugees (UNHCR), *Protecting and Supporting the Displaced in Syria: UNHCR Syria End of Year Report 2015* (United Nations, 2015).

[83] Judge, female.

[84] Youth and community practitioner, female.

Despite this grim picture, these tribal mechanisms could have the potential to provide an alternative to the dysfunctional youth justice systems that operate in Syria. While tackling this topic could lead to lengthy discussion, it is worth mentioning a few suggestions made by Syrian practitioners during interviews, who spoke of their reservations regarding reliance upon tribal mechanisms. First, it is worth keeping in mind that these mechanisms are different from restorative justice. Distinguishing them is important not only on conceptual level, but also to avoid duplicating a principle that may not be fit for the needs of Syria at this moment in its history.[85] It is also worth starting a dialogue with those who oversee and deliver these mechanisms on the way forward, and how they feel that they could be supported:

> This support should protect the form in which they were founded [tribal mechanisms]. It should also protect it from being institutionalised based on Western institutional principles. We have big crisis today. Let me explain. Western countries understand institutions in certain way and this understanding is based on their experience during the last 50 years or so. They decided that this is how institutions should look. Now when you take this perception to environments where the basics of institution are missing, you end up creating structures rather than institutions. It is difficult to design a uniform approach to institutional capacity and then impose it on other societies. Developing countries are really suffering from this particular situation, and Syria is no exception. This approach would have decided that we should build a five-story building for Arfeh or Hamayel. Well, how about asking them first what they need and how can we empower them? They know what they need. We don't. So we should be informed by their needs rather than the donor's vision [referring to the non-governmental organisations that concern themselves with Syria]. They need to speak to people. We should protect the authenticity of such mechanisms. We should not mess with its DNA.[86]

On the other hand, there is a potential risk of those mechanisms and the dignitaries behind them becoming an oppressive tool in the hand of the tribal leaders, since the concept of individual freedoms in society and in state laws is not fully developed in Syria.[87] Young people, and females in particular, expressed their concerns, arguing that these mechanisms are akin to sweeping the dust under the carpet, which cast doubts on the ability of these tribal mechanisms to provide meaningful and effective access to justice in rural areas. They also expressed their concerns that these mechanisms may strengthen the existing traditional and stereotypical views on women and young people:

> I don't want to sound judgmental, but I personally won't resort to such mechanisms. We should have a strong and efficient justice system under one unified law which all Syrians appeal to, whether in cities or rural areas. In my town, in Sahnayah, Druze people take their disputes to Sheikh-Akel. Christians in my town, some of them seek the bishop as a mediator. We had a dispute with another family in the town, and the bishop visited

[85] Youth practitioner, female.
[86] Youth consultant, male.
[87] Youth practitioner, female.

> us acting as a mediator. I was like 'Who are you? And why you are involved?' These mediators invest a lot of time asserting their authority instead of trying to solve the problem. You know? Like 'oh I am a divine authority and listen to what I have to say' … They think that they can mediate. They are useless. Wisdom has no white hair … Young Syrians are fed up with adults' perspectives on right and wrong. We need young people who facilitate restorative sessions and promote it in youth clubs and other social institutions.[88]

These concerns were also echoed by a female youth practitioner who questioned whether women would be allowed to lead such mechanisms:

> Can you say that females will be involved, other than as a victim or perpetrator? Restorative practices will be implemented and facilitated by males who think we are subhuman. The problem is that we may end up with approaches designed for the needs of males and those will become an additional tool to the arsenal of oppressive mechanisms already used to oppress and supress Syrian women. No thank you. I prefer just laws and a strong criminal justice system.[89]

This reference to the formal justice system should not be mistaken for a belief in the current one, bearing in mind Dukhan's assertion that Syrians in rural areas are replacing their national identity and their faith in state institutions with their tribal identity and norms; rather it reflects the aspiration to a justice system that is fair and accessible for all Syrians (as Donson and Morgan-Williams have shown in chapter 7 of this volume, the justice system itself can provide a barrier to some in accessing justice). This probably responds to the social mood of Syrians, who aim for the certainty that may be found in state institutions over customary solutions, which may change subject to the social and culture development in a country that is exposed to an open crisis whose end is not in sight.

## V. Conclusion

To enable meaningful and effective access to justice for offences that are youth related, a radical change in the social and the political structure is required. This should be coupled with an awareness of the needs of young people and the serious impact of their offending on their welfare and the future development of the country. This is particularly the case among communities in rural areas, which are experiencing questions of identity, a high level of arms proliferation, and increasing reliance on tribal norms and mechanisms in the absence of the formal justice system that has been devastated in the course of the war. Arguably, these mechanisms have provided an alternative to the formal justice system and are capable of continuing to do so. However, they remain subject to the influence of tribal

[88] Youth practitioner, male.
[89] Community and youth practitioner, female.

concepts, customs and practices in rural Syria that may impede their (the mechanisms') capacity to provide an alternative form of justice.

Alternative access to justice in rural areas in Syria is a necessity today rather than a choice. While the basic infrastructure is there in customs and traditions, deep and meaningful reflection should take place on finding the way forward for the tangible and feasible implementation of these mechanisms. This must take into consideration the particular needs of young people, revisiting established concepts on crime and justice and encouraging enhanced female and youth participation in heading and moderating these mechanisms.

# 13

# A Retrospective on Rural Legal Service Provision: Lessons Emerging from International Research

KIM ECONOMIDES AND CHARLES WATKINS

## I. Introduction

In this chapter we adopt a retrospective and comparative approach to reviewing and analysing international developments in the provision of rural legal services over the last 30 years or so. Following the *Florence Access to Justice Project*, funded by the Ford Foundation in the late 1970s, which gave initial momentum to the international Access to Justice movement and global comparative studies of civil procedure, the authors worked together with Mark Blacksell on the ESRC-funded *Access to Justice in Rural Britain Project* (AJRBP), based at Exeter University in the 1980s.[1] The Exeter AJRBP project was the first to adopt an explicitly rural focus to legal service provision across the United Kingdom (UK) and included in-depth empirical surveys of rural legal practitioners, para-legal services and members of the public, the results of which were published in a series of working papers, articles and a monograph that summarised key findings.[2] Moreover, the AJRBP also represented one of the very first interdisciplinary collaborations between academic lawyers and human geographers, that laid foundations for subsequent developments in the budding sub-discipline of legal geography.[3] While the relationship

[1] We dedicate this essay to the memory of our dear friend and collaborator, Mark Blacksell. See N Roberts 'Obituary: Professor Mark Blacksell' (2008) 174 *The Geographical Journal* 179. We should also like to offer this as a modest contribution to Exeter law school's centennial celebrations. For an overview of the *Florence Access to Justice Project* and subsequent developments, see K Economides, 'Mauro Cappelletti's legacy: retrospect and prospects' (2016) *Annuario di Diritto Comparato e di Studi Legislativi* 245.

[2] See generally M Blacksell, K Economides and C Watkins, *Justice Outside the City: Access to Legal Services in Rural Britain* (Longman, 1991); K Economides and M Blacksell, 'Access to Justice in Rural Britain: Final Report' (1987) 16(4) *Anglo-American Law Review* 353.

[3] K Economides, M Blacksell and C Watkins, 'The Spatial Analysis of Legal Systems Towards a Geography of Law? (1986) 13(2) *Journal of Law and Society* 161; M Blacksell, C Watkins and

between law and geography has blossomed over the past three decades, particularly in terms of theoretical sophistication explaining law's 'spatial turn', it is fair to say that much of this scholarship has explored the boundaries of legality in terms of abstract spatial metaphor rather than explaining, through established anthropological or cartographical techniques, limitations on how geographically remote citizens physically tread a pathway to, or experience, law and legal institutions.[4]

Our aim here is to track the evolution of international research on legal service provision in rural, regional and remote (RRR) settings, drawing on a selection of studies, both academic and policy-oriented, that update the work of the earlier Florence project.[5] We do not attempt to summarise all previous research but instead reflect on the impact of select studies that illustrate a range of perspectives on the provision of rural legal services within and beyond the UK. These studies draw upon both socio-legal and geographical research methods, but also are not confined to either, and show how rural communities both experience and influence legal services and institutions of justice in ways that contrast with how law behaves in the metropolis. We also note how current UK policy potentially impacts on inclusion and resilience for different kinds of rural communities and policy options that could improve overall access to justice for remote rural, coastal and island communities.

## II. Evolution of Research on Legal Services in Rural Areas

The AJRBP represented one of the first major interdisciplinary collaborations between academic lawyers and geographers, and began by applying established cartographical techniques to the physical distribution of solicitors throughout England and Wales, building on earlier work of Ken Foster who two decades earlier

K Economides, 'Human Geography and Law: A Case of Separate Development in Social Science' (1986) 10(3) *Progress in Human Geography* 371; K Economides, 'Law and Geography: New Frontiers' in PA Thomas (ed), *Legal Frontiers* (Dartmouth, 1996) 180.

[4] See collections on legal geography: N Blomley, D Delaney and R Ford (eds), *The Legal Geographies Reader* (Blackwell, 2001); J Holder and C Harrison (eds), *Law and Geography: Current Legal Issues 2002*, vol 5 (Oxford University Press, 2003)[reviewed by K Economides (2005) 2 *International Journal of Law in Context* 209]; I Braverman et al (eds), *The Expanding Spaces of Law: A Timely Legal Geography* (Stanford University Press, 2014); T O'Donnell, DF Robinson and J Gillespie (eds), *Legal Geography: Perspectives and Methods* (Routledge, 2020). See A Philippopoulos-Mihalopouolos, 'Law's Spatial Turn: Geography, Justice and a Certain Fear of Space' (2010) 7 *Law, Culture and the Humanities* 187; and A Philippopoulos-Mihalopouolos, *Spatial Justice: Body, Lawscape, Atmosphere* (Routledge, 2015). See also Margaret Davies' synoptic overview of the 'geo-legal' literature in *Asking the Law Question*, 4th edn (Lawbook Co, 2017) 436–50 and her discussion of 'pathfinding' in *Law Unlimited: Materialism, Pluralism and Legal Theory* (Routledge, 2017) ch 9.

[5] See especially latest reports in the current *Global Access to Justice Project* (GA2JP) at www.globalaccesstojustice.com.

had gathered data on, but without actually mapping, the location of solicitors.[6] Our research revealed, counter-intuitively, that rural areas in England and Wales were not in fact suffering from a paucity of solicitors and, bearing in mind the density of the rural population, were generally 'rather well served in terms of access to legal services'.[7] However, while legal services may have retained a physical presence in rural areas, when one looked beyond superficial distributions and considered the precise scope and nature of legal work actually covered by solicitors in private practice, a different picture came to light in which gaps in areas of their legal work were exposed, some of which, but by no means all, were being partially covered by para-legal services. In some instances, because of the increasingly specialised and routine nature of legal work in private practice, fully qualified solicitors were not infrequently consulting unqualified non-lawyers about technical, unprofitable and unfamiliar areas of law, such as social welfare law, that fell outside their normal sphere of work. Our analysis of the market for rural legal services focused on factors determining supply and demand for both private professional and para-legal services and generated three key hypotheses to help guide and predict the location, mobilisation and development of legal services in rural areas.[8] This first phase of our research reported detailed empirical findings on supply and demand that gave original and deeper insight into the mind-set and operation of country solicitors,[9] para-legal services[10] and rural communities' stated legal needs.[11] Our approach was to explain the complex networks and interactions between providers and users of legal services by focusing on southwest England, but we also collaborated with research teams in other parts of the UK who produced control studies to ensure our findings were not confined to what happened in Devon and Cornwall.[12] We also looked briefly at the delivery of rural legal services overseas – especially in North America, Australia, New Zealand and parts of Europe – to see what models might be relevant to the UK, but at this time

[6] See Blacksell et al, *Justice Outside the City* (n 2) ch 2; C Watkins, M Blacksell, K Economides, 'The Distribution of Solicitors in England and Wales' (1988) 13 *Transactions of the Institute of British Geographers*, 39; K Foster, 'The location of solicitors' (1973) 36 *MLR* 153.

[7] Blacksell et al, *Justice Outside the City* (n 2) 51. M Blacksell, 'Social Justice and Access to Legal Services: A geographical perspective' (1990) 21(4) *Geoforum* 489.

[8] K Economides, C Watkins and M Blacksell, 'Studying Rural Lawyers: Research strategy and context', AJRBP Working Paper 4 (University of Exeter, 1985) 42–48.

[9] M Blacksell, K Economides and C Watkins, 'Country Solicitors: Their Professional Role in Rural Britain' (1987) 25 *Sociologia Ruralis* 181.

[10] M Blacksell et al, 'Legal Services in Rural Areas: Problems of Access and Local Need' (1988) 12 *Progress in Human Geography* 47.

[11] C Watkins, K Economides and M Blacksell, 'The use of legal services in three remote, rural parishes', AJRBP Working Paper 14 (University of Exeter, 1986); M Blacksell, K Economides and A Dixon, 'Knowledge and opinion of law and legal services in remote rural areas', AJRBP Working Paper 15 (University of Exeter, 1989). See further Blacksell et al, *Justice Outside the City* (n 2) chs 3–6.

[12] M Slatter and M Moseley, 'Access to legal services in rural Norfolk', AJRBP Working Paper 7 (University of Exeter, 1986); P Thomas, 'Access to legal services in rural Dyfed, Wales', AJRBP Working Paper 11 (University of Exeter, 1986); A Paterson and S Bain, 'Access to legal services in rural Scotland', AJRBP Working Paper 13 (University of Exeter, 1986).

there was little experience and few lessons available to draw upon, and despite severe isolation found in many parts of North America and Australia, with hardly any exceptions, delivering legal services to remote or rural communities had yet to be identified as a serious access problem by researchers, government or the legal professions.[13] This was perhaps just one more example of what the pioneering access to justice scholar, Deborah Rhode, called the 'no-problem' problem: marginalised rural communities and their legal needs were, for the most part, off the legal radar prior to, and during, the 1980s.[14]

In the 1990s, following publication of *Justice Outside the City*, a new phase of research began that built upon earlier AJRBP findings. Within the UK, a few doctoral research projects were published that drew upon broader theoretical perspectives and looked more closely at the impact of rural courts, technology and private practice on (para-)legal service provision, especially in rural communities.[15] As we shall explain later, these perspectives were themselves to be taken further with the advent of remote justice, particularly given advances in technology and more flexible working practices that currently are being accelerated by the response to the Covid-19 pandemic. The AJRBP concentrated mainly on the work of solicitors in private practice who had direct contact with clients, and therefore to some extent neglected the work of barristers whose work (with a few exceptions in rural areas) was based in metropolitan higher courts, but Blacksell and Fussell partly remedied this omission by looking specifically at the geographical distribution and work of barristers.[16]

[13] See Blacksell et al, *Justice Outside the City* (n 2) ch 7; C Britt, 'The delivery of public legal services to rural areas: The American experience', AJRBP Working Paper 5 (University of Exeter, 1986). Don Landon's research in the United States (US) was a notable exception, and from the early 1980s his research focused on country lawyers, particularly in Missouri, and how rural communities shaped their professionalism: DD Landon, 'Lawyers and localities: the interaction of community context and professionalism' (1982) 7(2) *American Bar Foundation Research Journal* 459; DD Landon, 'Clients, colleagues and community: the shaping of zealous advocacy in a country law practice' (1985) 10(1) *American Bar Foundation Research Journal* 81; DD Landon, *Country Lawyers: The Impact of Context on Professional Practice* (Praeger, 1990). See also review by J Johnsen, 'Rural Justice: Country Lawyers and Legal Services in the United States and Britain' (1992) 17(3) *American Bar Foundation Research Journal* 415.

[14] But see the brief reference to rural legal needs in Benson, *Report of the Royal Commission on Legal Services*, vol 1 (Cmnd 7648, 1979) 89. D Rhode, 'The "No-Problem" Problem: Feminist Challenges and Cultural Change' (1991) 100(6) *Yale Law Journal* 1731.

[15] See the two ESRC-linked studentships that formed part of AJRBP: F Harris, 'Courts and Dispute Processing in Rural Area' (PhD, University of Exeter, 1994); and A Clark 'Advances in Information Technology and the Growth of Para-Legal Services in Britain' (PhD, University of Exeter, 1994) and associated publications: F Harris, 'The Development of Court Architecture, its effect on Utilization of the Law Courts with Specific Reference to the Court Houses of Truro, Cornwall', AJRBP Working Paper 16 (University of Exeter, 1991); A Clark and K Economides, 'Technics and Praxis: Technological Innovation and Legal Practice in Modern Society' (1990) 4 *Yearbook of Law, Computers & Technology* 16. See also J Marshall, 'A Post-Structuralist Analysis of the Practices and Processes of Lawyering in a Small Town' (PhD, University of Lancaster, 1999); J Marshall, 'Are small-town lawyers positivist about the law?' in M Freeman (ed), *Law and Sociology* (Oxford University Press, 2006) 279.

[16] M Blacksell and C Fussell, 'Barristers and the Growth of Local Justice in England and Wales' (1994) 19(4) *Transactions of the Institute of British Geographers* 482. See also research on rural courts: EK Stott, TJ Fetter and LL Crites, *Rural Courts: The Effect of Space and Distance on the Administration of Justice* (National Center for State Courts, 1977); P Branco, 'The geographies of justice in Portugal: redefining the judiciary's territories' (2019) 15 *International Journal of Law in Context* (2019) 442.

At this time we can also detect signs of a growing interest in various dimensions of rural justice in Wales, which began in the 1990s and continues through to the present day with the work of Daniel Newman of Cardiff University in editing this volume, no doubt prompted by Phil Thomas's pioneering work on access to justice in rural Dyfed.[17] Cardiff Law School also produced valuable postgraduate research examining the legal needs of itinerant groups living in rural areas, such as gypsies and the *Roma*, that were overlooked by the AJRBP and were either invisible to, or effectively excluded from, traditional legal services.[18] The collection of essays edited by Christopher Harding and John Williams (of the Centre for Law in Rural Areas based at Aberystwyth) nominally covered legal services, criminal justice and welfare provision in rural Wales, but most essays were focused on various aspects of criminal justice (such as the work of Crown courts, magistrates, the police and non-statutory support for victims and offenders and community care), all topics overlooked by the AJRBP, which focused on civil justice.[19] A key point to emerge from the Aberystwyth volume was that both legal and welfare policy for rural Wales was largely determined centrally and within the constraints of a metropolitan mind-set that had little comprehension of rural legality or local legal cultures. Work on cultural embeddedness in Wales continued well into the twenty-first century with further studies that examined the extent of the use of the Welsh language in courts, the sustainability of rural legal services as well as attitudes of Welsh rural communities to these services.[20]

But not everyone working on access to justice at this time shared an interest in rural justice. In common with earlier national reports on access to justice prepared for the Florence project, this rural dimension hardly featured at all in the major *Paths to Justice* (P2J) research led by Dame Hazel Genn, supported by the National Centre for Social Research, published on the cusp of the new millennium and which later spawned several other similar 'large-scale' national surveys of legal need.[21] This first study reported survey findings in England and Wales collected during the mid-1990s yet totally ignored the variable of rurality as a key factor determining access to civil justice, although this did feature in passing in a

[17] Thomas (n 12).

[18] PN Wheeler, 'Gypsy Travellers in England and Wales: Access to Justice and Primary Services' (MPhil, Cardiff Law School, University of Wales, 1999); S Campbell, 'Gypsy Travellers in England and Wales: Political and Civic Participation' (MPhil, Cardiff Law School, University of Wales 1999); RC Morris, 'Roamaphobia: The Invisibility of Travelling People in the United Kingdom' (PhD, Cardiff Law School, University of Wales 2003).

[19] C Harding and J Williams (eds), *Legal Provision in the Rural Environment: Legal Services, Criminal Justice and Welfare Provision in Rural Areas* (University of Wales Press, 1994).

[20] CF Huws, 'An Empirical Study of the Use of the Welsh Language in the Courts in the Twenty First Century' (PhD, Aberystwyth, University of Wales, 2005); A Franklin and RG Lee, 'The Embedded Nature of Rural Legal Services: Sustaining Service Provision in Wales' (2007) 34 *Journal of Law and Society* 218; D Newman, 'Attitudes to justice in a rural community' (2016) 36(4) *Legal Studies* 591. See also S Nason, *Justice in Wales* (Senedd Cymru/Welsh Parliament. March 2021) at https://business.senedd.wales/documents/s500007077/Adroddiad%20Cynghorydd%20Arbenigol%20y%20Pwyllgor%20Mai%202020%20Saesneg%20yn%20unig.pdf.

[21] H Genn, *Paths to Justice: What people do and think about going to law* (Hart Publishing, 1999).

parallel Scottish study that noted 'substantial variations in the delivery of advice and assistance in the social welfare field in different parts of rural Scotland' and, in a footnote, the impact of physical distance: 'the greater rurality of Scotland entails that those wanting to consult a CAB [Citizens Advice Bureau] in rural Scotland may have to travel greater distances than their counterparts south of the border'.[22] Moreover, a review of 26 legal need surveys conducted across 15 separate jurisdictions, and within the P2J tradition, acknowledged that 'geography' can influence (legal) advice-seeking ('Proximity to legal services appears to influence mode of access more than the fact of access to advice, with telephone becoming more prominent with distance …') but again did not particularly highlight rurality as a significant factor influencing the demand for legal and advice services, or explore sub-national spatial impacts of the justice system in any great depth, possibly reflecting an urban bias of researchers physically based in the metropolis.[23]

However, outside the UK from around 2010, we begin to see a new, third phase in rural justice research gaining momentum as research teams in Australia, North and South America, and elsewhere start to build on earlier studies to focus explicitly on the peripheral legal needs of rural populations. Many of these studies focus on complex interactions between law, lawyers and local communities, and show how law and legal processes are far from autonomous but rather, as in the case of China, become embedded and absorbed as an integral part of the moral economy in the countryside.[24] These studies not only consider how well the supply of rural legal services meets demand, but also set out implications for policymakers, particularly where gaps in provision may result, and also the underlying determinants of that demand. They also highlight ambivalent impacts of law on rural communities, as well as how the nature and scope of legal professionalism, of both lawyers and para-legals, may be shaped by these same communities.

[22] H Genn and A Paterson, *Paths to Justice Scotland: What people in Scotland do and think about going to law* (Hart Publishing, 2001) 17, 95. This second study referred to research undertaken for the Scottish Legal Aid Board: A Paterson and P Montgomery, *Access to and Demand for Welfare Legal Services in Rural Scotland* (Scottish Legal Aid Board, 1996) but not to the control study prepared for the AJRBP: Paterson and Bain (n 12).

[23] P Pleasence, NJ Balmer and RL Sandefur, *Paths to Justice: A Past, Present and Future Roadmap* (UCL Centre for Empirical Legal Studies/Nuffield Foundation, 2013) 38, 63. The bibliography of this report cites Blacksell et al, *Justice Outside the City* (n 2) and two other studies sensitive to spatial variations in advice-seeking: E Michelson, *Popular Attitudes towards Dispute Processing in Urban and Rural China* (The Foundation for Law, Justice, and Society, 2008); and A Patel, NJ Balmer and P Pleasence, 'The Geography of Advice Seeking' (2008) 39(6) *Geoforum* 2084.

[24] For ethnographic research on rural justice in China, see Michelson (n 23); X Ying, 'Barefoot lawyers and rural conflicts' in Y Hsing and CK Lee (eds), *Reclaiming Chinese Society: The New Social Activism* (Routledge, 2009) ch 4; K Li, 'Relational embeddedness and socially motivated case screening in the practice of law in rural China' (2016) 50(4) *Law & Society Review* 920. See also the award-winning film by Zhang Yimou, *The Story of Qiu Ju* (1992), based on C Yuanbin's short story, *The Wan Family's Lawsuit*, tr A Walling (Chinese Literature, 1992).

## III. Impacts of and on the Justice System in Rural and Remote Areas

In 2009, the Law Council of Australia (LCA) conducted a national survey of lawyers that exposed serious shortages of lawyers serving triple 'R' ('RRR') areas, highlighting problems of lawyer recruitment and retention in these areas.[25] The following year Australia convened its first biennial *National Rural Regional Law and Justice Conference* in Warrnambool, Victoria, and several papers drew upon the AJRBP findings by applying its methodology to explain both the demand for legal services and the work of Bush lawyers.[26] Kim Economides' contribution to this conference also applied insights from the AJRBP with a view to advancing strategy that might better meet rural legal needs, and in 2012, at the next meeting of the *National Rural Regional Law and Justice Conference* in Coffs Harbour, NSW, he delivered a keynote address that sought to challenge dominant assumptions about the way legal theory, education and practice structurally exclude perspectives and interests of legal communities beyond the metropolis.[27] Other Australian scholars followed through to rectify this exclusion, and in 2017 Trish Mundy, Amanda Kennedy and Jennifer Nielsen co-edited a volume, *The Place of Practice*, examining how well – from ethical and efficiency standpoints – lawyering in rural and regional Australia served the legal needs of Aboriginal and other communities, as well as the sustainability of these services, both public and private.[28] This research, which also reported findings from in-depth doctoral studies of private legal practices in country settings, noted the diversity of rural and regional communities and the educational and ethical resources required by rural and regional legal practitioners, who need not only technical legal skills, IT resources and knowledge, but also tools of resilience and wellbeing, in order to survive – if not thrive – in these diverse and challenging environments.[29]

[25] See RRRLaw at http://rrrlaw.com.au/. In March 2021, the LCA launched its *Rural, Regional and Remote (RRR) National Strategic Plan 2021–2023* at the Cooma Court House, NSW.

[26] 'Special Issue: Essays from the First National Rural Regional Law and Justice Conference' (2011) 16(1) *Deakin Law Rev*; see especially S Rice, 'Access to a Lawyer in Rural Australia: Thoughts on the Evidence We Need' ibid 13; K McDougall and R Mortensen, 'Bush Lawyers in New South Wales and Queensland: A Spatial Analysis' ibid 75; and C Hart, 'Sustainable Regional Legal Practice: The Importance of Alliances and the Use of Innovative Technology by Legal Practices in Regional, Rural and Remote Queensland' ibid 225.

[27] K Economides, 'Strategies for meeting rural legal needs: lessons from local, regional and international experience' ibid, 47; K Economides, 'Core-periphery tensions in legal theory and practice. Can law and lawyers resist urban imperialism?' (2012) 1(2) *International Journal of Rural Law and Policy* 1.

[28] T Munday, A Kennedy and J Nielsen (eds), *The Place of Practice: Lawyering in Rural and Regional Australia* (Federation Press, 2017).

[29] See doctoral research on private legal practice in RRR areas by C Hart, 'The Prevalence and Nature of Sustainable Regional, Rural and Remote Legal Practice' (PhD, University of Southern Queensland 2014); H McGowan, 'Adapt, Improvise and Overcome: Engaging with Conflicts of Interest in the Bush' (PhD, ANU College of Law, 2018); C Hart, *The Seven Elements of Successful Country Law Firms* (Federation Press, 2018).

As Lisa Pruitt and Kelly Beskin note, about a decade ago US researchers, expanding on insights from Don Landon's earlier studies in rural Missouri, started to examine not only the specific nature of rural lawyers' work but also its overall scope, highlighting limitations of male dominance and the problem of rural access by exposing so-called 'legal deserts' when assessing the range of difficulties affecting the provision of access to justice in rural America from the point of view of both lawyers and their clients.[30] The challenge is not simply to map these deserts but rather to develop and coordinate national policies to effectively halt, if not reverse, the drought in legal service provision, perhaps along the lines of the Law Council of Australia's RRR National Strategic Plan.[31]

The US has also initiated schemes that seek to attract and encourage new young lawyers into rural areas, the first of which was *Project Rural Practice* established in South Dakota in 2013. This scheme allowed up to 16 law graduates to receive annual payments for five years as long as they opened a full-time office in a rural county with a population of less than 10,000 for the period concerned.[32] The following year Lisa Pruitt and Bradley Showman explored a range of legal access issues faced by rural Americans.[33] Quoting from *Access across America: First Report of the Civil Justice Mapping Project* (2011),[34] which noted that 'geography is destiny: the services available to people from eligible populations who face civil justice problems are determined not by what their problems are or the kinds of services they may need, but rather by where they happen to live', they argue that rural Americans are poorly provided with lawyers and courts. They identify specific problems facing rural lawyers, including the lack of networking and career opportunities and relatively low levels of pay. They also argue that rural residents may be more likely than those in cities to have an 'ethic of law avoidance'. More practically, of course, rural residents may well have difficulty reaching lawyers' offices and courts because of transport problems. In addition, rural clients are less likely than urban ones to benefit from free pro bono legal advice because urban lawyers provide more pro bono hours per capita than rural lawyers. This is not to say that *existing* rural clients may not be provided with reduced fee advice by a local

[30] See LR Pruitt and KV Beskin, ch 2 in this volume; Landon (n 13); see also LR Pruitt, 'Gender, Geography, and Rural Justice' (2008) 23 *Berkeley Journal of Gender, Law & Justice* 338; LR Pruitt et al, 'Legal Deserts: A Multi-State Perspective on Rural Access to Justice' (2018) 13 *Harvard Law & Policy Review* 15.

[31] LCA (n 25). See also *Recruitment and Retention of Legal Practitioners to Rural, Regional and Remote Areas Strategy: Discussion Paper* (Canberra, LCA Recruitment and Retention Working Group Working Draft, 2009) ch 2, recommending various government, profession and employer-based initiatives such as bonuses, tax breaks, subsidised housing and scholarships/placements to stimulate recruitment (and retention) of lawyers in RRR areas, at www.lawcouncil.asn.au/publicassets/c5ed33af-de39-e711-93fb-005056be13b5/Recruitment%20and%20Retention%20of%20Legal%20Practitioners%20ro%20Rural,%20Regional%20and%20Remote%20Areas%20Strategy%20Discussion%20Paper.pdf.

[32] D Gilbertson 'Reflections on the rural practice of law in South Dakota: past, present and future' (2014) 59(3) *South Dakota Law Review* 433.

[33] LR Pruitt and BE Showman, 'Law stretched thin: access to justice in rural America' (2014) 59(3) *South Dakota Law Review* 466.

[34] RL Sandefur and A Smyth, *Access across America: First Report of the Civil Justice Infrastructure Mapping Project* (American Bar Foundation, 2011) v at https://ssrn.com/abstract=1962790.

lawyer, especially if the lawyer 'has a personal sense of duty and connection' to the local community. However, potential new pro bono legal clients, especially if controversial legal issues are involved, may find rural lawyers reluctant to provide advice.[35] More recent work by Lisa Pruitt and her team of researchers examined the landscape of rural access to justice across six States: California, Georgia, North-eastern Minnesota, Northern Wisconsin, Maine and South Dakota. They mapped rural lawyers and examined the institutional framework, community needs and shortfalls in provision. They also considered policy responses and the role of legal education in the different States. Overall, their findings are bleak, and they argue that '[r]ural America faces an increasingly dire access to justice crisis, which serves to exacerbate the already disproportionate share of social problems afflicting rural areas'.[36]

Similarly, researchers elsewhere in both North and South America have begun to look more closely at access issues, and beyond rural and regional contexts, to consider obstacles to justice experienced by those residing at the very periphery of society (particularly those confronting remote, as well as Indigenous, communities), with a view to overcoming barriers of physical distance and exploring novel methods of proactive delivery that include various forms of itinerant justice.[37] Global developments with itinerant courts, community legal clinics, technology and increasing recognition of First Law – especially in Australia, Brazil and Canada – have been analysed within the context of a new 'counter-wave' of the access to justice movement.[38] This latest 'counter-wave' seeks to avoid imposing solutions on remote and Indigenous communities through schemes often conceived in cities by instead encouraging those delivering legal services to be far more inclusive of diverse perceptions of what constitutes a just outcome, for example by establishing new channels of communication that allow for dialogue and consensual agreement regarding the objectives and priorities of justice policy.[39]

[35] Pruitt and Showman (n 33) 519.

[36] Pruitt et al, 'Legal Deserts' (n 30) 16.

[37] J Baxter and A Yoon, 'No Lawyer for a Hundred Miles – Mapping the New Geography of Access of Justice in Canada' (2014) 52 *Osgoode Hall Law Journal* 9; N Aylwin and L Moore, *Rural and remote access to justice. A literature review* (Canadian Forum on Civil Justice/Rural and Remote Access to Justice Boldness Project, 2015); RS Moreira, 'Do acesso à justiça para a cidadania à construção da cidadania para a justiça: decodificando o potencial da justiça itinerante' ['From access to justice for citizenship to the construction of citizenship for justice: decoding the potential of itinerant justice'] (PhD, Universidade Federal Fluminense, Rio de Janeiro, 2017); LS Ferraz (ed), *Repensando o Acesso à Justiça: Estudos Internacionais* [*Rethinking Access to Justice: International Studies*] (Evocati, 2016); CT Gaulia, *A experiência da Justiça Itinerante: o espaço de encontro da magistratura com a população brasileira* [*The itinerant justice experience: where the judiciary meets the Brazilian population*] (Mauad, 2020); K Economides, 'Itinerant Justice and Proactive Legal Services: Origins, Achievements and Future Directions' (2020) 18(3) *Direito em Movimento* 176.

[38] K Economides, A Timoshanko and LS Ferraz, 'Justice at the Edge: Hearing the Sound of Silence' (2020) 41(1) *Adelaide Law Rev* 39, 51–68 (see also the accompanying explanatory video at https://youtu.be/MwVLN8dxICM). For a discussion of this latest wave, see VAB da Silva (ed), *Access to Justice in the Americas* (Justice Forum Project, 2021) 16–21 at doi.org/10.53080/forjus-ajam.

[39] See F Allison and C Cunneen, 'The Role of Indigenous Justice Agreements in Improving Legal and Social Outcomes for Indigenous People' (2010) 32 *Sydney Law Review* 645 and ch 5 of this volume; Economides (n 37) 189–90.

## IV. Structural Determinants of Future Rural Justice Policy

Most previous research examining and explaining gaps in legal service provision has focused on the supply side of the equation: the provision of high quality, face-to-face legal advice to clients by lawyers in their offices within small country towns. This is the way that legal advice has been dispensed for generations. There has been considerable debate over several decades concerning the potential impact of the digital revolution and Internet on the legal profession and the provision of legal advice, but until very recently there had been little change in the way that advice was provided.[40] The impact of Covid-19 has brought about changes in the provision of many services in rural areas, including shopping for food and household goods, virtual religious services and virtual viewing of houses for sale. In terms of access to justice, court hearings, the making of wills and the signing of legal documents have all, to some extent, become virtual.[41] But we do not yet know the extent to which virtual meetings with lawyers, as with doctors, are likely to remain commonplace. Moreover, the problems caused by lack of access to broadband – the so-called 'digital divide' – remain significant in many rural areas. In addition, lack of ownership of computers and tablets, or familiarity with their use, remains a significant issue for many people in need of legal advice. In this section we raise questions about how we may need to prepare for less visible changes in the underlying structure of society, particularly in a post-Covid world and post-Brexit Britain, and how this new environment in turn presents novel challenges, and research agendas, particularly for justice policy serving rural and remote areas.

It is has long been noted that changes in the commitment to the welfare state impact directly on access to justice, and this will be even more so in an age of austerity (as considered in Jess Mant's contribution to this book).[42] Assumptions underpinning the post-war Beveridge reforms and access to welfare no longer apply in the UK, if ever they applied in the free-market US, and yet Covid-19 has compelled even the most right-wing governments to introduce wage subsidies and social(ist?) investment in infrastructure, affordable housing and social care – even if only temporarily – in order to keep the economy afloat while global economic activity shrinks. A recent paper by Roxanna Dehaghani and Daniel Newman has

[40] R Susskind, *The Future of Law: Facing the Challenges of Information Technology* (Oxford University Press, 1996); R Susskind, *Tomorrow's Lawyers: An Introduction to your Future* (Oxford University Press, 2013). See also, M Hagan, 'The User Experience of the Internet as a Legal Help Service: Defining standards for the next generation of user-friendly online legal services' (2016) 20(2) *Virginia Journal of Law and Technology* 394.

[41] D Nicholson and E Fisher-Frank, 'Legal Advice in the Covid-19 Lockdown: Making Do or Brave New World?' in C Ferstman and A Fagan (eds), *Covid-19, Law and Human Rights: Essex Dialogues* (University of Essex, 2020) 229.

[42] M Cappelletti (ed), *Access to Justice and the Welfare State* (Sijthoff, 1981); Economides (n 1) 249–50; and J Mant, ch 9 of this volume.

examined the impact of cuts in public funding in England and Wales, 'in both overall legal aid spending and the fees paid to lawyers', on the criminal defence profession.[43] In addition to the reduction of funding of legal aid, the Law Society of England and Wales noted in 2019 that the average age of criminal duty solicitors is rising, and that this is particularly true in rural areas.[44] The report noted that rural areas were likely to be particularly affected by the low numbers of criminal defence lawyers. For example, in parts of west and mid-Wales, and some rural English counties such as Worcestershire, Cornwall and Dorset, over 60 per cent of duty solicitors were aged over 50, and there were fewer firms of solicitors and greater travel distances. In mid-Wales there were only 11 criminal defence lawyers of whom 64 per cent were over 50 and only one was aged under 35. Interestingly, although the legal system in Wales remains part of the single jurisdiction of England and Wales, there has been considerable debate about the implications of this position, especially relating to differences in political culture between the two countries. Moreover, the authors argue that greater levels of poverty and unemployment in Wales, the widespread importance of the Welsh language and very poor transport links across the country provide a very different context for the provision of legal services. They interviewed 20 lawyers and legal representatives from across rural and urban South Wales and aimed 'to investigate the co-constitutive relationships between people, place, and the law'. They found that there was a 39 per cent decline in criminal legal aid firms, from 146 in 2010/11 to 89 in 2018/19, and in offices of 32 per cent from 186 to 126. One of their respondents noted that in the small town of Abergavenny there were around 10 firms of solicitors when they first started practising, and that this had fallen to three firms. The study found that as older lawyers in rural areas and small country towns retired, they were unlikely to be replaced, as 'there was a lack of will for younger lawyers to take on relatively low paying criminal practices'. Established criminal lawyers found it difficult to recommend criminal legal aid as a career as the pay was so low; some felt that consequently the role would only attract less capable solicitors. They conclude that there has been a considerable decline in the morale of criminal legal aid practitioners in south and west Wales, and a danger that this will lead to the loss of criminal legal aid provision and the creation of 'justice deserts'.

Other fundamental changes in UK policy, most notably Brexit, will have a major impact on the local economy and, indirectly, on future demand for rural legal services, particularly in the devolved nations and Cornwall. In 2007, the Legal Services Commission noted that in Cornwall not only rural but also coastal communities were suffering from deprivation, which became more apparent during the winter months when tourism declined.[45] Remote island communities, whether

[43] R Dehaghani and D Newman, 'The crisis in legally aided criminal defence in Wales: bringing Wales into discussions on England and Wales' (2020) 41(2) *Legal Studies* 234.

[44] Law Society, *Criminal Duty Solicitors: A Looming Crisis* (Law Society, 2019).

[45] Legal Services Commission Conference Report 'Legal Advice – The Way Ahead for Rural and Coastal Communities' (Eden Project, Bodelva, Cornwall, March 2007).

in the Shetlands, Outer Hebrides or Pacific islands, also generate particular legal needs.[46] Brexit, which has now removed EU subsidies, is at the same time changing the behaviour of tourism, as indeed has Covid-19, and therefore areas that once experienced under-investment from one source may possibly be compensated by investment from another. Similarly, developments in IT and remote working are likely, especially post-Covid, to encourage population dispersal from urban to rural and remote areas. A key point to remember is that there are many different types of rural area, and these will be affected very differently by the medium- and long-term implications of Brexit and Covid-19. Martin Phillips' valuable research on changing class complexions in the British countryside, published in 2007, demonstrated the very high proportion of what he terms the petit bourgeoisie, including small-scale family farmers, builders, self-employed tradesmen, etc in rural areas such as Devon and Cornwall, mid-Wales, Herefordshire and Shropshire, and northern upland Britain compared to other rural areas. In contrast, higher-grade professionals were very well represented in attractive rural areas within 60 to 70 miles of London and major cities.[47] Additional research by Philip Lowe and Neil Ward identified seven distinctly different types of rural areas, including 'Deep Rural' areas with sparsely populated farming communities, 'Retirement Retreat' areas with large populations of retired people, and 'Dynamic Rural' areas with a large number of professional and knowledge workers.[48] In 2015, a study of commuting emphasised that rural residents 'depend on urban labour markets for employment, specialized services and cultural activities'; in addition, the benefits of living in the countryside were 'sufficiently attractive to many professionals and managers to justify relatively long commutes'.[49] There is no doubt, however, that rural deprivation, including access to legal services, remains a major concern. A recent study by Jon May and co-researchers emphasises that 'new geographies of austerity are overwriting and compounding problems of rural poverty in the UK'.[50] They demonstrate how rural poverty and deprivation are often disguised by the almost overwhelming appearance of prosperity and affluence in many small villages and market towns. Other valuable research has demonstrated the impact of the 'digital divide' in rural Britain, and the continuing, critical importance of access to transport.[51] All this evidence points to an uncertain, diverse

[46] See S Najafi et al, *Between State and Nonstate Systems: Access to Justice in Rural Solomon Islands* (Reach Alliance, 2021).

[47] M Phillips, 'Changing class complexions on and in the British countryside' (2007) 23 *Journal of Rural Studies* 283. A phenomenon also noted in our earlier study of the distribution of solicitors in England and Wales: Watkins et al (n 6) 52–53.

[48] P Lowe and N Ward, 'England's Rural Futures: A Socio-Geographical Approach to Scenarios Analysis' (2009) 43 *Regional Studies* 1319.

[49] DL Brown et al, 'The Migration-commuting nexus in rural England. A longitudinal analysis' (2015) 41 *Journal of Rural Studies* 127.

[50] J May et al, 'Still bleeding: The variegated geographies of austerity and food banking in rural England and Wales' (2020) 79 *Journal of Rural Studies* 409.

[51] L Philip et al, 'The digital divide: Patterns, policy and scenarios for connecting the "final few" in rural communities across Great Britain' (2017) 54 *Journal of Rural Studies* 386; N Black, K Scott and M Shucksmith, 'Social inequalities in rural England: Impacts on young people post-2008' (2019) 68 *Journal of Rural Studies* 264.

and challenging future for rural legal services. Rural deprivation exists side by side with wealthy tourist hot spots. The subtle, complex and often tense interactions between wealthy second homeowners, who often let their cottages to other wealthy holidaymakers, and former residents who still live nearby, was very effectively portrayed in the 2019 British film *Bait*, written and directed by Mark Jenkin, set in a Cornish fishing village. The very recent upsurge in home working and the consequent desire for larger houses and gardens means that there could well be an increased demand for conveyancing work by rural solicitors. Criminal legal aid provision may indeed be bleak, but this needs to be set in the context of changes in rural crime.

## V. Conclusion: Future Priorities for Policy on Rural Justice

If any one lesson emerges from previous research on rural justice over the past three decades it is that no single approach guarantees success, and what works in urban settings may not be transferable to all rural, regional or remote communities where social relationships, networks and legal needs may fundamentally differ. These communities may nurture more cooperative styles of legal practice that adhere to distinctive cultural understandings of professional responsibility unfamiliar, if not totally unknown, to more competitive urban-based lawyers.[52] By way of conclusion, we focus not so much on lawyers' future behaviour but on policy initiatives and strategies that governmental agencies and professional bodies could take across three areas that should broaden public awareness of law through extending the reach of proactive legal service delivery: remote courts, digital inclusion and rural-proofing.

We have already referenced instances where rural courts and itinerant justice reach out to disputants in diverse rural and remote communities, but remote courts, based almost anywhere, only have the capacity to resolve disputes between parties and decision-makers that are physically separated so long as there is Internet or telephone coverage to bring them together.[53] Technological solutions, apart from raising concerns about the privacy and security of information, suffer from a number of drawbacks, most notably when it comes to sustained contact with nomadic traveller communities, the homeless and those socially or spatially

[52] Regional Legal Practitioners Workshop (Toowoomba, University of Southern Queensland, October 2009). See also R Mortensen, 'The Moralities of Australian Bush Lawyers' in Mundy et al (n 28) ch 2; and H McGowan and R Coverdale, 'Access to Justice in Rural and Regional Communities' in Mundy et al (n 28) ch 7; Hart (n 26).

[53] See Harris (n 15); research on rural courts (n 16) and itinerant justice (n 37). On remote justice, see R Susskind, *Online Courts and the Future of Justice* (Oxford University Press, 2019) and examples drawn from all over the globe at https://remotecourts.org. See also M Rossner, 'Remote rituals in virtual courts' (2021) 48(3) *Journal of Law and Society* 334.

excluded at or beyond the margins of society.[54] These groups and communities, even if within the reach of broadband, often lack access to mobile phones or tablets and therefore remain effectively excluded from the justice system.

To overcome this barrier, bodies such as *Talk-Meet-Resolve*, an independent New Zealand dispute resolution agency that provides conciliation services for injured persons wishing to resolve disputes arising from the Accident Compensation Scheme (ACC), has developed digital inclusion strategies that enable disputants to engage in remote conciliation by uploading documents to iPads that have been sent by courier to remote locations, and then removing documents and locking the iPads before they are picked up by courier for return.[55] This cost-effective service preserves both privacy and security of information, and has produced remarkably high levels of consumer satisfaction and trust and with no loss of iPads.[56]

These types of administrative and technological challenges must be understood within very contrasting types of rural area. In some southern European countries, most notably in Spain, Italy and Greece, rural areas continue to suffer from very high rates of depopulation, to the extent that many rural settlements have become largely abandoned creating so-called 'ghost towns'.[57] This has prompted various initiatives designed to breathe life back into these abandoned communities through introducing ecotourism and the provision of financial incentives, such as buying a house in Italy for as little as €1.[58] Other areas, with good transport links and Internet connections, are likely to become more prosperous. There are many challenges for central and local government in facilitating the provision of legal services in these rapidly changing and dramatically diverse types of rural area.

Another approach is for central government to provide policymakers with guidance on 'rural-proofing', with the aim of ensuring that rural communities enjoy a higher quality of life, access to social and economic opportunities, and can realise their full potential as do their urban counterparts.[59] So far as legal

[54] See studies mentioned at n 18 and n 37 above.

[55] See further Talk-Meet-Resolve at https://talkmeetresolve.co.nz; and radio interview with barrister and researcher Warren Forster at www.rnz.co.nz/national/programmes/ninetonoon/audio/2018788193/a-new-approach-to-resolving-acc-claims.

[56] See also recent reports from Talk-Meet-Resolve, *Overcoming Digital Exclusion in Aotearoa New Zealand: Using a Digital Inclusion Strategy* (Wellington, 2020), which also discuss standards for dispute resolution; W Forster, T Barraclough and C Barnes, *Making Aotearoa New Zealand Accessible: A Design for Effective Accessibility Legislation* (New Zealand Law Foundation, 2021) chs 5–6.

[57] V Llorent-Bedmar, VC Cobano-Delgado Palma and M Navarro-Granados, 'The rural exodus of young people from empty Spain. Socio-educational aspects' (2021) 82 *Journal of Rural Studies* 303; M May, 'Community-led approaches and interventions for abandoned towns in southern Italy' (2016) 2(1) *Ecocycles* 18; K Ntassiou, 'Studying abandoned settlements' renaissance in the context of rural geography: perspectives for Prespes, Greece' (2021) *European Planning Studies*, doi:10.1080/09654313.2021.1957085.

[58] See, eg, Case A 1 Euro at https://casea1euro.it.

[59] The New Zealand Government has invested in this kind of approach: Ministry for Primary Industries, *Rural proofing: guidance for policymakers* at www.mpi.govt.nz/legal/rural-proofing-guidance-for-policymakers/.

services are concerned, it is essential that legal policymakers, in local and central government as well as the professions, remain responsive to meeting local needs and both national and international standards. Our own research, and that of others, suggests this is best done through independent regional legal services committees (that should include lay and local, and wherever feasible, Indigenous representation) able to apply research to make informed judgements that balance ever-changing local and national expectations. The approach therefore needs to be both 'top-down' and 'bottom-up', and future research will need to identify not only gaps in provision, but also how best to fill these gaps considering local conditions and available resources.

# 14

# Access to Rural Justice: Domestic Violence in Rural America

ZIWEI QI AND CHRISTY CRAIG

Domestic violence is an inherently gendered phenomenon that has profound effects on victims. Domestic violence in American rural communities is prevalent, and research continually indicates it is a significant public-health problem in rural areas.[1] Women living in rural areas experience higher rates of domestic violence and greater frequency and severity of physical abuse than their urban counterparts.[2] Due to culturally constructed gender roles, social and familial networks, the stigma of abuse, poverty, and a lack of access to housing and services, among many other challenges, victims in rural and isolated areas face unique and complex obstacles when experiencing gender-based family violence.[3] Escaping abuse is perilous, leaving many survivors unable to disengage from abusive households, or forced to return to their abusers.[4] Therefore, it is crucial to provide adequate access to a full spectrum of resources and services for survivors. This chapter focuses on the experiences of rural victimhood, addresses some of the causes and outcomes of gender-based family violence in rural communities, and specifically examines the law, criminal justice system and legal response to domestic violence in rural areas in order to more fully understand these impacts on rural victims.

[1] M Black et al, 'National intimate partner and sexual violence survey: 2010 summary report' (The National Center for Injury Prevention and Control of the Centers for Disease Control and Prevention, 2011).

[2] C Peek-Asa et al, 'Rural Disparity in Domestic Violence Prevalence and Access to Resources' (2011) 20(11) *Journal of Women's Health* 1743.

[3] In a related vein, Gordon and Brown's contribution (ch 8 of this volume) explores the problems that older people can experience as victims of crime in rural areas.

[4] AZ Chavis and MS Hill, 'Integrating multiple intersecting identities: A multicultural conceptualization of the power and control wheel' (2008) 32(1) *Women & Therapy* 121; KO DuBois, 'Rural isolation, small towns, and the risk of intimate partner violence' (2020) 37 *Journal of Interpersonal Violence* at doi.org/10.1177/0886260520943721; J Little, 'Understanding domestic violence in rural spaces: a research agenda' (2017) 41(4) *Progress in Human Geography* 472; CM Rennison, WS DeKeseredy and M Dragiewicz, 'Intimate relationship status variations in violence against women: Urban, suburban, and rural differences' (2013) 19(11) *Violence against Women* 1312.

Domestic violence is a pattern of coercive, controlling behaviour that can include physical, emotional/psychological, sexual and/or financial abuse that occurs in a close relationship.[5] Domestic violence is a significant public-health epidemic in need of more attention from the field of research and public services both nationally and globally.[6] Domestic violence in rural areas is not limited to physical abuse, forced isolation and financial abuse: a vast majority of abused women experience emotional abuse while in abusive relationships, and more than 90 per cent experience both sexual and physical abuse.[7] In light of men's verbal and physical abuse, women in abusive relationships report fear of retaliation as a strong barrier to leaving.[8] Indeed, this concern has been realised for women who have had restraining orders against their former partners, yet still experienced ex-partners' acting upon threats of harm even in the face of protective orders.[9] Domestic violence is a form of 'intimate terrorism' that impacts every element of victims' lives, and which deserves increased recognition and resources at both the interpersonal and community level.[10] It is crucial to recognise the prevalence and significance of domestic violence – not only to society as a whole but also in the personal experiences of the survivors.

According to the National Coalition Against Domestic Violence, an average of 20 people experience intimate partner violence per minute in the United States, which equates to more than 10 million victims annually.[11] One in four women and one in nine men experience severe physical violence from abusive partners with wide-ranging impacts, such as injury, fearfulness, post-traumatic stress disorder and loss of financial resources.[12] Although both men and women are victims, an estimated 85 per cent of American domestic violence victims are female.[13]

[5] Centers for Disease Control and Prevention, and Centres for Disease Control and Prevention, 'Intimate partner violence: Definitions' *Injury Centre: Violence Prevention* (2010); Little (n 4); World Health Organisation. *Understanding and addressing violence against women: Intimate partner violence*, WHO/RHR/12.36 (World Health Organisation, 2012).

[6] E Salinsky, 'Domestic Violence: A Public Health Priority' *Grantmakers in Health* (July, 2017) at www.gih.org/publication/domestic-violence-a-public-health-priority/.

[7] KM Anderson, LM Renner and TS Bloom. 'Rural women's strategic responses to intimate partner violence' (2014) 35(4) *Health Care for Women International* 423; K Bosch and MB Bergen, 'The influence of supportive and nonsupportive persons in helping rural women in abusive partner relationships become free from abuse' (2006) 21(5) *Journal of Family Violence* 311; K Roush and A Kurth, The lived experience of intimate partner violence in the rural setting' (2016) 45(3) *Nursing: Journal of Obstetric, Gynecologic, and Neonatal* 308; Peek-Asa et al (n 2).

[8] PB Teaster, KA Roberto and TA Dugar, 'Intimate partner violence of rural ageing women' (2006) 55(5) *Family Relations* 636.

[9] Roush and Kurth (n 7).

[10] MP Johnson, *A Typology of Domestic Violence: Intimate terrorism, violent resistance, and situational couple violence* (Upne, 2010); R Pain, 'Everyday terrorism: Connecting domestic violence and global terrorism' (2014) 38(4) *Progress in Human Geography* 531.

[11] *Domestic violence* (National Coalition Against Domestic Violence, 2020) at https://assets.speakcdn.com/assets/2497/domestic_violence-2020080709350855.pdf?1596811079991.

[12] JL Truman and RE Morgan, *Nonfatal domestic violence* (US Department of Justice, Bureau of Justice Statistics, 2014).

[13] L Garcia, C Soria and EL Hurwitz, 'Homicides and intimate partner violence: A literature review' (2007) 8(4) *Trauma, violence, & abuse* 370.

Women who are physically abused by an intimate partner experience higher rates of assaults and suffer more injuries than their male counterparts.[14] Therefore, domestic violence should be considered, predominantly, a crime against women, and prevention strategies and victim services should reflect gender-specific features of victimisation.

## I. Impacts of Domestic Violence: Rural Realities

Rural victims of gender-based family violence face complex issues that influence their experiences and outcomes of victimisation. Research on domestic violence has historically focused on urban settings; it was not until recently that published studies began to focus heavily on the prevalence of victimisation in rural areas.[15] For the purpose of this chapter, 'rural' is defined as a location with fewer than 50,000 people that is not an urbanised area.[16] Due to geographical isolation, victims in rural areas are disproportionately underrepresented in domestic violence literature.[17] Overall, women in rural and isolated areas report a higher rate of victimisation of domestic violence compared to women in urban areas, and experience significantly higher occurrences of physical abuse.[18] It is estimated that at least 20–28 per cent of rural women are currently victims of domestic violence, with 50 per cent of rural women experiencing some type of violence in their households in their lifetime.[19] Compared to those in urban areas, women in rural communities have fewer adequate intervention resources.[20] Rural women face unique obstacles when leaving abusive relationships because of geographical isolation, limited resources and services, lack of employment opportunities, lack of housing, insufficient transportation, psychological trauma and cultural tolerance towards violence in intimate partner relationships.[21]

Examining traditional gender ideologies in the rural context, and specifically the role of masculinity, is also important in conceptualising rural domestic violence. Domestic violence, like a great deal of gendered crime, is inherently

[14] SL Miller, *Victims as Offenders* (Rutgers University Press, 2005).

[15] K Beyer, A Baber Wallis and LK Hamberger, 'Neighbourhood environment and intimate partner violence: A systematic review' (2015) 16(1) *Trauma, Violence, & Abuse* 16; WS DeKeseredy et al, 'Intimate violence against women in rural communities' in J Donnermeyer (ed), *The Routledge International Handbook of Rural Criminology* (Routledge, 2016) 171.

[16] US Health Resources & Services Administration, *Defining Rural Population* (5 October 2021) at www.hrsa.gov/rural-health/about-us/definition/index.html.

[17] WS DeKeseredy, *Woman Abuse in Rural Places* (Routledge, 2021).

[18] Peek-Asa et al (n 2).

[19] A Clifford, 'Intimate partner violence in rural women' (2003) 51(4) *Kentucky Nurse* 9.

[20] Peek-Asa et al (n 2).

[21] BJ Eastman et al, 'Exploring the perceptions of domestic violence service providers in rural localities' (2007) 13(7) *Violence against Women* 700; SF Grossman et al, 'Rural versus urban victims of violence: The interplay of race and region' (2005) 20(2) *Journal of Family Violence* 71; Roush and Kurth (n 7).

linked to patriarchal social structures in which men have more power than women.[22] Violence cannot be separated from structures of gendered power relationships; the role of hegemonic masculinity and cultural ideologies relating to manhood cannot be ignored when examining domestic violence, as research indicates that rural masculinity is often constructed with particularly rigid expectations about strength, power and control, and closely linked to conservative political ideology.[23] Research indicates that violence is more likely to occur when traditional/hegemonic patriarchal ideals are challenged, or in situations where men feel their masculinity is challenged.[24] Many rural women experience sexual abuse during and after ending abusive relationships, and women cite male peer support as being a large part of what equipped and promoted their former partners' abusive tendencies, especially as related to physical and sexual violence and the enforcement of gendered roles.[25] After a relationship ends, or a partner attempts to end an abusive relationship, men in rural areas may be influenced by a perceived loss of social status with other men to use abusive, controlling behaviours against their female partners.[26] About four out of five male ex-partners who committed post-separation sexual assault held rigid gender-role beliefs rooted in misogynistic attitudes toward women, and most or all of the male friend peer groups that women's ex-partners socialised with vocally shared these beliefs.[27] Gun ownership rates are higher in rural areas than in urban areas, and abusive men control and intimidate women with threats of gun violence, creating a significant factor for abuse and a barrier to escape.[28] Websdale's (1998) seminal work on women battering in rural areas depicted the importance of patriarchal family values in rural communities, wherein men are considered the head of the household and maintain power over their wives and children; in this context, victims

[22] R Dobash, R Emerson and RP Dobash, 'When Women are Murdered' in F Brookemen, ER Mcguire and M Mcguire (ed), *The Handbook of Homicide* (Wiley-Blackwell, 2017) 131; L Hamberger et al, 'Coercive control in intimate partner violence' (2017) 37 *Aggression and Violent Behavior* 1.

[23] K Carrington and J Scott. 'Masculinity, rurality and violence' (2008) 48(5) *The British Journal of Criminology* 641; L Mshweshwe, 'Understanding domestic violence: masculinity, culture, traditions' (2020) 6(10) *Heliyon* e05334.

[24] S Hautzinger, 'Researching men's violence: personal reflections on ethnographic data' (2003) 6(1) *Men and Masculinities* 93; JW Messerschmidt and S Tomsen. 'Masculinities and Crime' in WS Dekeseredy and M Dragiewicz (eds), *Routledge Handbook of Critical Criminology* (Routledge, 2018) 83; R Jewkes and R Morrell, 'Hegemonic masculinity, violence, and gender equality: Using latent class analysis to investigate the origins and correlates of differences between men' (2018) 21(4) *Men and Masculinities* 547.

[25] AK Hall-Sanchez, 'Male peer support, hunting, and separation/divorce sexual assault in rural Ohio' (2014) 22(4) *Critical Criminology* 495.

[26] W DeKeseredy et al, 'Thinking critically about rural gender relations: Toward a rural masculinity crisis/male peer support model of separation/divorce sexual assault' (2007) 15(4) *Critical Criminology* 295.

[27] WS DeKeseredy et al, 'Separation/divorce sexual assault: The contribution of male support' (2006) 1(3) *Feminist Criminology* 228.

[28] JB Averill, AO Padilla and PT Clements. 'Frightened in isolation: Unique considerations for research of sexual assault and interpersonal violence in rural areas' (2007) 3(1) *Journal of Forensic Nursing* 42; Teaster, Roberto and Dugar (n 8).

hesitated to report their abuse to family, friends or officials for fear of challenging this patriarchal family structure.[29] DeKeserdy's (2021) research demonstrates that 'good ol'boy' networks and male peer support systems socially legitimise violence against women. These networks permeate all types of social arenas in rural communities, including families, churches and law enforcement.[30] Overall, research indicates that abusive men rely on cultural constructions and expectations about masculinity in framing, rationalising and perpetuating abusive behaviour.[31] Rural communities are generally socially cohesive, pride themselves on sharing consensus in values and have little tolerance for behaviours perceived as detrimental to traditional values.[32] Rural women are likely to share these beliefs and values, and consequently may feel reluctant to disclose domestic violence, to seek help or to leave an abusive relationship.

## II. Physical and Social Isolation in Rural Communities

While experiences of rurality differ, victims of domestic violence in rural locales experience both physical and social isolation that restricts access to social services. Discrepancies in affordable care and health services between rural and urban communities impact women seeking services to address domestic violence.[33] Rural and remote areas often have less available services and lower quality, quantity and funding for those services.[34] Healthcare services are often ill-equipped or non-existent in rural areas, with a shortage of resources and staff members.[35] Rural healthcare facilities regularly lack comprehensive training to respond to domestic violence, and rural hospitals are less likely to use standardised screening measures or provide regular clinician training.[36] Significantly fewer rural hospitals staff an onsite full-time victim advocate compared to urban facilities.[37]

[29] N Websdale, *Rural Women Battering and the Justice System: An ethnography*, vol 6 (Sage, 1998).

[30] DeKeseredy (n 17); H Jakobsen, 'Community Law Enforcement in Rural Tanzania' in Donnermeyer (ed) (n 15) 409.

[31] KL Anderson and D Umberson, 'Gendering violence: Masculinity and power in men's accounts of domestic violence' (2001) 15(3) *Gender & Society* 358.

[32] J Hornosty and D Doherty, 'Responding to wife abuse in farm and rural communities: Searching for solutions that work' in R Blake and A Nurse (eds), *The Trajectories of Rural Life: New perspectives on rural Canada* (Saskatchewan Institute of Public Policy, 2003) 37.

[33] EK Choo et al, 'Rural-urban disparities in emergency department intimate partner violence resources' (2011) 12(2) *Western Journal of Emergency Medicine* 178.

[34] Eastman et al (n 21); KM Edwards, 'Intimate partner violence and the rural–urban–suburban divide: Myth or reality? A critical review of the literature' (2015) 16(3) *Trauma, Violence, & Abuse* 359; Roush and Kurth (n 7).

[35] American Psychological Association, 'Rural Health' (nd) at www.apa.org/practice/programs/rural; Averill, Padilla and Clements (n 28).

[36] Roush and Kurth (n 7).

[37] MF Shepard and AK Hagemeister, 'Perspectives of rural women: Custody and visitation with abusive ex-partners' (2013) 28(2) *Affilia* 165.

Geographic isolation additionally restricts access to local domestic violence shelters. In rural areas, more than 25 per cent of victims must travel 40–75 miles or more to access domestic violence shelters, a stark contrast to women in urban areas, where fewer than one in 100 women must travel this distance to access services.[38] Lack of transportation is an additional barrier for victims seeking help, accessing quality service and reporting their abusers.[39] In addition, due to severely limited resources, rural service providers turn away more requests for assistance than urban providers, and rural shelters are not well equipped to provide long-term and transitional housing, despite a demonstrated need for these services.[40] Social and physical isolation limits victims' access to transportation and adequate health services.

Recognising the role of isolation of victims by abusers is essential to understanding the impact of domestic violence; this isolation is more easily perpetuated in rural areas with lower population density and fewer opportunities for social interaction on a day-to-day basis.[41] A vast majority, up to 97 per cent, of rural female survivors experience forced isolation.[42] Rural women are faced with minimal alternatives when abusers exacerbate isolation through tactics such as disabling or destroying transportation options.[43] The consequences of social isolation are far-reaching. Women experience depression and hopelessness, but fear partner retaliation if they reach out to their social networks for help.[44] Over time, rural victims report feeling they have no choice but to remain with their abusive partner.[45] In fact, many women report their partners threatened murder if they spoke to others about their abuse;[46] threat of murder is a common tactic among abusers.[47] Indeed, rural victims of abuse in the United States are more often murdered by abusive partners, or former partners, than suburban and urban victims.[48]

[38] Bosch and Bergen (n 7); Peek-Asa et al (n 2).

[39] Peek-Asa et al (n 2).

[40] AL Few, 'The voices of black and white rural battered women in domestic violence shelters' (2005) 54(4) *Family Relations* 488; R Iyengar and L Sabik. 'The Dangerous Shortage of Domestic Violence Services: An analysis suggests that more than one in ten victims in a twenty-four-hour period asked for – but didn't get – help' (2009) 28 Supp 1 *Health Affairs* w1052.

[41] Averill, Padilla and Clements (n 28).

[42] K Bosch and WR Schumm. 'Accessibility to Resources: Helping rural women in abusive partner relationships become free from abuse' (2004) 30(5) *Journal of Sex & Marital Therapy* 357.

[43] WS DeKeseredy and MD Schwartz, 'Thinking Sociologically About Image-Based Sexual Abuse: The Contribution of Male Peer Support Theory' *Sexualization, Media, & Society* (December 2016); Websdale (n 29).

[44] Bosch and Schumm (n 42).

[45] WS DeKeseredy, 'Bringing Feminist Sociological Analyses of Patriarchy Back to the Forefront of the Study of Woman Abuse' (2021) 27(5) *Violence against Women* 621.

[46] Teaster, Roberto and Dugar (n 8).

[47] DeKeseredy and Schwartz (n 43).

[48] DeKeseredy (n 45); A Reckdenwald et al, 'The Effectiveness of a Coordinated Response Toward Nonfatal Strangulation in Facilitating Evidence-Based Prosecution' (2021) 32(8) *Criminal Justice Policy Review* 816.

It is not only lack of access to social services that is problematic for rural victims; social connections with family and friends can be limited and potentially confining. Often tightly-knit, rural networks play an important role in women's ability to leave an abusive situation.[49] Women in rural communities recognise they would be even further isolated if they were to leave their community and social networks.[50] While rural victims experience a great deal of social isolation as an integral element of intimate violence, they recognise leaving or reporting abuse can create a schism in their community and social networks.[51]

Conceptualising this violence as 'intimate terrorism', wherein abusers rely on domination and violence to control their intimate partners, can be a particularly useful framework when examining rural domestic violence.[52] In rural settings, the system of abuse includes isolation, control and dependency in ways that are present in many, if not most, abusive scenarios, but that lead to unique consequences for rural victims of domestic violence.[53] As Jo Little's (2017) research indicates, victims of domestic violence are often controlled by partners inside the home, particularly in terms of ability to move about freely both within the home, or outside the home in the social world.[54] Technology provides additional avenues for intimate terrorists to monitor and control the behaviours of their victims, even in the absence of physical presence.[55] Bowstead's (2011) work emphasises how the consistent surveillance becomes internalised and normalised for victims who begin to limit their interactions with others to avoid further abuse. In addition, small, close-knit communities can serve to enhance surveillance of victims.[56] These close relationships can also make disclosing violence difficult, as victims fear being ostracised or not being believed.[57] Overall, geographic isolation significantly exacerbates difficulties accessing justice for victims in rural areas.

## III. Poverty

Poverty is generally considered one of the most relevant factors for determining an individual's risk of experiencing domestic violence.[58] The intersections of

[49] Averill, Padilla and Clements (n 28); Bosch and Schumm (n 42); Teaster, Roberto and Dugar (n 8).

[50] Eastman et al (n 21).

[51] ibid.

[52] MP Johnson and JM Leone, 'The differential effects of intimate terrorism and situational couple violence: Findings from the National Violence Against Women Survey' (2005) 26(3) *Journal of Family Issues* 322.

[53] Little (n 4).

[54] ibid.

[55] JA Dunlap, 'Intimate Terrorism and Technology: There's an App for That' (2012) 7 *University of Massachusetts Law Review* 10.

[56] J Bowstead, 'Space and place as constraints and resources in women's strategies to escape domestic violence' (2011) 1 *Metronome* 9.

[57] Little (n 4).

[58] WS DeKeseredy, MD Schwartz and S Alvi. 'Which women are more likely to be abused? Public housing, cohabitation, and separated/divorced women' (2008) 21(4) *Criminal Justice Studies* 283.

poverty, lacking housing options and financial abuse create unique circumstances for women experiencing domestic violence in rural areas. Approximately 25–48 percent of all victims are homeless after fleeing from an abusive relationship.[59] Due to limited access to domestic violence shelters or emergency housing, many women look for affordable housing. However, rural isolation and higher poverty rates restrict this option. Because poverty disproportionately impacts women in rural areas, women attempting to leave abusive situations often cannot afford even basic services, let alone live independently in areas that often lack affordable housing.[60] Access to affordable housing is instrumental in women's capacity to escape abusive situations; deficient affordable housing in rural communities creates a clear barrier for victims of domestic violence.[61]

Alongside lacking housing, many women struggle to find consistent employment due to limited job availability and lack of employment training. For victims who are employed, domestic violence has a significant economic effect: 75 per cent of employed battered women are harassed in their workplace by their abusers, and 54 per cent of these women lose their jobs as a result of the abuse;[62] 40 per cent of battered women reported that domestic abuse caused them to be late for work more than three times in the last month, and 34 per cent reported missing entire days of work; 23 per cent reported difficulties advancing in their careers, and 20 per cent reported difficulties keeping their jobs.[63] Domestic violence costs US employers approximately $100 million per year in lost wages, sick leave, absenteeism and non-productivity.[64] Victims of domestic violence lose a total of 8 million days of paid work each year.[65] Additionally, available jobs in rural areas are generally minimum wage, thus keeping women trapped in abusive situations.[66] Financial abuse further exacerbates impoverishment of victims and is an element of abuse for 89 per cent of victims, and is combined with additional controlling behaviours in both work and at home; abusive partners often control any money earned by their partners.[67] Overall, rural victims experience extreme socioeconomic distress not only within abusive relationships, but also when disclosing their abuse.

[59] National Research Council, *Understanding Violence against Women* (National Academies Press, 1996).

[60] Bosch and Bergen (n 7).

[61] Bosch and Schumm (n 42); BJ Eastman and S Grant Bunch, 'Providing services to survivors of domestic violence: A comparison of rural and urban service provider perceptions' (2007) 22(4) *Journal of Interpersonal Violence* 465; T Riddell, M Ford-Gilboe and B Leipert, 'Strategies used by rural women to stop, avoid, or escape from intimate partner violence' (2009) 30 *Health Care for Women International* 134.

[62] National Research Council (n 59).

[63] S Lloyd, 'The Effects of Domestic Violence on Women's Employment' (2002) 19(2) *Law & Policy* 139.

[64] Centers for Disease Control and Prevention, 'Intimate partner violence: Definitions' *Injury Center: Violence Prevention* (2010).

[65] EF Rothman et al, 'How employment helps female victims of intimate partner violence: A qualitative study' (2007) 12(2) *Journal of Occupational Health Psychology* 136.

[66] Shepard and Hagemeister (n 37).

[67] Bosch and Schumm (n 42).

## IV. Problematic Law Enforcement Response

The standard handling of domestic violence cases by law enforcement in rural areas often leads to detrimental consequences for victims who report crime and seek help from the criminal justice system. A key problem with the traditional criminal legal system's approach is that the arrest, investigation, court process and plea bargaining often happen behind closed doors and fail to address the needs of survivors and community members.[68] Survivors' lack of confidence in the criminal justice system may affect victims' decisions to report their abusers to the formal legal system, reinforcing the message that what happens between significant others is a private matter.[69] The sociocultural context in rural areas is distinct, with diminished anonymity and physical isolation, where victims of domestic violence already face significant challenges to reporting their abuse to officials. Victims risk ridicule, ostracism and possible loss of the sole income of the household.[70] In rural and remote areas, both physical isolation and resource scarcity prevent victim reporting and effective police response to domestic violence.

Law enforcement in rural areas face unique challenges in covering vast distances in a short period of time in rural counties, especially in those areas that have extremely low population density.[71] In addition to delayed response time, victims in rural and remote areas may lack access to Internet and phone services that severely limits their opportunities to reach for help.[72] Smaller police departments, like those in rural areas, demonstrate a higher likelihood of inadequate domestic violence response policy.[73] Larger agencies are more likely to have clear domestic violence policies, have more extensive response requirements for their 911 dispatchers, and are more likely to have domestic violence special units with victim advocates working inside the police department. Rural local enforcement agencies rarely have the resources to afford such structures.[74]

Common practices of rural policing are particularly problematic in domestic violence cases.[75] These approaches often ignore the intimate nature of the relationship between victims, perpetrators and the community, as well as the trauma

[68] K Van Wormer, 'Restorative justice as social justice for victims of gendered violence: A standpoint feminist perspective' (2009) 54(2) *Social Work* 107.

[69] S Wendt and B Cheers, 'Impacts of rural culture on domestic violence' (2002) 7(1) *Rural Social Work* 22.

[70] ST Young, 'Wild, Wonderful, White Criminality: Images of "White Trash" Appalachia' (2016) 25(1) *Critical Criminology (Richmond, BC)* 103.

[71] Websdale (n 29).

[72] J Lai and NO Widmar, 'Revisiting the Digital Divide in the COVID-19 Era' *Applied Economic Perspectives and Policy* (3 October 2020) at doi:10.1002/aepp.13104.

[73] AR Klein and United States Office of Justice Programs, *Practical Implications of Current Domestic Violence Research for Law Enforcement, Prosecutors and Judges* (Office of Justice Programs, US Dept of Justice, 2009).

[74] B Deans et al, 'Victims of Domestic Violence: Improving Law Enforcement Response to Domestic Violence to Prevent Revictimization' (2018) 9(1) *Journal of Marketing and Management* 1.

[75] DM Blumberg et al, 'New Directions in Police Academy Training: A Call to Action' (2019) 16(24) *International Journal of Environmental Research and Public Health* 4941.

and barriers experienced by victims themselves.[76] Rural victims experience fear of retaliation from abusers, ineffective responses of police, potential failure to protect charges, and fear of losing home and child custody; thus, rural victims of domestic abuse are less likely to report and cooperate with local law enforcement and victim advocates.[77] In rural places, gender stereotypes and patriarchal values impact law enforcement response. A survey of rural county sheriffs revealed a connection between regressive beliefs about abused women among sheriffs and what policies are enacted to address domestic violence.[78] Law enforcement officers who reject stereotypical beliefs of women are more inclined to enforce stricter protective policies, while officers with negative views of women and victims of domestic abuse are more likely to arrest both the abuser and victim.[79] Detrimental attitudes towards women and their experiences of abuse are widely upheld by male law enforcement officers, which both explicitly and implicitly impact the ways they respond to domestic violence calls.[80] In addition, rural law enforcement often lacks diversity in gender and ethnicity. Federal statistics indicate that 14.1 per cent of officers in metropolitan areas were women while 8.1 per cent in non-metropolitan areas were women.[81] These statistics may over-represent the actual number of women in the police force in extremely rural and remote areas.[82] The lack of representation of officers with a diverse cultural and racial background as well as a lack of female police officers may further exacerbate the patriarchal culture and gender stereotypes in policing.[83] Due to the lack of resources and funding, rural law enforcement faces constraints to facilitate victim-centred and trauma-informed approaches in domestic violence intervention.[84]

Law enforcement is commonly the first responding party during an emergency crisis and criminal incidents. However, problematic procedures and biased attitudes towards victims in domestic violence cases disrupt the trust between victims and law enforcement and minimise support provided to victims. While

[76] A Millar, J Devaney and M Butler, 'Emotional Intelligence: Challenging the Perceptions and Efficacy of "Soft Skills" in Policing Incidents of Domestic Abuse Involving Children' (2018) 34(6) *Journal of Family Violence* 577.

[77] N Youngson et al, 'Challenges in Risk Assessment with Rural Domestic Violence Victims: Implications for Practice' (2021) 36(5) *Journal of Family Violence* 537.

[78] EM Farris and MR Holman, 'Public officials and a "private" matter: Attitudes and policies in the county sheriff office regarding violence against women' (2015) 96(4) *Social Science Quarterly* 1117.

[79] EG Lambert et al, 'The impact of officer and agency characteristics on the likelihood of arrest in domestic violence situations among rural law enforcement officers' (2007) 22(2) *Journal of Police and Criminal Psychology* 91.

[80] H Huhtanen, *Gender Bias in Sexual Assault Response and Investigation* (End Violence Against Women International, 2017).

[81] Federal Bureau of Investigation, 'Full-time law enforcement employees' (nd) at https://ucr.fbi.gov/crime-in-the-u.s/2018/crime-in-the-u.s.-2018/topic-pages/tables/table-74.

[82] CM Rennison, M Dragiewicz and WS DeKeseredy, 'Context Matters: Violence Against Women and Reporting to Police in Rural, Suburban and Urban Areas' (2012) 38(1) *American Journal of Criminal Justice* 141.

[83] Rennison, DeKeseredy and Dragiewicz (n 4).

[84] A Jolin and CA Moose. 'Evaluating a Domestic Violence Program in a Community Policing Environment: Research Implementation Issues' (1997) 43(3) *Crime and Delinquency* 279.

recognising these problematic issues exist in both urban and rural police forces, the effect on the survival and recovery of domestic violence victims in rural areas is complex. Victims in rural communities lack both formal and informal social support to escape abuse, have limited available resources and lack transportation to seek help from victim services. Patriarchal beliefs and gender stereotypes upheld by local police forces along with police staff under-equipped in domestic violence intervention and trauma-informed care intensify obstacles for abused women accessing victim services.

## A. Failure to Protect

Police officers often have the discretion to decide to arrest, separate or provide mediation during domestic violence calls.[85] Victims may request a court-issued order to protect them from direct contact with their abusers when police officers arrest alleged abusers during disturbance calls.[86] Victims of domestic violence, already in vulnerable positions, face particular difficulties obtaining protection orders from the court when police departments fail to arrest abusers.[87] More often, victims fear being punished for reporting violence, with consequences of legal charges and possible loss of child custody.[88] When it comes to protective orders issued for victims, rural victims experience difficulties obtaining orders and having them enforced.[89] Rural victims rate law enforcement as a barrier to protection at double the rate of urban victims, have more limited knowledge regarding options available during the legal process and report protection order violation rates at three times the rate of urban victims, with violators facing minimal, if any, consequences.[90]

Failure to Protect (FTP) laws were developed so that caretakers and other mandated reporters would be more likely to report suspected or known child abuse, in an attempt to minimise the risk of violence against children.[91] Similar to domestic violence, which was long ignored by the Government and criminal justice system, laws on child abuse and neglect were not established until the late 1960s when child welfare services were expanded and required by the States.[92] Related

[85] LB Gezinski, '"It's Kind of Hit and Miss with Them": A Qualitative Investigation of Police Response to Intimate Partner Violence in a Mandatory Arrest State' (2020) 37(1) *Journal of Family Violence* 99.

[86] ibid.

[87] D Hirschel et al, 'Domestic Violence and Mandatory Arrest Laws: To What Extent Do They Influence Police Arrest Decisions?' (2007) 98(1) *The Journal of Criminal Law & Criminology* 255.

[88] CT Benitez, DE McNiel and RL Binder, 'Do protection orders protect?' (2010) 38(3) *Journal of the American Academy of Psychiatry and the Law* 376.

[89] N Hawkins, 'Perspectives on Civil Protective Orders in Domestic Violence Cases: The Rural and Urban Divide' *National Institute of Justice Journal* (25 May 2010) 4.

[90] ibid.

[91] ibid.

[92] A Mahoney, 'How failure to protect laws punish the vulnerable' (2019) 29 *Health Matrix* 429.

charges may be prosecuted through criminal court, the child welfare system or both, and can lead to penalties ranging from incarceration to loss of parental rights. Unfortunately, these laws have been unfairly applied to mothers who experience abuse.[93] Although FTP laws are ostensibly written to be gender-neutral, women are the primary defendants charged in these cases.[94] The disparity between fathers and mothers involved with child abuse/neglect cases demonstrates the impact of heteropatriarchal expectations of mothers to take care of their children regardless of abuse. This outcome may be explained by the societal belief that mothers are believed to be the primary caretakers responsible for protecting their children.[95] Even when a history of battering of the mother is taken into consideration, the criminal justice system still expects abused women to overcome various barriers to reporting abuse and leaving an abuser to protect their children.[96] In addition, these court orders often require that women negotiate continued contact with their abusive partners to maintain children's relationships with abusive fathers, and post-separation joint-custody arrangements remain unsafe for women as well as their children.[97] The actions an abused woman takes, such as protecting her children from the violence, seeking services to aid them and planning an escape, are rarely taken into consideration by the court when FTP charges are brought against an abused mother.[98]

Being charged with and convicted of child abuse may cause significant consequences for rural women experiencing domestic violence. One of the consequences is the loss of parental rights. Victims are more often charged with and convicted of FTP than their abusive partners in domestic violence situations, as mothers are unable to protect their children from witnessing and experiencing abuse from fathers.[99] This discriminatory and biased approach makes victims more vulnerable in reporting domestic violence incidents and less likely to cooperate with prosecutors in criminal charges.[100] Such punitive sentiment may be even more exaggerated in rural places when gendered social norms prescribe the caring responsibilities related to motherhood. While losing child custody is particularly detrimental to the victims, loss of parental rights may not be the only consequence of being

[93] K Ahearn, 'Charging Battered Mothers with "Failure to Protect": Still Blaming the Victim' (2000) 27 *Fordham Urban Law Journal* 849; Mahoney (n 92).

[94] A Bierria and C Lenz, 'Battering Court Syndrome' in J Stoever (ed), *The Politicization of Safety* (New York University Press, 2019) 91.

[95] Ahearn (n 93); Mahoney (n 92).

[96] JL Hardesty and GH Chung, 'Intimate partner violence, parental divorce, and child custody: Directions for intervention and future research' (2006) 55(2) *Family Relations* 200.

[97] C Varcoe and LG Irwin, '"If I killed you, I'd get the kids": Women's survival and protection work with child custody and access in the context of woman abuse' (2004) 27(1) *Qualitative Sociology* 77.

[98] Bierria and Lenz (n 94).

[99] K Ballou, 'Failure to Protect: Our Civil System's Chronic Punishment of Victims of Domestic Violence' (2017) 31(2) *Notre Dame Journal of Law, Ethics & Public Policy* 355.

[100] S Singh, 'Punishing Mothers for Men's Violence: Failure to Protect Legislation and the Criminalisation of Abused Women' (2021) 29(2) *Feminist Legal Studies* 181.

prosecuted for FTP. In some States, life sentences have been reported as a sentencing option.[101] The consequences of abused mothers' being charged with FTP also impact children, who may have to participate in the prosecutorial process and thus experience re-traumatisation through reliving previous family violence. Children also face the possibility of being placed in foster care.[102] Petitions of neglect are often brought against abused (non-abusive) mothers, with the allegation that they were unable to support or protect their children as a victim of domestic abuse; this can be exacerbated when parental kidnapping laws fail to sufficiently accommodate the fact that abused mothers may try to escape with their children in order to protect them and avoid prosecution under FTP.[103] Knowledge of FTP laws may actually result in mothers' deciding not to seek help for fear of being prosecuted.[104] These problematic FTP laws demonstrate the power imbalance between abusers and victims, and within the criminal justice system, especially when the court scrutinises survivors' reactions to abuse.[105]

## B. Mandatory Arrest

Mandatory arrest policies require an arrest if there is probable cause to believe an assault occurred during a domestic violence incident. There is a long debate regarding the effectiveness of mandatory arrest in domestic violence situations. On the one hand, studies show that mandatory arrest reduces the recidivism rates of offenders who are married and employed, and increases the likelihood of prosecutors' pressing charges against abusers.[106] On the other hand, mandatory arrest may be less effective in families where the abusers are the main economic resources, as victims rely on their partners' incomes to survive.[107] Mandatory arrest policies also increase the likelihood of retaliation against victims.[108] Additionally, rates of reporting decrease after implementation of mandatory arrest policies.[109] Fear of being misidentified as the abuser and arrested in mandatory arrest scenarios, fear of losing child custody and fear of retaliation are the main reasons victims

[101] ibid 182.

[102] C Cross, 'Criminalizing battered mothers' (2018) 2 *Utah Law Review* 259.

[103] Ahearn (n 93).

[104] Mahoney (n 92).

[105] C Cross, 'Harm Reduction in the Domestic Violence Context' in Stoever (ed) (n 94) 332.

[106] AM Zelcer, 'Battling Domestic Violence: Replacing Mandatory Arrest Laws with a Trifecta of Preferential Arrest, Officer Education, and Batterer Treatment Programs' (2014) 51(2) *The American Criminal Law Review* 541.

[107] SB Starr and MM Rehavi. 'Mandatory Sentencing and Racial Disparity: Assessing the Role of Prosecutors and the Effects of Booker' (2013) 123(1) *The Yale Law Journal* 2.

[108] L Dugan, DS Nagin and R Rosenfeld, 'Exposure Reduction or Retaliation? The Effects of Domestic Violence Resources on Intimate-Partner Homicide' (2003) 37(1) *Law & Society Review* 169.

[109] ibid.

do not report.[110] In locations with mandatory arrest policies, arrests for women during domestic violence situations have risen by 25–35 per cent, although only 1–7 per cent arrested are estimated to be actual primary batterers.[111]

Rural victims of domestic violence are especially impacted by mandatory arrest policies. Patriarchal ideology reinforces structures of male power and control, which often impact officers' response towards domestic violence incidents.[112] Officers' beliefs in the form of biases and stereotypes of what makes a 'good' victim also contribute to victim arrests.[113] The perception of a 'good' victim is inherently gendered, and such gendered bias is observed more often in rural law enforcement.[114] Heightened gendered expectations of rural women in the family setting often include financial dependence on their male partners, primary caretaker responsibilities and sociocultural inferiority of women compared to men.[115] In rural areas, victims who do not conform to these traditional female gender roles are more at risk of arrest, especially in rural areas where these beliefs are firmly held.[116] Mandatory arrests may also occur more frequently when abusers know how to manipulate the criminal justice system, especially when responding officers lack domestic violence-specific training.[117]

Agency responding policies, such as mandatory arrests, problems obtaining and/or issuing protection orders, and delayed police response create significant obstacles to rural survivors' reporting to and seeking help from the formal criminal legal system. Due to concerns with anonymity and potential for familial and social repercussions, victims are afraid to report to or seek help from local law enforcement. Battered women report that rural police fail to take domestic violence seriously because local police believe domestic violence is a private family matter, or place blame on victims of violence.[118] In addition, the punitive nature of many of above-mentioned policies jeopardises the safety of survivors and their children, and upends the lives of survivors socially and economically.[119] Finally, the barriers to reporting for rural women disguise the actual number of incidences of domestic violence and repercussions associated with victimisation for both survivors and communities.[120]

[110] MA Novisky and RL Peralta, 'When Women Tell: Intimate partner violence and the factors related to police notification' (2015) 21(1) *Violence against Women* 65.

[111] ibid.

[112] M Rajan and KA McCloskey, 'Victims of intimate partner violence: Arrest rates across recent studies' (2007) 15 *Journal of Aggression, Maltreatment & Trauma* 27.

[113] ibid.

[114] D Greco and S Dawgert, 'Poverty and Sexual Violence: Building prevention and intervention responses' (Pennsylvania Coalition Against Rape, 2007) at www.pcar.org/sites/default/files/pages-pdf/poverty_and_sexual_violence.pdf.

[115] LK Sudderth, 'An Uneasy Alliance' (2006) 1(4) *Feminist Criminology* 329.

[116] Rajan and McCloskey (n 112).

[117] ibid 42.

[118] Websdale (n 29).

[119] A Kellie, JD Riffe-Snyder and SJ Reel, 'Intimate Partner Violence Stories of Appalachian Women' (2022) 31(2) *Clinical Nursing Research* 261.

[120] M Perez Trujillo and S Ross, 'Police Response to Domestic Violence' (2008) 23(4) *Journal of Interpersonal Violence* 454.

# V. Domestic Violence in Rural Immigrant Communities

Immigrant victims of domestic violence are subject to unique social, legal and economic abuse compared to victims with US citizenship.[121] Some of the major challenges immigrant victims commonly face are fear of deportation, language barriers and extreme poverty.[122] Immigrant victims also report fear of direct contact with police due to their immigration status.[123] The threat of deportation is a powerful deterrent for immigrants to report their abusers, especially when children are involved in the relationship.[124] This threat is exacerbated when a victim lacks information about her rights and options because the victims are isolated at home or face language barriers to accessing victim services.[125] The process to request and receive legal protections for both legal and undocumented immigrants from US government are highly complex, and require hiring legal professionals, often at high personal expense, or requiring referral from comprehensive victim advocacy organisations, which are demonstrably lacking in rural areas.[126] Without readily available income and resources, immigrant victims are stranded in the cycle of abuse.[127]

The experience of isolation is particularly prevalent in immigrant victim populations when their legal status relies on their spouses' work visas. Even though refugees reside legally in the United States, abusers use the threat of deportation as an effective control tactic, because many refugee victims lack accurate information about their legal resident status.[128] Immigrant victims in rural areas may face additional challenges in seeking help from others. Immigrant women may be harassed or abused in uniquely demeaning ways in their own culture, in which family members and communities see these victims as traitors for exposing family issues to outsiders.[129] Cultural backgrounds also shape how women experience and respond to violence, including reporting, seeking services, and gaining family and

[121] E Erez, N Ammar and LE Orloff, 'Violence against immigrant women and systemic responses: An exploratory study', *A report submitted to the National Institute of Justice, Washington, DC: US Department of Justice* (2003).

[122] ibid.

[123] M Runner, S Novick and M Yoshihama, 'Intimate partner violence in immigrant and refugee communities: Challenges, promising practices and recommendations' (Robert Wood Johnson Foundation, 2009) at www.futureswithoutviolence.org/userfiles/file/ImmigrantWomen/IPV_Report_March_2009.pdf.

[124] ibid.

[125] ibid.

[126] E Erez, M Adelman and C Gregory, 'Intersections of Immigration and Domestic Violence' (2009) 4(1) *Feminist Criminology* 32.

[127] E Sellers, 'Access to Justice for Undocumented Immigrant Victims of Domestic Violence' (2015) 84(2) *UMKC Law Review* 543.

[128] K James, 'Domestic Violence Within Refugee Families: Intersecting Patriarchal Culture and the Refugee Experience' (2010) 31(3) *Australian and New Zealand Journal of Family Therapy* 275.

[129] A Raj and J Silverman, 'Violence Against Immigrant Women: The roles of culture, context, and legal immigrant status on intimate partner violence' (2002) 8(3) *Violence against Women* 367.

community support.[130] These cultural differences may make immigrant victims less likely to report violence or may otherwise impact their choice to seek help.[131]

As previously mentioned, an impediment commonly faced by immigrant victims is language inefficiency.[132] Abusers often exploit limited English proficiency skills to limit the movement of victims or control what victims can or cannot do; perpetrators who possess greater English language skills silence their victims by serving as the family's sole communicator in the United States.[133] Commonly faced with a shortage of affordable and comprehensive healthcare and services, rural immigrant victims are rarely able to access culturally and linguistically appropriate services while experiencing mounting racial and ethnic disparities in rural areas.[134]

Immigrant women working in the agriculture industry are subject to high rates of victimisation, including sexual assault and domestic violence.[135] Farming industries are heavily occupied by male farmworkers, where women workers experience isolation in a male-dominated field with pervasive cultural patriarchy, gender stereotypes and violence.[136] Trying to survive in male-dominated industries and working and living in remote and isolated areas, while experiencing economic discrimination, sexual harassment, sexism and racism, impact immigrant women farm workers' lives and well-being. These women encounter the same challenges that rural victims commonly face, but these challenges are exacerbated by lack of access to resources, and fear of retaliation and deportation.[137] Thus, abuse, sexual violence and trauma are largely under-reported among immigrant women.[138]

Foreign-born women who experience socioeconomic inequalities in their marriages and relationships with their partners are especially vulnerable, especially when their legal status is at stake.[139] Immigrant victims commonly experience economic abuse when they are unable to obtain or maintain stable employment with liveable wages.[140] Most employment opportunities in rural communities are

[130] M Abraham, 'Isolation as a form of marital violence: The South Asian immigrant experience' (2000) 9(3) *Journal of Social Distress and the Homeless* 221.

[131] H Bauer et al, 'Barriers to Health Care for Abused Latina and Asian Immigrant Women' (2000) 11(1) *Journal of Health Care for the Poor and Underserved* 33.

[132] Raj and Silverman (n 129).

[133] James (n 128); Raj and Silverman (n 129).

[134] Yu Xu et al, 'Health-Seeking Behaviors and Barriers to Health Care of Southeast Asian Immigrants: Implications for the Home Health Nurse' (2001) 14(1) *Home Health Care Management & Practice* 22.

[135] ML Ontiveros, 'Lessons from the fields: Female farmworkers and the law' (2002) 55 *Maine Law Review* 157.

[136] National Farm Worker Ministry, *Health and Safety* (2020) at http://nfwm.org/farm-workers/farm-worker-issues/health-safety/.

[137] IM Waugh, 'Examining the Sexual Harassment Experiences of Mexican Immigrant Farmworking Women' (2010) 16(3) *Violence against Women* 237.

[138] G Meng, Human Rights Watch, 'Cultivating fear: The vulnerability of immigrant farmworkers in the US to sexual violence and sexual harassment' (2019) at https://searchworks.stanford.edu/view/9637873.

[139] Raj and Silverman (n 129).

[140] AM Stylianou, 'Economic abuse within intimate partner violence: A review of the literature' (2018) 33(1) *Violence and Victims* 3.

for low-paying, low-skill and labour-intensive jobs, providing few opportunities for advancement and economic comfort.[141] Many immigrants and refugee women experience domestic violence in the context of language difficulties, confusion over their legal rights, and the overall stress of adaptation to new cultural and social structures.[142] Immigrant women in rural communities experience family violence at the nexus of language and culture differences, which can be compounded by issues related to legal status.

## VI. Conclusion

Rural victims of domestic violence face complex issues that influence their experiences and outcomes of victimisation. Sociocultural systems contribute to an overall gendered narrative of women that perpetuates domestic violence and uniquely impacts rural victims. Compared to those in urban areas, women in rural communities often encounter distinct obstacles to accessing adequate intervention resources. The lack of domestic violence-specific and trauma-informed criminal justice response compounds barriers to victims' reporting abuse.

Domestic violence is a serious and reoccurring health issue globally and within the United States; this remains true for rural victims of abuse. While the domestic violence movement has made great strides, there continues to be an intense need for social, institutional and political change. Practitioners and policymakers must address effective strategies to enhance victim safety and intervention programmes to prevent the cycle of violence in rural areas. Domestic violence-specific training must be mandatory for rural police departments. Community-level collaboration between victim advocacy agencies, law enforcement agencies and legal professionals should prioritise the needs of victims and their family members. Legal services and support for underrepresented populations, such as immigrant communities, should be expanded to include language assistance, affordable housing and accessible legal services. Eradicating domestic violence requires continual analysis and development of robust policies addressing the needs of rural victims of domestic violence.

[141] RM Adelman et al, 'Using estimates of undocumented immigrants to study the immigration-crime relationship' (2020) *Journal of Crime and Justice* 1 at www.tandfonline.com/doi/abs/10.1080/0735648X.2020.1819375?journalCode=rjcj20.

[142] Runner, Novick and Yoshihama (n 123).

# 15

# Rural Access to Justice and Beyond: Dimensions of Access as a Criterion for Understanding Lay Users' Satisfaction with Remote Justice

OLUMIDE ADISA, SUE JAMES AND DANIEL NEWMAN

## I. Introduction: Dysfunctionalities and Blockages and the Greater Use of Technology in Courts

The court reform programme in England and Wales has, since 2010, closed more than half of all courts,[1] as it shifted away from court buildings and hearings in person and focused instead firmly on the use of technology. This process could impact all who come into contact with the justice system, but most prominently removed courts from many rural areas and fundamentally changed the experience of the legal system for many rural residents. Such trends were impacted – and exaggerated – by the arrival of the Covid-19 pandemic. By the start of April 2020, all possession claims had been stayed in the courts and 90 per cent of all hearings were remote, with 33 per cent conducted by video, 45 per cent by audio and the remaining 12 per cent on paper.[2] Before the initial closure of the magistrates' courts, and as part of its consultation outlining proposals, the Ministry of Justice conducted an impact assessment into operational and geographical constraints.[3] While travel time impacts were briefly discussed, the

[1] G Sturge, 'Court statistics for England and Wales' (House of Commons Library, 23 December 2021) at https://commonslibrary.parliament.uk/research-briefings/cbp-8372/ (accessed 17 January 2022).

[2] HM Courts and Tribunal Service, 'HMCTS weekly use of remote audio and video technologies May 2020 to May 2021' (10 June 2021) at www.gov.uk/government/statistical-data-sets/hmcts-weekly-use-of-remote-audio-and-video-technologies-may-2020-to-april-2021 (accessed 17 January 2022).

[3] Ministry of Justice, 'Decision Impact Assessment on Her Majesty's Court and Tribunal Service proposals on the provision of courts tribunal services in England and Wales' (Ministry of Justice, 2016) at https://assets.publishing.service.gov.uk/government/uploads/system/uploads/attachment_data/file/800874/hmcts-fit-for-the-future-consultation-response.pdf (accessed 17 January 2022).

Ministry of Justice accepted generally that national average travel times would slightly increase, but there was no mention of the travel costs or the value of this time on court users now having to make longer journeys to court. The travel times included and used in the assessments were at the time based on travel by both car and public transport using the (now defunct) Transport Direct Journey Planner tool, and calculated assuming an individual goes to court to arrive at 10am and leaves at close of business. Furthermore, based on this tool, the Ministry of Justice concluded that those living in the catchment area of the closing magistrates' courts will see their average public transport journey travel time increase by around 35 minutes under the preferred option.[4] Aside from the assumptions made around capability, capacity and confidence to travel implicit in such moves, subsequent empirical research into the court closures has shown that estimates on the travel time impacts were grossly underestimated.[5]

The Association of District Judges wrote in their submission to the Justice Select Committee 'What might be viewed by some as a minor inconvenience of extra travel appears to have a disproportionate effect on court attendance.'[6] Based on evidence from the County Court in Sheffield – when Oldham County Court was closed, and work transferred there – fewer defendants turned up to court, even when the stakes were as high as to save their homes. One of the original driving forces for the digital reforms was to mitigate the challenges of geographical access by using modern information and communications technology to improve access to justice. For remote physical locations, technology can aid and hinder, as we have seen during the Covid-19 crisis, which thrust new challenges upon us almost overnight. For example, the affordability issue persists, as there are a lot of assumptions being made about Internet connectivity and digital equality in relation to legal advice in England and Wales during the Covid-19 pandemic.[7]

The Covid-19 pandemic saw a greater use of technology in people's daily lives. According to Ofcom, by June 2020, more than seven in 10 adults were making video calls weekly during the Covid-19 crisis, compared to 35 per cent before the first UK lockdown in March 2020.[8] However, what this estimate does not tell us is the extent to which that technology was being used and intergroup differences based on differing needs and geography, which then lead us to consider wider issues of access that have implications for remote justice during and (presumably) after the pandemic.

[4] ibid 16.

[5] O Adisa, *Access to Justice: Assessing the Impact of the Magistrates' Court Closures in Suffolk* (University of Suffolk, 2018).

[6] R Lumb, *Written submission from The Association of Her Majesty's District Judges* (The Association of Her Majesty's District Judges, 2019).

[7] See D Newman, J Mant and F Gordon, 'Vulnerability, legal need and technology in England and Wales' (2021) 21(3) *International Journal of Discrimination and the Law* 230.

[8] Ofcom, 'UK's internet use surges to record levels' (24 June 2020) at www.ofcom.org.uk/about-ofcom/latest/media/media-releases/2020/uk-internet-use-surges (accessed 17 January 2022).

Similarly, while we now have remote ways of adjudicating on cases via audio or video facilities, questions remain unanswered around how appropriate those uses of technology are for all lay users. Coupled with this are the ongoing concerns from practitioners (and their clients) around the risk involved in the loss of the client's voice in the court process, which was often the first (and only) time they had an opportunity to have their voice heard. With the loss of voice comes the loss of effective participation for lay court users in particular. As individuals, we do not engage and participate in the same way remotely as we do in person. Something we have all been able to relate to during the pandemic – meeting friends, family and colleagues online – is not the same as physically being together. We do not feel as present, we do not have the same connection. Advocates might get better at understanding the nuances of remote hearings, but for the client it will be their one chance, if they do have the technical equipment, the ability to use it and enough data. There is also a risk of loss of empathy, not just between judge and litigant but also between solicitor and client. A large part of what advocates do is to sit with clients, listen and stand alongside them – throughout their case, building rapport, getting to understand one another. Lastly, there is also the risk to open justice – ensuring accountability of the state in the way it adjudicates between individuals as well as a check and balance on its own powers. We have a shared culture of the courtroom. What do we lose when we shift the arena to online spaces – when we no longer have our day in court but, rather, have it in someone's front room.

As the distance between courts becomes greater, and the use of video and telephone technology become the norm, what is the impact? This chapter argues that this question ought to be considered in relation to five equity concepts drawn from the work of Penchansky and Thomas: availability, accessibility, accommodation, affordability and acceptability.[9] Using three England and Wales case studies from our cross-disciplinary research and practice experiences, we highlight pertinent issues around remote justice that have implications for lay user satisfaction, and in particular implications for rural access to justice. As such, we address the impact that changes in policy have had on the justice system for rural areas, highlighting some of the differential impacts between rural and urban areas. As Qi and Craig show in chapter 14 of this volume, the United States and England and Wales have different levels of services as between rural areas and urban areas; there is a different experience of living and engaging with the state in rural and urban areas. The move to remote justice highlights one aspect of this. We briefly consider pressing challenges, such as the impact of physical distances and infrastructure in rural communities, greater use of technology and Covid-19, as well as austerity. While each of these case studies takes place in different timeframes and settings, they all provide useful examples when reflecting on the blockages and dysfunctionalities that are likely to impede remote justice. And they help us to understand

[9] R Penchansky and W Thomas, 'The concept of access: definition and relationship to consumer satisfaction' (1981) 19(2) *Medical Care* 127.

how all, but most pertinently rural dwellers, are impacted by the shift away from face-to-face justice.

## II. Defining 'Remote Justice' and What 'Good' Access to Justice Looks Like

Remote justice is typically used to mean virtual justice and includes the use of technology via online hearings in higher and lower courts to achieve just outcomes.[10] When thinking about why remote justice has become important in the context of England and Wales, a good place to start is the Government's digital reform programme (DRP), which started in 2016. Pinning down the impact of remote justice is a challenging task given its recent widespread and (ongoing) use in the legal system of England and Wales. While much has been said by commentators on the pitfalls of the DRP, not much research has been undertaken in uncovering the experiences and impacts of remote justice in a comprehensive manner, particularly for lay users. During the Covid-19 pandemic, a handful of rapid reviews and consultations undertaken by non-governmental agencies underscored this point to put a spotlight on the issue, but these findings have yet to stall the staunch supporters and implementers of the DRP.[11]

The slogan for the Government's DRP is an interesting one – 'a justice system for those who need it most'.[12] From a human rights framework, one would hope that the justice system that is fit for purpose is one that is accessible to all rather than just those who need it the most. We opine that to take into account the needs of users – and in particular victims, witnesses and those who are vulnerable – we need an equity lens to further assess the extent to which remote justice works.

The Government goes on to state that they have a responsibility to ensure that a justice system that is fair is one that is accessible to everyone:

> Our justice system defends our fundamental rights and freedoms. It is a cornerstone of our modern society and it must serve all those who call on it, when they call on it. From some of the most vulnerable people in our society, to families in crisis, victims of crime, claimants and commercial businesses – we have a responsibility to administer a justice system that is accessible to everyone and operates efficiently.[13]

[10] For a discussion, see G McKeever, 'Remote Justice? 'Litigants in Person and Participation in Court Processes during Covid-19' [2020] MLRForum 005 at www.modernlawreview.co.uk/mckeevers-remote-justice/ (accessed 17 January 2022).

[11] N Byron, S Beardon and A Kendrick, *The Impact of COVID-19 Measures on the Civil Justice System* (Civil Justice Council, 2020); Fair Trials, 'Justice under lockdown (England & Wales)' (25 June 2020) at www.fairtrials.org/articles/publications/justice-under-lockdown-england-wales/; M Ryan et al, 'Remote hearings in the family court post-pandemic' (Nuffield Family Justice Observatory, 2020) at www.nuffieldfjo.org.uk/resource/remote-hearings-post-pandemic.

[12] HM Courts and Tribunals Service (HMCTS), 'The HMCTS reform programme' (9 November 2018) at www.gov.uk/guidance/the-hmcts-reform-programme.

[13] ibid.

Nonetheless, what constitutes success for remote justice remains unclear for the DRP.[14]

## A. What 'Good' Looks Like for Remote Justice

In 2021, the Ministry of Justice published its evaluation framework on the HMCTS reform programme, five years after the reform programme had commenced.[15] The framework is based on a theory-driven approach (theory of change), whereby the reform programme's activities and the expected results are examined, but whether this would yield convincing evidence of impact, particularly for lay users, remains to be seen. The lack of baseline data is telling:

> Similarly, the scoping of the overarching evaluation began after the implementation of some aspects of reform. While this is often difficult to avoid in policy evaluation, a consequence is that baseline data was not collected prior to the start of the reform programme.[16]

Nonetheless, the Government are clearly optimistic about the DRP and have recently made some interesting but unsubstantiated claims of impact as there is a lack of publicly available data on user satisfaction.

> Reform is already well under way and having a huge impact for the public … Over 426,000 people have used our online services, keeping simple claims out of court and reserving judges and court space for the most difficult cases.[17]

Grand claims aside about the impact, there is plainly a dearth of research and evidence on remote justice, limiting our understanding of what works. Therefore, there is an opportunity to consider equity aspects to further develop the remote justice research and evaluation agenda, particularly in relation to user satisfaction – and with a consideration of rural experiences. In the next subsection, we propose and consider the dimensions of accessibility using the case studies.

# III. The Dimensions of Access and its Potential Application to Improving Remote Justice

In the 1980s, two scholars, Roy Penchansky and William Thomas, developed a theory on access and consumer satisfaction in the health policy and health services research fields.[18] These conceptual ideas on access and consumer satisfaction in

[14] See McKeever (n 10).

[15] Ministry of Justice, *HCTMS Reform: Evaluation Framework* (2021) at www.justice.gov.uk/publications/research-and-analysis/moj.

[16] ibid 13.

[17] HM Courts and Tribunals Service (n 12).

[18] Penchansky and Thomas (n 9).

the health fields have come to be known as the five dimensions of access. Access is conceptualised as a set of dimensions that closely connect users to the healthcare system. In the same way, one can apply these concepts to the DRP and courts services. Going back to the Government's claim that over 400,000 people may have used the services, the five dimensions of access help to move the conversation from one solely about being faster and more efficient to deeper issues that relate to the differing needs of court users, which are likely to impact on user satisfaction and access to justice.

These dimensions of access can be a useful framework for assessing impacts, and exemplar questions to explore in future work are:

- *Availability.* Here we can consider issues like how adequate the supply of legal advice and representation in the system is. This is an important dimension, particularly in relation to lay participation where one is more likely to encounter non-professional court users navigating the remote court system. There have been urgent calls by the legal profession to address the evidence gap for litigants in person (LIPs) at remote hearings,[19] and for those now described as Living outside of Legal Aid (LOLAs).[20] For LIPs and LOLAs, the availability of legal advice and representation becomes paramount.
- *Accessibility.* One question around understanding impact is to assess whether access and effective participation has improved because of remote justice. Here we can discuss the physical location of clients and the geographical distribution of remote hearing centres. Additionally, how the availability of technology infrastructure affects remote justice outcomes. For example, in cases where clients are offered a remote hearing centre, rather than connecting via their front rooms, how accessible is the location in terms of travel time costs; and if using their front rooms and personal devices, how robust is the Internet connectivity – an issue in many rural areas.
- *Accommodation.* How adaptable is the use of technology to the needs of vulnerable lay users, and what are lay users' perceptions and experiences of the adaptations, particularly for those with protected characteristics. Linked to this issue are concerns around the loss of client voice and the loss of empathy from virtual proceedings, particularly in sensitive cases. Building more empathy in the remote justice system calls for an understanding and a willingness to accommodate and listen to the experiences of lay users. While the reform programme has attempted to engage with stakeholders in evidence gathering, the majority of these stakeholders are often professional court users.[21] Robust evidence gathering on remote justice calls for a reimagining of stakeholder engagement and a participative approach. There is available good practice on co-production and stakeholder participation in health justice partnerships as an example.

[19] McKeever (n 10).
[20] Newman, Mant and Gordon (n 7).
[21] Ministry of Justice (n 15).

- *Affordability*. A key question here is the costs involved in accessing the remote justice arrangements and whether these costs disproportionately affect some lay users over others. Assumptions around ownership of the appropriate technology or the relevant fees to utilise it (such as subscriptions) might be made for all court users, despite the reality being more diverse and complicated. It is important to understand whether access to remote hearings affects lay users' ability and willingness to pay to use the system.
- *Acceptability*. This involves thinking through the attributes of lay users and whether the allowances are considered acceptable by those with protected attributes and characteristics. Not everyone has the same experience of using technology or of communicating remotely. Certain health conditions and disabilities, for example, might have a known effect on telephone or video chat proficiency amongst users. It needs to be probed how willing people would be to accept these difficulties for something as fundamental as justice services.

Now that we have presented these equity principles, we use the three case studies to buttress our points about the need to expand our understanding of accessibility to better and more fully capture the impacts of remote justice.

## A. Case Study 1

The first case study, which is based in the English county of Suffolk, highlights the legal geography and infrastructure issues that persist with rural access to justice and court closures. Such considerations are also likely to impact users' experiences of remote courts.

Research on rural access to justice is sparse.[22] The notion of rural neglect in the academic literature on studies relating to access to justice has been paid less attention than other areas of access to justice. Studies examining remote justice through a legal geography lens are even rarer. While there is a vast literature that examines spatial implications for public services such as hospitals and schools, to our knowledge, adequate consideration has not been given to the availability of infrastructure for remote justice in rural communities. Researching rural access to justice in a challenging socio-economic climate engenders a need for theoretical and empirical innovations. This is a view that we all share as scholar-activists.

One of the authors (Adisa) examined impacts of court closures in Suffolk in 2018. The county of Suffolk had lost two out of its three courts (Bury St Edmunds and Lowestoft), which closed in 2016. Suffolk was then left with only one magistrates' court, the Ipswich Magistrates' Court, which serves the whole of the county. Suffolk is a large rural county,[23] covering nearly 1,600 square miles, contains

[22] See D Newman, 'Attitudes to Justice in a Rural Community' (2016) 36(4) *Legal Studies* 591.

[23] Rural is defined as those areas that surround settlements of over 10,000 people. In England, these areas account for 85% of the land area and 18% (9.3 million) of the population. Of these, 4.5 million live in rural towns and their fringes, 2.7 million in rural villages, and 1.6 million in rural hamlets and isolated dwellings (Government Statistical Service, 2017).

over 480 villages and hamlets as well as the large towns of Ipswich, Lowestoft and Bury St Edmunds, and has a population of around 750,000. Using a generalised transport cost model, Adisa estimated travel time costs impacts for users of magistrates' courts – victims, defendants, witnesses, some members of the general public, and legal professionals who use public transport to get to magistrates' courts. Generalised costs, defined as the sum of both the time and money cost for a journey, were expressed in units of time. Monetary costs include bus and train fares, or fuel costs. Non-monetary costs include overall opportunity costs (eg, time spent undertaking the journey, unreliability of bus/train times, frequencies of buses, ease and convenience of the journey, and so on). Non-monetary costs may consist of a larger part of the overall journey costs,[24] and can deter users from turning up to court.

The two dimensions of accessibility of greatest relevance here are affordability and accessibility. One of the key findings from this 2018 study was that the Suffolk court closure had significant travel cost impacts on defendants and their defence advocates. For example, following the Bury St Edmunds court closure, the generalised time costs of a defendant coming from a remote location daily doubled in almost all cases. For those living in rural areas, additional travel time and costs incurred in accessing magistrates' courts, following the closures of nearby courts, could help explain why there are vastly different experiences of the criminal justice system, either as a defendant or as a witness, compared to those living in large towns and cities.

Furthermore, the role of infrastructure (in this case public transportation) cannot be underestimated in getting to courts on time. Rural areas are very car dependent, as public transport is perceived as inadequate; however, many low-income households find it challenging to own or maintain a car. Research by the RAC Foundation showed the significant impact on low-income households of having to run a car. In 2012 it estimated that 800,000 car-owning households spent at least 31 per cent of their disposable income on buying and running a vehicle.[25]

Use of video and telephone technologies was then proposed by the Government as a solution to reducing travel time burdens and other associated costs in getting to court even before the pandemic.[26] This is a solution that has now been propelled further, partly through necessity brought on by the pandemic and as part of the digital reform programme. However, ignoring issues about infrastructure for remote hearings is likely to create perverse outcomes for remote justice. The issues of affordability and Internet connectivity are very specific issues that need addressing for those in rural communities, and for the poorest in society.

[24] K Button, *Transport Economics* (Edward Elgar Publishing, 2010) 142–43.

[25] RAC Foundation, 'Poorest households sink deeper into transport poverty' (6 February 2014) at www.racfoundation.org/media-centre/transport-poverty (accessed 17 January 2022).

[26] P Gibbs, *Defendants on video – conveyor belt justice or a revolution in access?* (Transform Justice, 2017).

These concerns were echoed in the research that underpins this case study, as exemplified by the following observation from a member of the judiciary:

> These reforms don't seem to consider real people. The huge majority of those that come to the courts are likely to not have Iphones, tablets etc. They are typically those that cannot afford to buy these things. Not having money and taking unlawful actions to gain it is often why they are in court in the first place. For example, say someone depends heavily on drugs and alcohol and resorts to repetitive shoplifting, asking them to plead online by going on the internet or calling a number is likely to not going to lead to compliance.

What emerges, then, are dangers for court users, which will apply across their experiences with the legal system while remote courts are in operation. Those in rural areas are likely to be most obviously affected.

## B. Case Study 2

The second study considers the use of video and telephone technology in a real-life remote hearing case to which one of the authors (James) was privy. The Covid-19 crisis provided a window through which to view the use of video and telephone technology by court users, and an opportunity to assess its impact.

David Renton, a housing and employment barrister, describes a remote hearing he conducted during the pandemic and documents the impact it had on one of his clients (Mr Curlew):

> Geoff explained to his father [Mr Curlew] the options (video on and off, mute) which were available on his phone. But how was Mr Curlew supposed to send messages to me if his only means of communication was through the same phone by which he would be listening?
>
> Mr Curlew told me he would attend the hearing from his own car, with his mobile phone charging from its engine. At least, he would have peace and quiet there, he said.[27]

The venue for this significant event was not a court but a car. If there is no court for you to attend, the court users may be reduced to such informal, unceremonious and fundamentally inadequate engagement. Renton unpicks how the remote hearing plays out, which provides a flavour of how disjointed and inadequate such hearings can be:

> The court sent out advice on how to conduct an online hearing 'While a remote hearing may seem less formal than a conventional hearing', it began, before reminding participants of the need to approach the hearing in an appropriate spirit. 'All participants should ensure they are in a quiet room free from distractions and ensure that telephones are off or muted.' A sentence in bold warned us that recording a court hearing was a criminal offence.

[27] D Renton, *Jobs and Homes* (Legal Action Group, 2021) 57.

> There was an awkward moment before the hearing began when half a dozen people had joined the call but neither Mr Makk nor Mr Curlew. My opponent connected. She had been trying through her computer but could not get it to work and joined us via her mobile. The image was clear but the sound cut in and out.
>
> The last to join was my client. 'Hello,' Mr Curlew said, 'hello, sorry I'm late, I couldn't' – before the clerk muted him. It was the last part he played in the hearing: although, of course, it was his family which was at stake, the future of his children.[28]

The issues of availability, accessibility, accommodation, affordability and acceptability come into play in this one case study alone. The warning from the court suggests that a participant will have private space, a computer and a phone. However, Geoff did not have either private space or a computer. He had to sit in his car and use his phone to access his hearing. This meant he was not able to communicate with his legal advisor, nor could he participate in the hearing in a relevant way. The hearing was only partially available and accessible to him, and was completely unacceptable as a vehicle to deliver justice, as his circumstances describe.

Most County Courts did not have video-conferencing technology when the pandemic commenced and were ill-prepared for the management of remote hearings at scale. Social media were awash with lawyers reporting on their remote hearings, often presenting a positive transition to home and remote working and congratulating themselves on their success. Common themes included savings on travel, cost and efficiency. Most lawyers welcoming the new medium did not refer to their clients at all. In contrast, the guest blog of Professor Ceila Kitzinger for the Transparency Project[29] brought the effect of remote justice sharply into focus for one court user, Sarah,[30] whom Kitzinger had been assisting for just over a year in a serious medical treatment case concerning Sarah's father.

The lawyers involved wrote their own account, stating how 'comfortable and familiar' it felt relatively quickly; they thought that witnesses might feel 'less intimidated … as they sat in their homes, responding to the questions, but not having the full glare of the court on them'.[31] Their conclusion: 'What did we miss? In truth, nothing that mattered'[32] jars markedly with the feelings expressed by Sarah:

> Skype took away from me the ability to look these people in the eyes – these people who have their opinions about my Dad and only knew him through third-hand notes. I wanted to look them in the eyes and make them hear the truth but I was looking at a computer screen.

[28] ibid 58.

[29] C Kitzinger, 'Remote justice: a family perspective' (Transparency Project, 29 March 2020) at www.transparencyproject.org.uk/remote-justice-a-family-perspective/ (accessed 17 January 2022.

[30] The name referred to in the blog post but not her real name.

[31] Kitzinger (n 29).

[32] N Khalique and Sophia Roper, 'Skype in the Court of Protection: The courts in the time of coronavirus' *Local Government Lawyer* (27 March 2020) at www.localgovernmentlawyer.co.uk/adult-social-care/307-adult-care-features/43223-skype-in-the-court-of-protection-the-courts-in-the-time-of-coronavirus (accessed 17 January 2022).

> In a court room people can see body language. They can feel the pain and emotion when you speak about that moment of utter desperation that you went through. But I was in a little one-inch box on a screen and being honest I bet half of them weren't even engaged in looking at it – as the judge couldn't monitor them to make sure they were paying attention.[33]

Sarah noted how she felt like an outsider, which made her nervous and insecure; for Sarah, 'It felt like a second-best option. It didn't feel professional. It didn't feel like justice.'[34]

Court often gives the opportunity of being heard, a novel and powerful experience for many. Sarah felt this was denied to her. She was invisible to the court: her camera off. This created a distance; a remoteness and a lack of the empathy that might usually be present. Housing solicitor Simon Mullings notes 'A person facing a court hearing for the first time in whatever role has a vast amount of culturally acquired knowledge to support them in finding their own place in the setting and narrative of court proceedings.'[35] He concludes that the introduction of new technologies into legal proceedings should only proceed if those technologies can be made to work to reduce structural power imbalances in society. The danger is that such technologies are deployed in a manner that enshrines and worsens such power imbalances.

If we consider the principles of availability, accessibility, accommodation, affordability and acceptability in relation to Sarah's case, we might conclude that the hearing was available and accessible and affordable in principle but it was not acceptable to Sarah.

Possession cases were stayed by the introduction of *Practice Direction 51Z: Stay of Possession Proceedings, Coronavirus* by the Master of the Rolls in March 2020; however, this was challenged in the case of *Arkin v Marshall*.[36] In April 2020, the representative body for housing lawyers, Housing Law Practitioners Association, put out an urgent call for evidence to its members included in the schedule of responses to the case and asked what the effect would be if cases were allowed to continue. The responses are relevant not only to the case itself, but also for the wider, more general, remote access to justice issues, as in the following example:

> Face to face interaction facilitates both trust and effective and clear communication which is vital to vulnerable and often chaotic clients in stressful situations where their home is at stake. The use of other media, skype, or zoom can be outside of our client's capability whether this is due to their digital skills, digital media may not be available to them because of the cost and also the fact that Wi-Fi is not always stable. Our clients are more likely to have a phone but not necessarily a smart phone, and even if they do,

[33] Kiztinger (n 29).

[34] ibid.

[35] S Mullings, 'Fairness in new-tech court proceedings in the era of Covid-19' *The Justice Gap* (23 March 2020) at www.thejusticegap.com/court-drama-genre-familiarity-and-fairness-in-new-tech-court-proceedings-in-the-covid-19-crisis/ (accessed 17 January 2022).

[36] *Arkin v Marshall* [2020] EWCA Civ 620.

> they may not have access to scanning and printing. Our clients are amongst the poorest in society.[37]

Other responses discussed the high levels of clients with a mental-health diagnosis, for whom it could be difficult to engage in case management directions without their support worker or social workers present to assist them. The lack of such support was shown to make it hard for some clients to complete even rudimentary tasks, so put them in an unfair position. Further, some responses highlighted the challenges attending court hearings remotely: for example in a rural area, where a phone or Internet connection is unreliable and the signal frequently gets lost; or when clients are also apparently less likely to show up for the hearing due to nerves, when they lack the comfort of a lawyer's physical presence that they get in person.

Prior to the pandemic, video and telephone technology had been seen as part of a drive towards efficiency savings, as well as supposedly introducing convenience for court users. It has impacted rural court users most of all. It is now more widely experienced – and has thus become a more prominent issue due to the pandemic. And as more people are drawn into remote justice, the impact is clear: the personal accounts of court users and lawyers show that a great deal is lost when justice is remote. The case of *R (Unison) v Lord Chancellor*[38] established the principle that changes to the justice system should be assessed according to their likely impact on behaviour in the real world. The same principle applies here. Perhaps rural court users were easily ignored as this was not the experience of the majority; with remote justice increasingly mainstream, the flaws are more obvious for all to see.

## C. Case Study 3

The third case study brings into sharp focus issues of social welfare that intersect with dimensions of access to legal aid and remote justice. One of the authors (Newman) looked at the impact of austerity on access to justice for social welfare law.[39] The study captured a diversity of experiences and purposively included rural areas and smaller towns, as well as the better-studied large cities. This case study includes original quotes from those working in or around these rural areas and smaller towns to give a flavour on remote justice. We include detail from those working in the advice sector, working variously in services funded by grants and local authorities as well as in pro bono capacities.

[37] *Arkin v Marshall*, CA B2/2020/0620 & B2/2020/0621, 122, at www.hlpa.org.uk/cms/wp-content/uploads/2020/05/Arkin-v-Marshall-HLPA-evidence.pdf.

[38] *R (Unison) v Lord Chancellor* [2017] UKSC 51.

[39] The quotations reproduced in this case study are unused material from a larger project conducted with Jon Robins. See J Robins and D Newman, *Justice in a Time of Austerity* (Bristol University Press, 2021).

One key finding was that many people struggling with social welfare problems do not qualify for legal aid after the enactment of the Legal Aid, Sentencing and Punishment of Offenders Act 2012, and thus may never see a lawyer. Additionally, it was found that, outside of the large cities, the decline of a local advice sector and the move to remote provision were hurting those going through the justice system and experiencing social welfare problems.

Coupled with concerns around the replacement of a local advice sector with remote provision were questions around literacy. There were anxieties around digital literacy, but underpinning that, a more fundamental worry about literacy in and of itself. For example, this comment by an advisor sets out the fundamental issue literacy presents:

> I have no doubt that literacy is the biggest problem for litigants-in-person now, for us, for here. But not only filling in the forms but understanding the forms. Writing statements coherently and legibly. They just wouldn't be able to do it.

Understanding the forms relating to a case should be seen as essential to any notion of access to justice. But if LIPs are having to manage their cases alone and cannot even comprehend the information they are reading, attempting to fill out or are providing to the court, their active participation in the justice system is going to be undermined.

The principles of availability, accessibility, accommodation, affordability and acceptability interweave with this concern. At the start, we mentioned that issues of availability, relating to how adequate the supply of legal advice and representation in the system is, are likely to affect outcomes for court users. The research upon which this case study is based demonstrates that this is already manifesting as an obstruction in the system.

The timing of this research has meant that it captured the roll-out of Universal Credit as a new way of claiming welfare benefits, which required claimants to have access online. Some areas had just piloted the scheme, others were just starting, while a few were anticipating it coming online. Those we talked to at all stages were disturbed – and were having to deal with worried clients – as a result of Universal Credit, with the online aspect of the benefit cited as the most common concern. Such fear is captured in this account from an advisor:

> I've got a client who is just a man who has just had to go onto Universal Credit, and he's a very, very anxious client, so he's there absolutely in tears because he can't make any sense, because now all Universal Credit is done online. And he just can't do that. He can't manage getting onto the website, putting in some information, finding the right page, it's just impossible. So he tries to get his daughter to do it and he was distraught really, actually, trying to make it work.

This client was not confident enough to manage his own case. He had to rely on a family member to help him, who, luckily for the client, was willing and able to support him. Not everyone would have someone there for them.

What the dependency on support to take part in the benefit process speaks to is the coalescing of digital literacy with literacy in and of itself, which links to the principle of accommodation. This was evident from the report provided by the following advisor:

> We're already seeing the impact because of the introduction of Universal Credit … everything is expected to be on the Internet. We're already seeing people failing to complete their journals and then being sanctioned. Failing to apply for Universal Credit, housing costs in time, which means … their rent is straight into arrears because the housing benefit – what was housing benefit has not been paid. Although people are digitally excluded, they're also digitally not literate. So there's people that have literacy and numeracy problems anyway, but then they're expected to immediately know how to use the computer and access, and find their way around computer systems, and whatever sites they need to go on to.

Underpinning this case study on the intersections of social welfare and remote justice is the question of equity. The result of being unable to engage with the system for welfare benefits claims is to be sanctioned. There was a real risk of clients' losing essential entitlements due to an inhospitable system that fails to consider differences in experience and ability when it comes to using digital technology or filling out forms.

We were told that those living outside larger cities faced an additional burden in the shift to online access – connectivity issues. The following advisor outlines the problem:

> The big problem in rural areas is the digital exclusion as well, because there isn't fast broadband, there isn't 4G – everything is expected to be done on the Internet these days. People are expected, if they haven't got Internet at home that they can access their local library, but their local libraries … no longer exist. They're only in the three main towns: Brecon, Newtown and Welshpool – oh, and Llandrindod Wells. And if you look at a map, you can see lots and lots of villages and towns around it, they have to try and find their own way into one of those town to access the Internet.

The changing landscape of the advice sector has been affected by the issue of accessibility. For some clients, it was hard enough to find a library in which to access the internet; harder still to find an expert to guide someone through the process. The local advice eco-system has shrunk under austerity measures, so that towns such as the above have no legal aid lawyers, no Citizens Advice Bureaux, and no law centres.

Some providers were running outreach programmes into rural areas, which would otherwise leave residents lost in advice deserts. In the following example, one such advisor highlights some of the benefits of these services:

> A lot of the clients we take on from those rural areas have got a number of problems when they first come to us. It's not just, 'Oh, I've got this form I can't fill in, can you help me?' It's, 'Well, actually I have got a form that I need filled in, but I can't get even to the outreach venue. Is it possible to have a home visit?' Even though, perhaps, it's still in the town itself for example. And then when you go there you find their housing is totally unsuitable for them. And then before you go, they start telling you about how much council tax they're paying. Well, actually, they should be paying quite a bit less.

> Or they haven't heard of pension credit, so they haven't really got very much income, although, you know, they've just got the state pension which isn't really adequate and below the level of … the income they should have. That's very typical of what we find in the rural areas.

Not only does an outreach service contact clients who might otherwise not get help, but the benefit of seeing clients in person rather than remotely is that the advisor can understand their wider context and the additional problems that the client may not mention but that might be important to their case (and general well-being). Through face-to-face meetings, the advisor may come understand the clustered injustices that could otherwise be missed through remote access.

What emerged across these interviews was how the loss of local advice, and shifts online, were deeply problematic to people's experiences of access to justice, especially outside of large cities. Through this case study, this loss of advice does not meet the accessibility, affordability, accommodation, availability and acceptability criteria – the supply of place-based legal advice and representation in the system is inadequate and this is having impacts on remote justice. Additionally, the shifts to online access failed to take into consideration the literacy levels of LIPs and the added costs to LIPs, which as a result is an unintended consequence of remote justice.

## IV. Learning from the Case Studies

One of the aims of this chapter was to expand the conversations about how the concept of 'access' in equity terms could be applied to tackling the dysfunctionalities and blockages in the system as use of technology in the courts and legal system become more the norm. We have highlighted the value of considering availability, accessibility, accommodation, affordability and acceptability in access to justice. The case studies deployed in this chapter have demonstrated that there is clearly a need to understand, and importance in understanding, the different experiences of lay users in order to fully comprehend the impact of remote justice: this was true before the pandemic, when we conceived the idea for this chapter with a sole focus on rural access to justice, but it is especially pertinent in the world as shaped by Covid-19. Much has been written about the challenges of remote court hearings during the pandemic, as well as the need to engage with lay users involved in remote hearings and using the courts' online services. We support the calls for a participative rather than a consultative approach, which take into consideration these equity principles. These should take account of rural experiences, where remote access may increasingly become the norm given policies such as the court closure programme in England and Wales.

This chapter has proposed an agenda for research on remote justice in general and rural access to justice in particular, which has at its core the principles of accessibility, affordability, accommodation, availability and acceptability; and these concepts deserve further exploration. We recommend that the Ministry of Justice's evaluation framework be augmented with these equity concepts to yield richer insights into user satisfaction. There is also scope for non-governmental organisations that are commissioning research in this area to consider the dimensions of access in their surveys, enquiring about lay user satisfaction and experiences of remote justice. As it stands, satisfaction survey participation for lay users remains low and the risks are high, meaning that more research is urgently needed in this area. Access to justice for all, and most particularly for those living in rural areas, risks being compromised by the shift to remote justice, so we need to take the threat more seriously and better understand how it impacts those brought into the justice system.

# AFTERWORD

MICHELE STATZ

In *Wisdom Sits in Places: Landscape and language among the Western Apache*, Keith Basso writes, '[A]nthropologists have paid scant attention to one of the most basic dimensions of human experience – that close companion of heart and mind, often subdued, yet potentially overwhelming, that is known as *sense of place*.'[1] As the contributors to this volume know, access-to-justice scholars have also largely overlooked the complex, intimate dimensions of place – and, more specifically, rural place. This is perhaps unsurprising, particularly when we consider rurality as consequentially disregarded and systematically marginalised[2] in policy and practice on a global scale. What results for anyone interested in the unique spatial dimensions of access to justice is a prevailing image of rural place as 'isolated', 'peripheralised', 'alienated' and 'socio-economically excluded', to draw on some descriptions listed throughout this volume.

These descriptors are not inaccurate, and yet we also know that justice is ultimately accessed, mobilised, deferred or forgone by *someone somewhere*, an individual with a distinct relationship to a place and all it implies. Understanding this lived relationship – the 'sense of place' of which Basso writes – is intrinsic to the efficacy of the ideas in this collection. It is a perspective that necessarily offers and demands an expansive regard for rural place as marginalised *as well as* differently contested, cherished, appraised, memorialised, valued and traversed. It allows us to take what we know about the institutions and policies that render rural places marginalised – which, thanks to the sustained efforts of many of this book's contributors, is a good deal – and further consider what occurs within these places as a result of (or in spite of) these structural realities. In turn, we can do something *more*, namely put forth proximate, spatially-accountable, responsive avenues for accessing justice in rural areas. This process is the heart of *Access to Justice in Rural Communities*, and it represents a monumental, urgent step forward.

Of course, as the reader has no doubt realised, there is no clear, single step forward when it comes to advancing rural access to justice. And this is appropriate: rurality is not homogeneous, and access-to-justice scholars' efforts must

[1] K Basso, *Wisdom Sits in Places: Landscape and language among the Western Apache* (University of New Mexico Press, 1996) 106.

[2] AM Eisenberg, 'Distributive justice and rural America' (2020) 61 *Boston College Law Review* 189.

be correspondingly dynamic and responsive to the particularities of place. This book offers a range of approaches. Both Beskin and Pruitt (chapter 2) and Kool and Haksgaard (chapter 11) centre largely on access to attorneys, with the latter contributors uniquely engaging a supply chain management framework to envision how we might get 'product' (lawyers and other legal services) to 'the destination' (rural communities). Drawing on health services scholarship, Adisa, James and Newman (chapter 15) offer us 'five dimensions of access' – availability, accessibility, accommodation, affordability and acceptability – to better assess the impacts and equitability of remote (telephonic or virtual) justice technologies in rural places. Maluleke (chapter 4) calls for rural infrastructural enhancements and geographically distinct access to justice policies and priorities. Moore (chapter 10) proactively steers us towards 'people-centered perspectives' of access to justice, which includes both the legal and non-legal dimensions of problems and recognises that people must be empowered to know where to go *if* a problem arises, not when. In other chapters, access to justice is understood most generally as a human right – that is, justice that is accessible not only to those who can afford it or 'need it most' (to draw on Adisa et al) but to everyone, regardless of social and spatial location.

It is important to pause here at Allison and Cunneen's contribution (chapter 6), for while the authors similarly draw on this human rights framing, and in particular the United Nations Declaration on the Rights of Indigenous Peoples, they also recognise that '[d]efinitions of access to justice are often framed by and within the dominant legal system', which often fails to reflect the needs and perspectives of those seeking justice. What follows is a renewed call for accountability to justice seekers, which critically includes a more deferential regard for justice seekers as those who engage, participate in and are well positioned to *lead* access to justice processes. It also involves a deeper examination of those dominant structures that powerfully shape access to justice needs and 'remedies'. And many of the contributors here do just that, with analyses spanning the legacies of settler colonisation and colonisation (Moore – chapter 10; Rono and Bunei – chapter 3), changes in national policy (Economides and Watkins – chapter 13), legal aid reforms (Mant – chapter 9), delayed professional attention to rural legal deserts (Beskin and Pruitt – chapter 2) and jurisdictional shifts (Donson and Morgan-Williams – chapter 7). Taken together, we are better equipped to identify how institutions, policies and paradigms contribute to the 'entrenched marginalisation' of diverse rural individuals – including those who no longer live in rural areas (Donson and Morgan-Williams – chapter 7) – and further impact rural community members' access to *and trust in* dominant legal systems and so many access to justice 'solutions'.[3]

[3] M Statz, R Friday and J Bredeson, '"They Had Access, but They Didn't Get Justice": Why Prevailing Access to Justice Initiatives Fail Rural Americans' (2021) 28 *Georgetown Journal on Poverty Law & Policy* 321.

Of course, there is something else that we must account for when it comes to access and trust, namely, the ways in which our own unique positionalities – our self-identifications, experiences of marginalisation or professional privileges[4] – influence the questions we ask and the answers we put forth in the context of rural access to justice. As Murat Madenüs reminds us (chapter 5), we are each differently situated along unequal spatial and socio-economic strata, a reality that causes people 'to have a different consciousness, and as a result they perceive the same event in different ways'. While the story Madenüs shares is a vital reflection on how local histories impact legal consciousness, it also challenges us to acknowledge our own unique perceptions of justice events, needs and solutions.

We know, for instance, that if the problem is defined by those who are legal practitioners, then the solution to rural legal deserts is often more attorneys/lawyers. If it is evaluated by policy makers and others who equate 'access to justice' with 'access to the courts', then the focus largely turns to regulatory reform and advancing the work of legal paraprofessionals, courthouse navigators, Citizens Advice workers and other 'non-lawyer' technicians. If court systems and other agencies need to take cost-saving measures and/or appeal to spatially- or pandemic-isolated populations, then technologies like smartphone apps, advice websites, courthouse self-service kiosks and fillable self-help forms tend to emerge as attractive forms of 'access'. None of these perspectives is entirely siloed, of course, but the patchwork nature of access-to-justice scholars' approaches likely has as much, if not more, to do with the positionalities of their champions as with the complex and deeply 'emplaced' justiciable needs they aim to address.

In a sense, this is precisely why access-to-justice scholars' initiatives that bring together a diverse range of voices, whether via workshops, local conversations or edited volumes like this one, are so important. Doing so facilitates a reorientation from access to justice 'solutions' that are overly determined by profession and positionality to allow something more transformative to occur. That, I think, is what is happening here. While none of the contributors to this volume ascribes to a nostalgic or idyllic image of rurality, it is their ultimate attention to sense of place as 'that close companion of heart and mind' that in turn creates a robust, urgent and strikingly cohesive call for *what must come next.* With a pervasive sense of impatience, the authors in this book put forth consistent demands for the field of access to justice, for policymakers, professional organisations and state agencies, and, at their best, for one another and for each of us.

First, there needs to be more equitable attention to rural access to justice generally and to the unique, often unconsidered consequences that laws and policies have on rural communities (Rono and Bunei – chapter 3) more specifically, and it must span institutions from the judiciary, policymakers, professional associations and higher education. This attention is not at the cost of denying the complex, often overwhelmingly fragmented nature of trying to access justice in urban

[4] MF Massoud, 'The Price of Positionality: Assessing the Benefits and Burdens of Self-Identification in Research Methods' *Journal of Law and Society* (2022) 49 *Journal of Law and Society* 51.

areas, as Mant thoughtfully notes in chapter 9, but instead signals a commitment to systematically recognise differences between – and disparities across – distinct spatial contexts. Beyond the obvious benefits to rural justice delivery, there are economic advantages to this institutional responsiveness. As Kool and Haksgaard point out in chapter 11, the resolution of legal needs enables rural residents to contribute to the economic health and vitality of a community more meaningfully, which in turn increases the attractiveness of that area for further investment (and more attorneys). There is also the matter of professional responsibility. Describing the markedly overdue professional attention to rural attorney shortages in the United States, in chapter 2 Beskin and Pruitt highlight the American Bar Association's 2020 'Profile of the Legal Profession' as the current 'apex of attention to the rural lawyer shortage'. Given this report relies on State bar associations to provide State-by-State data – some of which is outdated and inaccurate[5] – it is striking that the current 'apex' still misrepresents, and likely even underestimates, the true extent of rural attorney shortages. In the specific context of pandemic-related 'remote justice' in the United Kingdom, in chapter 15 Adisa et al similarly highlight the profound risks of professional and policy initiatives that lack strong empirical grounding or rigorous strategies for evaluation.

In other words, there is an urgent need for more, *and also better*, data on diverse rural realities. These include detailed census and mapping data as well as sustained, empirical studies of what diverse rural individuals 'expect, want or require' of justice systems (Moore – chapter 10) – and indeed, how these individuals actually *understand* 'justice'. This intrinsically calls for new ways of framing and presenting data, two of which are beautifully represented in Murat Madenüs's use of fictional narrative (chapter 5) and Witness Maluleke's engagement with legal pluralism to comparatively explore livestock farmers' experiences across distinct court settings (chapter 4). We cannot underestimate these different framing devices, as they uniquely offer deeper understandings of choice, trust, biography and history, and how each is implicated in 'rural access to justice'.

Second, and in this vein, *Access to Justice in Rural Communities* steers us toward a necessarily more nuanced understanding of rurality. For instance, while recognising its 'shared landscape of challenges', in chapter 10 Moore also highlights the many critical features that distinguish one rural place from another, among them availability of local services and supports, proximity to services in other communities, transportation options, educational and networking opportunities, pathways for professional development and availability of digital technologies. Drawing on typologies like 'deep rural' regions, 'retirement retreats' and 'dynamic rural' areas, Economides and Watkins similarly underscore differences across rural economies and socio-economic classes – while still reminding us that poverty and deprivation, including access to legal services, largely endures in even the wealthiest rural tourist hot spots.

[5] Data on file with the author.

Third, a more nuanced regard for rurality must also account for the ways in which *specific case types*, for instance family law (Mant – chapter 9), domestic violence (Qi and Craig – chapter 14), stock theft (Maluleke – chapter 4) or alcohol consumption (Rono and Bunei – chapter 3), both reflect and are impacted by the socio-spatial, digital, economic and jurisdictional barriers characteristic of rurality worldwide. It must also account for the legal *as well as* emotional and practical needs of rural individuals themselves. Here we find what are perhaps the most important questions of all. How are the current contours of rural access to justice – digital and advice deserts, distance, an absence of face-to-face services – along with broader legal aid reforms experienced by rural Litigants in Person with learning difficulties or mental-health issues (Mant – chapter 9)? How are domestic-violence supports accessed by physically and socially isolated rural individuals who have precarious legal status, fewer adequate intervention resources and who lack proficiency in the dominant language (Qi and Craig – chapter 14)? What would compel a rural Indigenous person, who is deeply and rightfully distrustful of colonial power structures and may daily experience the ongoing surveillance of the welfare state, to seek formal legal and non-legal supports (Allison and Cunneen – chapter 6)? Why would a once-rural member of the Traveller community seek justice from a system rife with exclusionary barriers that are steadily experienced as 'rediscrimination' (Donson and Morgan-Williams – chapter 7)? Turning the lens a bit, what sustains an attorney, health worker, librarian or other 'front-door service provider' as they attempt to address so many complex and urgent individual needs while simultaneously navigating ongoing socio-economic marginalisation and policy neglect?

These questions ultimately represent the 'heart' of 'the heart and mind' mentioned above, for even with the very best datasets and evaluation frameworks, there must still be an accounting for the emotions that persist through this book – and across the rural 'lawscape' more generally.[6] In the previous chapters, these emotions include the low morale of rural criminal legal aid practitioners; the overwhelm experienced by rural small-firm practitioners no longer eligible for civil legal aid clients; the hopelessness experienced by Indigenous individuals unable to locate basic legal information; the stress and confusion felt by rural immigrants trying to clarify their legal rights; and the shame and embarrassment of a Traveller who is not qualified for, or able to further access, legal advice and representation. These emotions are felt differently owing to rural individuals' unique positionalities and histories, and, as we know from this book, they are consistently shaped, compounded or mitigated depending on how and where one is rurally emplaced. Indeed, if there is one thing *Access to Justice in Rural Communities* most resolutely communicates, it is that rurality is deeply intersectional, and that rural place is intimately *sensed*. In response, we must insistently and rigorously attend to how it feels to seek, and to provide, access to justice in rural spaces.

[6] L Pruitt, 'The Rural Lawscape: Space Tames Law Tames Space' in I Braverman et al (eds), *The Expanding Spaces of Law: A Timely Legal Geography* (Stanford University Press, 2013) 190.

This, then, is an energetic call for more of what we find in this volume: more attention to structural dimensions of access to justice, to the nuances of distinct rural places, to legal and non-legal needs, case types, individual identities, emotions and to the ways they intersect in – and with – rural places. Overwhelmingly, it is also call for work that is systematically informed and enhanced by the voices of rural individuals themselves. Just as we know what is lost when rural perspectives are missing in policy or practice – namely, effective participation, due process, access,and empathy (Adisa et al – chapter 15) – so we know that the voices of rural community members 'must be part of the process that aims to improve their lives' (Maluleke – chapter 4).

This deliberate, systematic respect for rural voice complicates and expands prevailing access-to-justice approaches. As the contributors in this volume show us, it inevitably points to a definition of 'access to justice' as the ability of individuals to resolve and prevent justice problems in a way that feels equitable, empowering, fair, trustworthy, dignifying and accessible *to them*. It means access-to-justice efforts must engage the expertise and solutions of trusted community members, whether or not they are law trained. And it means that access-to-justice 'solutions' must consider the resources that diverse rural individuals need – whether housing, employment, education or other legal and non-legal supports – to participate fully in their communities. This requires a mindful shift, one in which we critically re-evaluate prevailing access-to-justice remedies, including the distinct positionalities from which they emerge, and instead prioritise those forms of access that are not 'prescriptive but rather reflective' of rural community members' own distinct voices, experiences and expertise (Allison and Cunneen – chapter 6). This is a just solution – a kind of access that is deeply attentive to *sense of place*.

# INDEX

www.ingramcontent.com/pod-product-compliance
Lightning Source LLC
LaVergne TN
LVHW011755200926
848484LV00003B/714